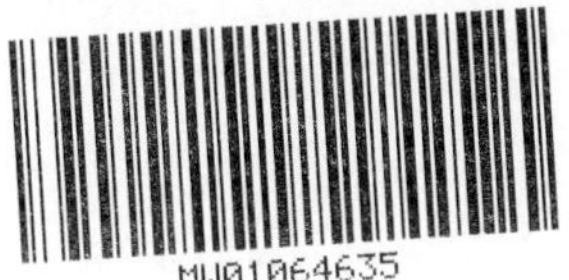

Aesthetics: *The Classic Readings*

PHILOSOPHY: *The Classic Readings*

This series of collections offers classic readings by philosophers ranging from ancient times to the first part of the twentieth century, and contains seminal writings from both Western and and non-Western traditions of philosophy. Combined with valuable editorial guidance, including a substantial Introduction to each volume as well as to individual pieces, they are intended to serve as core texts for historically orientated philosophy courses.

Forthcoming titles:

Ethics: *The Classic Readings*
Epistemology: *The Classic Readings*
Philosophy of Religion: *The Classic Readings*
Metaphysics: *The Classic Readings*
Political Philosophy: *The Classic Readings*

Aesthetics:

The Classic Readings

Edited by David E. Cooper

Advisory Editors
Peter Lamarque
Crispin Sartwell

BLACKWELL PUBLISHING
350 Main street, Malden, MA 02148-5020, USA
9600 Garsington Road, Oxford OX4 2DQ, UK
550 Swanston Street, Carlton, Victoria 3053, Australia

First published 1997 by Blackwell Publishers Ltd
Reprinted 1998 (twice), 2000, 2001, 2002, 2007

15 2011

Library of Congress Cataloging-in-Publication Data

Aesthetics: The Classic Readings / edited by David E. Cooper : advisory editors, Peter Lamarque, Crispin Sartwell.
p. cm. —(Philosophy: The Classic Readings).
Includes bibliographical references and index.
ISBN 978-0-631-19568-9 (hbk : alk. paper) — ISBN 978-0-631-19569-6 (pbk :)
1. Aesthetics. I. Cooper, David Edward. II. Lamarque, Peter. III. Sartwell, Crispin, 1958- . IV. Series.
BH39.C5794 1997 96–40885
111'.85—dc21 CIP

A catalogue record for this title is available from the British Library.

Set in 10.5 on 12pt Galliard
by Ace Filmsetting Ltd, Frome, Somerset

The publisher's policy is to use permanent paper from mills that operate a sustainable forestry policy, and which has been manufactured from pulp processed using acid-free and elementary chlorine-free practices. Furthermore, the publisher ensures that the text paper and cover board used have met acceptable environmental accreditation standards.

For further information on
Blackwell Publishers, visit our website:
www.blackwellpublishers.co.uk

Contents

Series Preface

Philosophers in the English-language world are becoming increasingly aware of the importance of the history of their subject. *Philosophy: The Classic Readings* is a series which provides students and teachers with the central historical texts in the main branches of philosophy. The texts selected range from ancient times to the first part of the twentieth century. In response to a growing and laudable interest in the contributions of non-Western philosophers, the volumes in the series will contain seminal writings from the Indian, Chinese and other traditions as well as the classics of Western philosophical literature.

Each volume in the series begins with a substantial introduction to the relevant area of philosophy and its history, and to the bearing of this history on contemporary discussion. Each selected text is prefaced by a discussion of its importance within the development of that area.

Taken individually, each volume will serve as a core text for courses which adopt a historical orientation towards the relevant branch of philosophy. Taken together, the volumes in the series will constitute the largest treasury of classic philosophical writings available.

The books in the series are edited and introduced by David E. Cooper, Professor of Philosophy at the University of Durham, England, and author of many books, including *World Philosophies: an historical introduction*, also published by Blackwell.

Introduction

In ill-chosen company, a philosopher who describes himself as an aesthetician is liable to be taken as laying claim to an exquisite taste in things, or perhaps as elevating matters of taste over the practical concerns of life, or even as endorsing Théophile Gautier's cheerful acceptance of a tyrant's return provided he 'brings me back a hamper of Tokay' wine.[1] This philosopher is, of course, being confused with an aesthete, and his calling (aesthetics) with aestheticism. To understand that calling, and the subject of this volume, it helps to go back two hundred years.

Since 'aestheticism' is a late nineteenth century coin, it was not out of fear of the above confusion that, early in that century, it was only with some grumpiness that Hegel agreed to employ the word 'aesthetics' in the title of his lectures on 'the philosophy of fine art' (see chapter 9, p. 139). The name had, he conceded, 'passed over into common speech' and he consoled himself that it was but a 'mere name'. Mere or not, the name was still fairly new in Hegel's time. Aesthetic issues have, as this reader shows, been discussed since classical times, but they would not then have been so described. 'Aesthetics', deriving from the Greek word *aesthesis* ('perception'), was coined by the German philosopher, Alexander Baumgarten, in the middle of the eighteenth century.[2] By it, he meant 'the science of sensory knowledge', though the term soon began to be confined to a particular area of such knowledge and understood as 'the science of sensory beauty', the examination of taste. In his *Critique of Pure Reason*, Immanuel Kant was still resisting this confinement, so that the part of that work called 'Transcendental aesthetic' is concerned with the conditions – space and time – of *all* sensory experience. By 1790,

[1] *Mademoiselle de Maupin*, Hardmonsworth: Penguin, 1981, Preface, p. 39.

[2] Baumgarten's main relevant work was *Aesthetica* (1750).

however, with the appearance of the most influential of all works on aesthetics, the *Critique of Judgement*, Kant had decided to follow the growing fashion: aesthetic judgement is now virtually equated with judgement of taste and beauty (see chapter 7).

It was only with reluctance, then, on the part of the two philosophers who have most shaped the concept and agenda of aesthetics that the term entered the lexicon in its present sense. Reflection on the very different ways in which Kant and Hegel nevertheless came to tolerate the term, and to impose their own meanings on it, is instructive in understanding the concept and agenda of aesthetics as a relatively discrete branch of philosophy. For Hegel, both 'the science of sensory knowledge' and even 'the science of beauty' were too broad to capture what interested him, namely the philosophy of art. After all, we appreciate plenty of things as beautiful – sunsets and swans, say – which are not artworks. In Hegel, therefore, aesthetics is equated with the philosphy of art, an equation reflecting his conviction that art and our responses to it are of a totally different order from nature and its appreciation. To lump together, under the umbrella heading 'aesthetics', questions about both art and nature is, in his view, to obliterate crucial distinctions. Hegel has, ever since, had his supporters – Clive Bell, for example (see chapter 12) – for whom art is indeed the only proper domain of aesthetics.

For Kant, on the other hand, distinctions between art and nature are secondary: what is crucial, and constitutes the central topic of aesthetics, is a distinctive kind of response, attitude and judgement which things, be they flowers or paintings of flowers, can elicit. Indeed, the favourite examples given to illustrate aesthetic judgement by Kant (not a man, it seems, with much of an eye or an ear for the arts) are taken from nature – snow-crystals for instance. Those who follow Kant here will deny, therefore, that there is an essential connection between aesthetics and art, even if they concede that in many works of art we find paradigmatic examples of things that are suitable for aesthetic appreciation. For such writers, the core topic, in all its ramifications, of aesthetics is aesthetic experience – that experience or range of experiences, be they those of an artist, his audience or a 'nature lover', which seems to be so peculiarly disengaged from the practical and prudential concerns of ordinary life.

The difference between the approaches inspired by Kant and Hegel should not be exaggerated. There are many issues in aesthetics, some with a long pedigree, which are more or less neutral with respect to these approaches – the question, for example, of whether beauty, a flower's or a painting's, is 'in the eye of the beholder'. Moreover, there are few philosophers today who would want to delimit the domain of aesthetics in quite the terms laid down by either of the two Germans – not least because of doubts as to the unity and viability of their respective major categories, art and aesthetic experience. Is it more than a historical accident that Victorian novels, classical sonatas, Ming vases, and Paduan frescoes are all labelled 'art'? And is there a single kind of experience which all these items, let alone the beauties of nature, are apt to inspire?

It remains, however, that there are issues which only the followers of one or other philosopher would admit into the aesthetics curriculum. Questions about the historical significance of an art genre figure in the Hegelian curriculum, but not the Kantian. Contemporary concerns with the aesthetic value of lakes or mountains will be catered for in the Kantian syllabus, but not the Hegelian. Whether it is because there are few such followers nowadays, or in order to avoid friction in the philosophy department's common-room, the current tendency is to understand the domain of aesthetics in a broad, relaxed way. Questions of both the kinds just mentioned appear on exam papers in aesthetics. And, in a ploy of a sort much used by philosophers, contentious issues about the real scope of aesthetics have become part of the subject itself. '"Natural objects cannot be *appreciated* in the sense artworks can." Discuss' is a question I have seen on more than one paper.

This liberal policy is adopted in this reader. Some of the texts, like Plato's (chapter 1) discuss art, but not aesthetic judgement; others, like Kant's, discuss aesthetic judgement, but not art. Several, unsurprisingly, discuss both.

My account, in terms of the influences exerted by Kant and Hegel, of how the subject matter of aesthetics came to be understood is a familiar and useful one.[3] It helps to explain the variety of issues covered and hence to locate that subject matter. To say that this subject matter is art and aesthetic experience is not intended, though, as a clear, sharp definition. It can only be as clear and sharp as the notions of art and aesthetic experience themselves are – that is, not very. It might seem that such lack of clarity impugns the integrity of aesthetics, but that is not so. For one thing, as implied above, reflection on such fuzzy notions and the attempt, perhaps, to sharpen them become part of the subject itself. Second, there are plenty of questions that can be raised in relation to art and aesthetic experience which do not presuppose that these are sharp, homogenous

[3] See the recent and useful survey articles on aesthetics by Sebastian Gardner, in N. Bunnin & E. Tsui-James (eds), *The Blackwell Companion to Philosophy*, Oxford: Blackwell, 1996, and by Christopher Janaway, in T. Honderich (ed.), *The Oxford Companion to Philosophy*, Oxford: Oxford University Press, 1995.

notions – questions about, say, music's capability to express feeling, or the respective responsibilities of artist and audience for the response to an artwork.

When, as in this reader, the concern is not with contemporary journal literature but with the classic historical texts, it is insufficient simply to demarcate, however crudely, the area of aesthetics. It is necessary, as well, to attend to why and how these earlier philosophers addressed issues in this area. In keeping with the general tenor of contemporary philosophy, today's aestheticians tend to operate with a fine scalpel, working on specific problems – about, for example, representation or expression – without invading the large areas which surround them. But when great metaphysicians like Kant and Hegel discuss art or aesthetic judgement, it is very much the larger scene which concerns them. For Hegel, the main questions about art relate to its status, in relation to religion and philosophy, as a vehicle of truth, and its place and significance within the culture of peoples. For Kant, aesthetic experience is important, first and foremost, for what it shows about the nature of human beings, their mental faculties, and their place in the universe. In this largeness of vision, not only Kant and Hegel, but many other philosophers represented in this volume, are engaged in a rather different enterprise from that of most contemporary aestheticians, even if both enterprises can be described as the philosophical questioning of art and aesthetic experience.

What will surely strike readers about many of the texts I have selected – from Plato and Hsun Tzu to Dewey and Heidegger – are the attempts their authors make to *place*, so to speak, art or aesthetic experience. By this, I mean the efforts made, *inter alia*, to explore the religious significance of art, to identify the role artworks can play within the life of a community, to gauge whether aesthetic experience is a natural continuation of other forms or something which enables human beings to transcend their natural condition, and to measure the value of art against other values, notably those of morality. To take one example, it is Friedrich Schiller's ambition to show that the activity of 'aesthetic play' is capable of harmonizing the cognitive and sensual aspects of our existence that are ordinarily in tragic conflict with one another (see chapter 8). To take a second, A. K. Coomaraswamy argues in the Indian tradition that aesthetic pleasure is intelligible only as indicative of the religious sense of a universe that is a beautiful whole (see chapter 13).

What many of the texts manifest is the conviction that art and aesthetic appreciation are at once profoundly important yet deeply puzzling – phenomena that really should not occur at all on familiar, 'naturalistic' pictures of human existence, and hence call for correspondingly deep explanation.

That people should want to titivate their surroundings or relax and enjoy themselves, is no great puzzle. But whatever the explanation of that desire, it does not go far in explaining the passions and energies dedicated to the making and interpretation of works of art, few of which are titivating or relaxing to behold, and whose connection with the practicalities and ornamentation of life is obscure. It explains even less the enormous significance that people in nearly every culture have attached to the creation of such objects and to the capacity to appreciate not only them, but the beauties and forms of the natural world as well.

Hence the efforts, alluded to above, to explain or 'place' the aesthetic by rooting it in some less puzzling, more obviously 'natural', dimension of life – the desire for order, say, as Dewey suggests (chapter 14) – or, alternatively, by construing it as indicative of our not being purely 'natural' creatures after all, but ones who also occupy a more exalted realm of which art and beauty offer us intimations (see, for example, Plotinus (chapter 4) and Bell (chapter 12)). Hence, too, the attempts to decide whether it is sensible to devote so much energy to art and its appreciation, and to assign them such importance, given the existence of other pressing demands on out attention, notably moral ones (see, for example, Plato (chapter 1), Mo Tzu and Hsun Tzu (chapter 3) and Tolstoy (chapter 11)).

Again, I do not want to exaggerate the difference between aesthetics as practised by the authors in this reader and as worked on by contemporary aestheticians. Not all of the latter, after all, are preoccupied with rather technical problems about representation or artistic intention at the expense of a larger vision of human existence.[4] And not all of the classic texts I have included are concerned with the relation of art and aesthetic experience to the human condition or the order of things. For example, in his discussion of the criteria for taste, Hume (chapter 6), as elsewhere in his philosophical writings, sounds as if he would be at home at any recent British or American philosophy congress. In these texts, moreover, issues which tend to preoccupy today's aestheticians are not ignored, even if they are touched upon more lightly – and some of those touches have been decisive in shaping the direction of contemporary debate. For instance, Tolstoy is primarily interested in questioning the esteem in which art is held, but in the course of doing so offers a brief analysis of artistic expression with which every subsequent analysis has had to engage. Again, Collingwood (chapter 16) would not have described himself as, primarily, engaged in ontology,

[4] Two contemporary philosophers of aesthetics who certainly cannot be accused of narrowness of vision are Richard Wollheim (see, e.g. his *On Art and the Mind*, Cambridge, Mass.: Harvard University Press, 1974) and Stanley Cavell (see e.g., his *Must We Mean What We Say?*, Cambridge: Cambridge University Press, 1976).

but in the course of discussing the distinction between art and craft, and the role of the imagination in understanding emotion, he proposes a view of the status of artworks – as mental entities – around which has revolved much subsequent discussion of ontological questions like 'What *is* a sonata? A score? Its performances? Or what?'

That said, there are certainly some issues debated in recent years which our classic authors do not touch upon at all, or too lightly to have made an impression. Shifts in philosophical priorities, or in the artistic activities which stimulate philosophical musings, have brought new questions to the fore. Thus, while Plato and Aristotle presuppose the representational or 'mimetic' function of art, neither they nor any of our other authors are taxed, in the way we are today, by problems about depiction, such as 'Is it due to an objective resemblance, or to mere convention, that blobs of paint can be said to depict this rather than that?' The prominence of such problems reflects the twentieth century 'linguistic turn' in philosophy and the consequent need to think about the analogies and disanalogies between linguistic and artistic representations of the world. Again, while several of our authors are not shy to provide a certain kind of heady persuasive definition of art – art as the opening up of truth, art as the synthesis of the intellect and the senses, and so on – few of them share present headaches over the criteria for counting something as a work of art, for having a reply ready to the question 'But is it art?' Indeed, the earlier of the writers represented did not even possess our general concept of art over which to have headaches, and even most of the later ones were writing before the episodes in modern art – Duchamps' 'Fountain', 'conceptual art', avant-garde jazz and electronic music, André's 'bricks', and so on – which have exerted pressure on earlier assumptions as to what constituted art.

But if some of today's favourite topics are barely to be found in the texts in this reader, there are many compensations – not only that largeness of vision exhibited in the efforts to 'place' art, to which I referred earlier, but reflection on matters, once deemed central, which have perhaps been too cavalierly marginalized in recent times. For example, from Plato and Plotinus on, it was generally assumed that the primary object of aesthetic appreciation, and indeed artistic production, was ***beauty***. In an age when that is quite clearly ***not*** what many artists try to achieve, and when we are told instead that art is essentially a means of communication or personal expression, this ancient conviction sounds desperately unfashionable. But maybe it deserves revisiting: maybe we have too quickly abandoned the sense of our forefathers that beauty, truth and the good are indissolubly related, so that beauty well deserves its former status as the aesthetic value ***par*** *excellence.*[5] The notion of sublimity, which Kant discussed (see chapter 7, pp. 117 ff), and the idea that the identity of a people is partly, but crucially, forged by its 'paradigmatic' artworks – first mooted by Herder in the eighteenth century, but taken up by Heidegger (chapter 15) – also invite more attention than they currently receive. One purpose of an anthology of historical texts is to remind us not simply of how we arrived where we are, but of what we might have forgotten on arrival.

Despite, or perhaps because of, the fact that aesthetics has occupied a relatively modest position within philosophy, as measured by the volume of words devoted to it, aesthetics is a subject that has attracted a disproportionate number of anthologists. Maybe they have viewed it as less daunting to sift through the literature on aesthetics than that on, say, ethics or epistemology. The present anthology differs from most by restricting the selection of texts to ones written before the middle of this century, thereby permitting a more generous selection of such texts than is usually possible. Some of these texts are self-selecting: it is impossible to imagine a volume meriting the title *Classic Readings* which did not include, for example, Plato on *mimesis*, Hume on taste and Kant on aesthetic judgement. But, in other cases, principles of selection have been at work, not just personal predilection. I doubt if mentioning some of these principles will appease all of those who will complain about the omission of certain texts or the inclusion of others, but it might help.

First, and most obviously, each text needed to be a 'classic' in the sense that it is both renowned and influential. All the texts I have selected certainly pass that test, and if the Chinese and Indian pieces are not known to Western readers, I can only assure these readers that they enjoy 'classic' status within their own traditions. This leads us to a second principle: in keeping with the general policy of this series of readings, selection was not confined to the Western tradition. It is, in my view, a matter for considerable regret that most British and American writers on, and anthologists of, aesthetics show no sign of recognizing that reflection on art and beauty also took place east of Suez. The Chinese tradition in aesthetics is a rich and continuous one, and I have included three Chinese pieces. The Indian tradition is less rich, perhaps, in this area than in others, and I did not judge any of the texts from the classical era of Indian aesthetics suitable for inclusion. Partial amends are made by adding two chapters by the influential twentieth century thinker, A. K. Coomaraswamy, written very much in the line of an ancient tradition.

[5] But maybe beauty is staging a comeback. See especially Mary Mothersill, *Beauty Restored*, Oxford: Clarendon Press, 1984.

Third, and within the constraint imposed by the first principle, I have aimed for maximum variety, in both the topics addressed and the approaches adopted. St Augustine on beauty, Francis Hutcheson on taste, Edmund Burke on the sublime, Nietzsche on tragedy and music, Benedetto Croce on intuition and expression – all these are 'classic' treatments, but would have too closely shadowed Plotinus, Hume, Kant, Schopenhauer and Collingwood respectively, whose treatments of the same topics, in my judgement, pipped their rivals' in importance or in suitability for textual extraction. In accordance with this aim, I have tried to ensure that each major artform is given its due, for of course the different forms give rise to their own distinctive problems. Thus, it is his remarks on music, not the visual arts, which have been chosen from Schopenhauer: otherwise this most philosophically intriguing of the arts would have been scantily covered. (The two Chinese pieces on 'music' are really about the arts in general.)

Finally, I have tried to avoid texts which, however historically and philosophically significant, are so full of technicalities or written in such obscure prose that my preambles to them would have had to dwarf the texts themselves in order to make sense of them for the non-specialist reader. Some of the authors represented – Kant, Hegel and Heidegger, for example – are notoriously difficult: fortunately, however, they tend to be on their least offensive stylistic behaviour when writing about aesthetics. While none of them is easy-going, neither, with the guidance of a lecturer, are they beyond the comprehension of students new to the subject.

The purpose of this volume, evidently, is to acquaint students with the classic texts in the *history* of aesthetics. That it has a history, in the sense of not having sprung up in living memory – in the manner, say, of the philosophy of technology or artificial intelligence – is apparent from the very existence of those texts. Aesthetics is also historical in the rather more interesting sense of allowing for narratives to be told, cogent stories of earlier theories and concepts being developed or disowned by later thinkers, traditions in which certain problems are seen to be central. Thus I have been at some pains in my preambles to the selected texts to indicate, wherever possible, a given philosopher's debt to and legacy to other philosophers. Sometimes the pains have not been especially intense: it hardly needs to be laboured, for instance, how indebted to Plato is Plotinus' account of the relation between beauty and the good, and how that account still resonates in an author like Schiller. Even when there is no actual debt or legacy, it is often illuminating to read a text *as if* it were a reply to an earlier one or helped to shape a later perspective.

I referred just now to narrative*s*, in the plural, for there are some genuinely radical breaks in the history of aesthetics, moments when problems arise or ideas are generated which were foreign to previous times. As I explain in my preambles to the Hume and Kant chapters, for example, their questions about the subjectivity versus objectivity of taste could only have arisen in anything like the form they did *after* the burgeoning of science and 'modern' philosophy in the seventeenth century. Those questions did not and could not have taxed the Greek writers represented. To take a very different example, Shih-t'ao's seventeenth century *Quotes on Painting* (see chapter 5), directed as they are against a long and, as he saw it, exhausted tradition of painting, raises questions about the role of the artist that could not have been salient for those who founded and continued that tradition.

In this sense, then, there is no single 'grand narrative' of aesthetics, no continuous story to be told, from the beginnings of philosophy to the present, of the fate of a single set of issues and concepts. One might guess as much, to return to an earlier point, from the fact that 'aesthetics' is a relatively recent coinage. For what this indicates is that it is only in the modern period that philosophers have thought of the many questions that can be raised about art, beauty, creativity, imagination, expression, and much else, as constituting even a relatively unified set of issues. Whether or not that thought is a sensible one is another matter. It can seem amazing to us that that eminently artisitic people, the Greeks, had no term remotely equivalent to our 'art'. (The nearest was *techne*, but this applied not only to the arts but to many other crafts and skills, including those of soldiering and horsemanship). Yet there are many writers today who find it extremely unnatural – the product of historical accident or, as Dewey suggests, of the bourgeoisie's urge to hive off its predilections from the pleasures of the masses – that such disparate creations as *The Ring of the Nibelungen*, *Hamlet*, *Guernica* and a Persian carpet should all be brought under a single category, art, and be divorced from rock songs, Mills & Boon novels, saucy postcards and 'flying ducks' above the mantelpiece. For these writers, art is an entirely artificial category and, therefore, so is the notion of the aesthetic. Fortunately for the future of aesthetics as a branch of philosophy, this view, even if true, is not threatening. For, to recall the ingenious Protean ploy mentioned above, debates about the artificiality or otherwise of the category have become part of the very subject.

Indeed, to judge from the number of writings appearing on aesthetics and the number of students signing up for aesthetics courses, aesthetics seems assured of a buoyant future. Certainly the subject suffered neglect, at least in the English-language world, for several decades earlier in this century, victim of the emaciated conceptions of philosophy broadcast by the logical positivists and the analysts of 'ordinary language'. If aesthetics were the study, simply, of aesthetic discourse, and if this discourse were 'cognitively meaningless', just a vocabulary of ejaculations of pleasure or disapproval, or if the philosopher's rightful interest in it were confined merely to reporting on the usage of that vocabulary, aesthetics would be a subject that could quicken few people's blood. Moreover, any interesting problems that such a study might throw up would be so similar to those generated by 'evaluative' discourse in general that there could be little point in attending to aesthetic discourse in contrast, say, to that of ethics. Indeed, what happened in practice is that aesthetic questions were simply lumped together with ethical ones.[6]

Those strange, emaciating conceptions of philosophy at large, and of aesthetics in particular, are no longer entertained by many philosophers. One fortunate result of that demise has been a renewed interest in the history of aesthetics, in the writings of men whose agenda was quite obviously both very different from and much richer than anything allowed by the positivists and analysts. And that renewed interest, for which the present reader caters, is, I like to think, an important factor in the recovery of aesthetics from its Cinderella status.

[6] For this treatment of aesthetics, see A. J. Ayer, *Language, Truth and Logic*, London: Gollancz, 1936.

Plato, *The Republic*, Book 10

1

From Plato, *The Republic*, trans. Robin Waterfield. Oxford: Oxford University Press, 1994, pp. 344–63 [2 short passages omitted].

This reader begins, appropriately, with a section from the most famous philosophical work of all, one which contains the first sustained discussion of art in Western literature and the most abidingly influential. Few subsequent discussions of artistic representation and the relations of art to psychology, ethics and politics have failed to engage with Plato on these, the two main topics of Book 10 (595a–608b). The great Athenian philosopher, pupil of Socrates and teacher of Aristotle, who lived from c.427 to 347 BCE, remains the most robust advocate of art's 'heteronomy', its answerability to standards outside itself, for Plato insists that 'artistic values be subject to the sovereignty of truth and morality'.[1] This insistence should not be confused with the demand of Tolstoy (chapter 11) and some Marxists that these values be *defined* in terms of moral or social ones. Plato's *subordination* of artistic to other values presupposes that they can be independently identified.

Book 10 is not the only place in *The Republic*, let alone Plato's dialogues as a whole, in which art and literature are discussed. Earlier, in Books 2–3, he has examined their role – or, rather, lack of one – in the education of the young, especially of the future 'guardians' of the ideal State which it is *The Republic*'s task to describe. By the end of Book 3, he has concluded that most representational poetry, and certainly the enactment of dramatic verse, should be kept out of education, primarily because of the 'lies' it tells and the baleful influence on the young of 'impersonating' evil or corrupt characters. The question is left open, however, as to whether there should be a more stringent, indeed universal, ban on poetry in the State.

The issue is resumed in Book 10, supposedly a conversation between Socrates ('I') and Plato's brother, Glaucon ('He'). By this stage Plato is armed with his

[1] Stephen Halliwell, 'Plato', in D. E. Cooper (ed.), *A Companion to Aesthetics*, Oxford: Blackwell, 1992, p. 327.

theory of the Forms (or 'types' in the present translation), and his accounts of the just State and its ideal citizens. The Forms, which constitute 'true' reality, are abstract entities, ideal exemplars to which everyday objects are at best approximations. The élite in the Republic are the 'philosopher-kings', whose supremely rational capacities afford them knowledge of the realm of the Forms. In ruling others, however, they do what everyone in the just State should do – that is, to stick to performing the socially beneficial task for which one is cut out by nature and education.

All these Platonic views play crucial roles in the Book 10 onslaught on art and literature. Thus the painter – whom Plato discusses before turning to the more important case of the poet – produces only a perspectivally constrained representation or imitation (*mimesis*) of, say, a bed which is itself merely a 'copy' of what is truly real, the Form of beds. Hence, 'representation and truth are a considerable distance apart'. Moreover, the argument continues, producing representations of representations is surely a trivial occupation, no serious and useful contribution to the State. Unlike the people who make and use things, after all, artists have no expert knowledge of what they represent. 'Those who can, do it; those who can't, paint it', so to speak. Worse still, artists trade in and pander to the least rational sides of human nature: the painter to perceptual capacities all too prone to illusion (which he exploits through devices like perspective and shadowing),[2] and the poet to emotions which are typically disreputable and which anyway detract from the controlled life of reason. That last point is behind Plato's 'most serious allegation against representational poetry': its 'terrifying capacity for deforming' people.

In assessing Plato's contemporary relevance, it is important to avoid anachronism: to recognize, for example, that the works of Homer and the tragedians whom he would 'banish' were not considered, as they are today, 'high-brow' art, but the popular literature of the time and, to boot, educational texts and conduits for the dissemination of information and the shaping of public opinion.[3] When like is compared to like, it is easy to understand why Plato should continue to attract or repel. Whether or not they recognize the debt, he should surely appeal to those who would censor pornography on the ground that it presents a false and corrupting image of women; to those who are worried by the modern trend to regard novelists and playwrights as founts of wisdom

[2] See John Hyman, *The Imitation of Nature*, Oxford: Blackwell, 1989, pp. 84ff. Hyman shows that a familiar criticism of Plato, that he regards art as merely reproducing likenesses of things, is misguided. Plato's complaint – itself, no doubt, open to criticism – is that artists produce 'semblances' which are 'deceptive'. For example, in order to depict a row of columns receding into the distance, the areas of paint used to represent the columns must become ever smaller – something that does not correspond to any real difference in the sizes of the columns themselves.

[3] See Alexander Nehemas, 'Plato and the mass media', *Monist*, 71 (1988), pp. 214–34.

on politics and the human condition at large; and to those who wonder if another modern fashion, for 'letting it all hang out' or emotional 'self-expression', is as healthy as its champions assume. Equally, Plato will surely repel those who feel that any strictures on the 'autonomy' of art have, as their logical conclusion, the dead hand clamped upon human creativity by Stalin or the ayatollahs.

'You know', I said, 'the issue of poetry is the main consideration – among 595a
many others – which convinces me that the way we were trying to found our community was along absolutely the right lines.'

'What are you thinking of?' he asked.

'That we flatly refused to admit any representational poetry.[1] I mean, its total unacceptability is even clearer, in my opinion, now that we've distinguished the different aspects of the mind.' 595b

'How is it clearer?'

'Well, this is just between ourselves: please don't denounce me to the tragic playwrights and all the other representational poets. But it looks as though this whole genre of poetry deforms its audience's minds, unless they have the antidote, which is recognition of what this kind of poetry is actually like.'

'What do you mean? What do you have in mind?' he asked.

'It's fairly clear', I said, 'that all these fine tragedians trace their lineage back to Homer: they're Homer's students and disciples, ultimately. And this makes it difficult for me to say what I have to say, because I've had a
kind of fascinated admiration for Homer ever since I was young. Still, we 595c
should value truth more than we value any person, so, as I say, I'd better speak out.'

'Yes', he said.

'And you'll listen to what I have to say, or rather respond to any questions I ask?'

'Yes. Go ahead and ask them.'

'Can you tell me what representation basically is? You see, I don't quite understand its point myself.'

'And I suppose I do!' he said.

'It wouldn't surprise me if you did', I said. 'Just because a person can't
see very well, it doesn't mean that he won't often see things before people 596a
with better eyesight than him.'

'That's true', he said. 'All the same, I'd be too shy to explain any views I did have in front of you, so please try to come up with an answer yourself.'

'All right. Shall we get the enquiry going by drawing on familiar ideas? Our usual position is, as you know, that any given plurality of things which have a single name constitutes a single specific type [Form. Ed.]. Is that clear to you?'

'Yes.'

'So now let's take any plurality you want. Would it be all right with you
596b if we said that there were, for instance, lots of beds and tables?'

'Of course.'

'But these items of furniture comprise only two types – the type of bed and the type of table.'

'Yes.'

'Now, we also invariably claim that the manufacture of either of these items of furniture involves the craftsman looking to the type and then making the beds or tables (or whatever) which we use. The point is that the type itself is not manufactured by any craftsman. How could it be?'

'It couldn't.'

'There's another kind of craftsman too. I wonder what you think of him.'

596c 'What kind?'

'He makes everything – all the items which every single manufacturer makes.'

'He must be extraordinarily gifted.'

'Wait: you haven't heard the half of it yet. It's not just a case of his being able to manufacture all the artefacts there are: every plant too, every creature (himself included), the earth, the heavens, gods, and everything in the heavens and in Hades under the earth – all these are made and created by this one man!'

596d 'He really must be extraordinarily clever', he said.

'Don't you believe me?' I asked. 'Tell me, do you doubt that this kind of craftsman could exist under any circumstances, or do you admit the possibility that a person could – in one sense, at least – create all these things? I mean, don't you realize that you yourself could, under certain circumstances, create all these things?'

'What circumstances?' he asked.

'I'm not talking about anything complicated or rare', I said. 'It doesn't take long to create the circumstances. The quickest method, I suppose, is to
596e get hold of a mirror and carry it around with you everywhere. You'll soon be creating everything I mentioned a moment ago – the sun and the heavenly bodies, the earth, yourself, and all other creatures, plants, and so on.'

'Yes, but I'd be creating appearances, not actual real things', he said.

'That's a good point', I said. 'You've arrived just in time to save the argument. I mean, that's presumably the kind of craftsman a painter is. Yes?'

'Of course.'

'His creations aren't real, according to you; but do you agree that all the same there's a sense in which even a painter creates a bed?'

'Yes', he said, 'he's another one who creates an apparent bed.' 597a

'What about a joiner who specializes in making beds? Weren't we saying a short while ago that what he makes is a particular bed, not the type, which is (on our view) the real bed?'

'Yes, we were.'

'So if there's no reality to his creation, then it isn't real; it's similar to something real, but it isn't actually real. It looks as though it's wrong to attribute full reality to a joiner's or any artisan's product, doesn't it?'

'Yes', he said, 'any serious student of this kind of argument would agree with you.'

'It shouldn't surprise us, then, if we find that even these products are obscure when compared with the truth.'

'No, it shouldn't.' 597b

'Now, what about this representer we're trying to understand? Shall we see if these examples help us?' I asked.

'That's fine by me', he said.

'Well, we've got these three beds. First, there's the real one, and we'd say, I imagine, that it is the product of divine craftsmanship. I mean, who else could have made it?'

'No one, surely.'

'Then there's the one the joiner makes.'

'Yes', he said.

'And then there's the one the painter makes. Yes?'

'Yes, agreed.'

'These three, then – painter, joiner, God – are responsible for three different kinds of bed.'

'Yes, that's right.'

'Now, God has produced only that one real bed. The restriction to only 597c
one might have been his own choice, or it might just be impossible for him to make more than one. But God never has, and never could, create two or more such beds.'

'Why not?' he asked.

'Even if he were to make only two such beds', I said, 'an extra one would emerge, and both the other two would be of that one's type. It, and not the two beds, would be the real bed.'

'Right', he said.

'God realized this, I'm sure. He didn't want to be a kind of joiner, 597d making a particular bed: he wanted to be a genuine creator and make a genuine bed. That's why he created a single real one.'

'I suppose that's right.'

'Shall we call him its progenitor, then, or something like that?'

'Yes, he deserves the name', he said, 'since he's the maker of this and every other reality.'

'What about a joiner? Shall we call him a manufacturer of beds?'

'Yes.'

'And shall we also call a painter a manufacturer and maker of beds and so on?'

'No, definitely not.'

'What do you think he does with beds, then?'

597e 'I think the most suitable thing to call him would be a representer of the others' creations', he said.

'Well, in that case', I said, 'you're using the term "representer" for someone who deals with things which are, in fact, two generations away from reality, aren't you?'

'Yes', he said.

'The same goes for tragic playwrights, then, since they're representers: they're two generations away from the throne of truth, and so are all other representers.'

'I suppose so.'

'Well, in the context of what we're now saying about representation, I've got a further question about painters. Is it, in any given instance, the
598a actual reality that they try to represent, or is it the craftsmen's products?'

'The craftsmen's products', he said.

'Here's another distinction you'd better make: do they try to represent them as they are, or as they appear to be?'

'What do you mean?' he asked.

'I'll tell you. Whether you look at a bed from the side or straight on or whatever, it's still just as much a bed as it ever was, isn't it? I mean, it doesn't actually alter it at all: it just *appears* to be different, doesn't it? And the same goes for anything else you can mention. Yes?'

'Yes', he agreed. 'It seems different, but isn't actually.'

598b 'So I want you to consider carefully which of these two alternatives painting is designed for in any and every instance. Is it designed to represent the facts of the real world or appearances? Does it represent appearance or truth?'

'Appearance', he said.

'It follows that representation and truth are a considerable distance apart, and a representer is capable of making every product there is only because

his contact with things is slight and is restricted to how they look. Consider
what a painter does, for instance: we're saying that he doesn't have a clue
about shoemaking or joinery, but he'll still paint pictures of artisans working at these and all other areas of expertise, and if he's good at painting he 597e
might paint a joiner, have people look at it from far away, and deceive them
– if they're children or stupid adults – by making it look as though the
joiner were real.'

'Naturally.'

'I think the important thing to bear in mind about cases like this,
Glaucon, is that when people tell us they've met someone who's mas-
tered every craft, and is the world's leading expert in absolutely every
branch of human knowledge, we should reply that they're being rather
silly. They seem to have met the kind of illusionist who's expert at repre- 598d
sentation and, thanks to their own inability to evaluate knowledge, ignorance, and representation, to have been so thoroughly taken in as to believe
in his omniscience.'

'You're absolutely right', he said.

'Now, we'd better investigate tragedy next', I said, 'and its guru, Homer,
because one does come across the claim that there's no area of expertise,
and nothing relevant to human goodness and badness either – and nothing 598e
to do with the gods even – that these poets don't understand. It is said that
a good poet must understand the issues he writes about, if his writing is to
be successful, and that if he didn't understand them, he wouldn't be able
to write about them. So we'd better try to decide between the alternatives.
Either the people who come across these representational poets are being
taken in and are failing to appreciate, when they see their products, that
these products are two steps away from reality and that it certainly doesn't 599a
take knowledge of the truth to create them (since what they're creating are
appearances, not reality); or this view is valid, and in fact good poets are
authorities on the subjects most people are convinced they're good at writing about.'

'Yes, this definitely needs looking into', he said.

'Well, do you think that anyone who was capable of producing both originals and images would devote his energy to making images, and would make out that this is the best thing he's done with his life?'

'No, I don't.'

'I'm sure that if he really knew about the things he was copying in his representations, he'd put far more effort into producing real objects than he would into representations, and would try to leave behind a lot of fine products for people to remember him by, and would dedicate himself to being the recipient rather than the bestower of praise.'

'I agree', he said. 'He'd gain a lot more prestige and do himself a great deal more good.'

'Well, let's concentrate our interrogation of Homer (or any other poet
599c you like) on a single area. Let's not ask him whether he can tell us of any
patients cured by any poet in ancient or modern times, as Asclepius cured
his patients, or of any students any of them left to continue his work, as
Asclepius left his sons. And even these questions grant the possibility that a
poet might have had some medical knowledge, instead of merely representing medical terminology. No, let's not bother to ask him about any
other areas of expertise either. But we do have a right to ask Homer about
the most important and glorious areas he undertakes to expound – war-
599d fare, tactics, politics, and human education. Let's ask him, politely, "Homer,
maybe you aren't two steps away from knowing the truth about goodness;
maybe you aren't involved in the manufacture of images (which is what we
called representation). Perhaps you're actually only one step away, and you
do have the ability to recognize which practices – in their private or their
public lives – improve people and which ones impair them. But in that
case, just as Sparta has its Lycurgus and communities of all different sizes
have their various reformers, please tell us which community has you to
599e thank for improvements to its government. Which community attributes
the benefits of its good legal code to you? Italy and Sicily name Charondas
in this respect, we Athenians name Solon. Which country names you?"
Will he have any reply to make?'

'I don't think so', said Glaucon. 'Even the Homeridae [devotees of Homer. Ed.] themselves don't make that claim.'

600a 'Well, does history record that there was any war fought in Homer's
time whose success depended on his leadership or advice?'

'No.'

'Well then, are a lot of ingenious inventions attributed to him, as they are to Thales of Miletus and Anacharsis of Scythia? I mean the kinds of inventions which have practical applications in the arts and crafts and elsewhere. He is, after all, supposed to be good at creating things.'

'No, there's not the slightest hint of that sort of thing.'

'All right, so there's no evidence of his having been a public benefactor,
but what about in private? Is there any evidence that, during his lifetime,
he was a mentor to people, and that they used to value him for his teaching
600b and then handed down to their successors a particular Homeric way of
life? . . .'

'No, there's no hint of that sort of thing either', he said. . . .

600c 'But, Glaucon, if Homer really had been an educational expert whose
products were better people – which is to say, if he had knowledge in this

sphere and his abilities were not limited to representation – don't you think
he'd have been surrounded by hordes of associates, who would have admired him and valued his company highly? . . . So if Homer or Hesiod had 600d
been able to help people's moral development, would their contemporar-
ies have allowed them to go from town to town reciting their poems?
Wouldn't they have kept a tighter grip on them than on their money, and
tried to force them to stay with them in their homes? And if they couldn't
persuade them to do that, wouldn't they have danced attendance on them 600e
wherever they went, until they'd gained as much from their teaching as
they could?'

'I don't think anyone could disagree with you, Socrates', he said.

'So shall we classify all poets, from Homer onwards, as representers of
images of goodness (and of everything else which occurs in their poetry),
and claim that they don't have any contact with the truth? The facts are as
we said a short while ago: a painter creates an illusory shoemaker, when not
only does he not understand anything about shoemaking, but his audience 601a
doesn't either. They just base their conclusions on the colours and shapes
they can see.'

'Yes.'

'And I should think we'll say that the same goes for a poet as well: he
uses words and phrases to block in some of the colours of each area of
expertise, although all he understands is how to represent things in a way
which makes other superficial people, who base their conclusions on the
words they can hear, think that he's written a really good poem about
shoemaking or military command or whatever else it is that he's set to
metre, rhythm, and music. It only takes these features to cast this powerful
a spell: that's what they're for. But when the poets' work is stripped of its 601b
musical hues and expressed in plain words, I think you've seen what kind
of impression it gives, so you know what I'm talking about.'

'I do', he said.

'Isn't it', I asked, 'like what noticeably happens when a young man has alluring features, without actually being good-looking, and then this charm of his deserts him?'

'Exactly', he said.

'Now, here's another point to consider. An image-maker, a representer,
understands only appearance, while reality is beyond him. Isn't that our 601c
position?'

'Yes.'

'Let's not leave the job half done: let's give this idea the consideration it deserves.'

'Go on', he said.

'What a painter does, we're saying, is paint a picture of a horse's reins and a bit. Yes?'

'Yes.'

'While they're made by a saddler and a smith, aren't they?'

'Yes.'

'Does a painter know what the reins and the bit have to be like? Surely even their makers, the smith and the saddler, don't know this, do they? Only the horseman does, because he's the one who knows how to make use of them.'

'You're quite right.'

'In fact, won't we claim that it's a general principle?'

'What?'

601d 'That whatever the object, there are three areas of expertise: usage, manufacture, and representation.'

'Yes.'

'Now, is there any other standard by which one assesses the goodness, fineness, and rightness of anything (whether it's a piece of equipment or a creature or an activity) than the use for which it was made, by man or by nature?'

'No.'

'It's absolutely inevitable, then, that no one knows the ins and outs of any object more than the person who makes use of it. He has to be the one to tell the manufacturer how well or badly the object he's using fares in actual usage. A pipe-player, for example, tells a pipe-maker which of his
601e pipes do what they're supposed to do when actually played, and goes on to instruct him in what kinds of pipes to make, and the pipe-maker does what he's told.'

'Of course.'

'So as far as good and bad pipes are concerned, it's a knowledgeable person who gives the orders, while the other obeys the orders and does the manufacturing. Right?'

'Yes.'

'Justified confidence, then, is what a pipe-maker has about goodness and badness (as a result of spending time with a knowledgeable person and
602a having to listen to him), while knowledge is the province of the person who makes use of the pipes.'

'Yes.'

'Which of these two categories does our representer belong to? Does he acquire knowledge about whether or not what he's painting is good or right from making use of the object, or does he acquire true belief because of having to spend time with a knowledgeable person and being told what to paint?'

'He doesn't fit either case.'

'As far as goodness and badness are concerned, then, a representer doesn't have either knowledge or true beliefs about whatever it is he's representing.'

'Apparently not.'

'How nicely placed a poetic representer is, then, to know what he's writing about!'

'Not really.'

'No, because all the same, despite his ignorance of the good and bad 602b
aspects of things, he'll go on representing them. But what he'll be representing, apparently, is whatever appeals to a large, if ignorant, audience.'

'Naturally.'

'Here are the points we seem to have reached a reasonable measure of agreement on, then: a representer knows nothing of value about the things he represents; representation is a kind of game, and shouldn't be taken seriously; and those who compose tragedies in iambic and epic verse are, without exception, outstanding examples of representers.'

'Yes.'

'So the province of representation is indeed two steps removed from 602c
truth, isn't it?' I said.

'Yes.'

'But on which of the many aspects of a person does it exert its influence?'

'What are you getting at?'

'Something like this. One and the same object appears to vary in size depending on whether we're looking at it from close up or far away.'

'Yes.'

'And the same objects look both bent and straight depending on whether we look at them when they're in water or out of it, and both concave and convex because sight gets misled by colouring. Our mind obviously contains the potential for every single kind of confusion like this. It's because 602d
illusory painting aims at this affliction in our nature that it can only be described as sorcery; and the same goes for conjuring and all trickery of that sort.'

'True.'

'Now, methods have evolved of combating this – measuring, counting, and weighing are the most elegant of them – and consequently of ending the reign within us of apparent size, number, and weight, and replacing them with something which calculates and measures, or even weighs. Right?'

'Of course.'

'And this, of course, is the job of the rational part of the mind, which is 602e capable of performing calculations.'

'Yes.'

'Now, it's not uncommon for the mind to have made its measurements, and to be reporting that *x* is larger than *y* (or smaller than it, or the same size as it), but still to be receiving an impression which contradicts its measurements of these very objects.'

'Yes.'

'Well, didn't we say that it's impossible for a single thing to hold contradictory beliefs at the same time about the same objects?' [436b, 439b. Ed.]

'Yes, we did, and we were right.'

603a 'So the part of the mind whose views run counter to the measurements must be different from the part whose views fall in with the measurements.'

'Yes.'

'But it's the best part of the mind which accepts measurements and calculations.'

'Of course.'

'The part which opposes them, therefore, must be a low-grade part of the mind.'

'Necessarily.'

'Well, all that I've been saying has been intended to bring us to the point where we can agree that not only does painting – or rather representation in general – produce a product which is far from truth, but it also forms a close, warm, affectionate relationship with a part of us which is, in its turn,
603b far from intelligence. And nothing healthy or authentic can emerge from this relationship.'

'Absolutely', he said.

'A low-grade mother like representation, then, and an equally low-grade father produce low-grade children.'

'I suppose that's right.'

'Does this apply only to visual representation', I asked, 'or to aural representation as well – in other words, to poetry?'

'I suppose it applies to poetry as well', he said.

'Well, we'd better not rely on mere suppositions based on painting,' I
603c said. 'Let's also get close enough to that part of the mind which poetic representation consorts with to see whether it's of low or high quality.'

'Yes, we should.'

'We'd better start by having certain ideas out in the open. We'd say that representational poetry represents people doing things, willingly or unwillingly, and afterwards thinking that they've been successful or unsuccessful, and throughout feeling distressed or happy. Have I missed anything out?'

'No, nothing.'

'Well, does a person remain internally unanimous throughout all this?
We found that, in the case of sight, there's conflict and people have contra- 603d
dictory views within themselves at the same time about the same objects. Is it like that when one is doing things too? Is there internal conflict and dissent? But it occurs to me that there's really no need for us to decide where we stand on this issue now, because we've already done so, perfectly adequately, in an earlier phase of the discussion [439c–441b. Ed.], when we concluded that, at any given moment, our minds are teeming with countless thousands of these kinds of contradictions.'

'That's right', he said.

'Yes,' I said. 'But that earlier discussion of ours was incomplete, and I
think it's crucial that we finish it off now.' 603e

'What have we left out?' he asked.

'If a good man meets with a misfortune such as losing a son or something else he values very highly, we've already said, as you know, that he'll endure this better than anyone else.' [387d–e. Ed.]

'Yes.'

'But here's something for us to think about. Will he feel no grief, or is that impossible? If it's impossible, is it just that he somehow keeps his pain within moderate bounds?'

'The second alternative is closer to the truth', he said.

'But now I've got another question for you about him. Do you think 604a
he'll be more likely to fight and resist his distress when his peers can see him, or when he's alone by himself in some secluded spot?'

'He'll endure pain far better when there are people who can see him, of course', he said.

'When he's all alone, however, I imagine he won't stop himself expressing a lot of things he'd be ashamed of anyone hearing, and doing a lot of things he'd hate anyone to see him do.'

'That's right', he agreed.

'Isn't it the case that reason and convention recommend resistance, while
the actual event pushes him towards distress?' 604b

'True.'

'When a person is simultaneously pulled in opposite directions in response to a single object, we're bound to conclude that he has two sides.'

'Of course.'

'One of which is prepared to let convention dictate the proper course of action, isn't it?'

'Can you explain how?'

'Convention tells us, as you know, that it's best to remain as unruffled as

possible when disaster strikes and not to get upset, on the grounds that it's
never clear whether an incident of this nature is good or bad, that nothing
positive is gained by taking it badly, that no aspect of human life is worth
604c bothering about a great deal, and that grief blocks our access to the very
thing we need to have available as quickly as possible in these circumstances.'

'What do you have in mind?' he asked.

'The ability to think about the incident', I replied, 'and, under the guidance of reason, to make the best possible use of one's situation, as one
would in a game of dice when faced with how the dice had fallen. When
children bump into things, they clutch the hurt spot and spend time cry-
ing; instead of behaving like that, we should constantly be training our
604d minds to waste no time before trying to heal anything which is unwell, and
help anything which has fallen get up from the floor – to banish mourning
by means of medicine.'

'Yes, that's the best way to deal with misfortune', he said.

'Now, our position is that the best part of our minds is perfectly happy to
be guided by reason like this.'

'That goes without saying.'

'Whereas there's another part of our minds which urges us to remember
the bad times and to express our grief, and which is insatiably greedy for
tears. What can we say about it? That it's incapable of listening to reason,
that it can't face hard work, that it goes hand in hand with being frightened
of hardship?'

'Yes, that's right.'

604e 'Now, although the petulant part of us is rich in a variety of represent-
able possibilities, the intelligent and calm side of our characters is pretty
well constant and unchanging. This makes it not only difficult to represent, but also difficult to understand when it is represented, particularly
when the audience is the kind of motley crowd you find crammed into a
theatre, because they're simply not acquainted with the experience that's
being represented to them.'

605a 'Absolutely.'

'Evidently, then, a representational poet has nothing to do with this part
of the mind: his skill isn't made for its pleasure, because otherwise he'd
lose his popular appeal. He's concerned with the petulant and varied side
of our characters, because it's easy to represent.'

'Obviously.'

'So we're now in a position to see that we'd be perfectly justified in
taking hold of him and placing him in the same category as a painter. He
resembles a painter because his creations fall short of truth, and a further
605b point of resemblance is that the part of the mind he communicates with is

not the best part, but something else. Now we can see how right we'd be to refuse him admission into any community which is going to respect convention, because now we know which part of the mind he wakes up. He destroys the rational part by feeding and fattening up this other part, and this is equivalent to someone destroying the more civilized members of a community by presenting ruffians with political power. There's no difference, we'll claim, between this and what a representational poet does: at a personal level, he establishes a bad system of government in people's minds by gratifying their irrational side, which can't even recognize what
size things are – an object which at one moment it calls big, it might call 605c
small the next moment – by creating images, and by being far removed from truth.'

'Yes.'

'However, we haven't yet made the most serious allegation against representational poetry. It has a terrifying capacity for deforming even good people. Only a very few escape.'

'Yes, that *is* terrifying. Does it really do that?'

'Here's my evidence: you can make up your own mind. When Homer or another tragedian represents the grief of one of the heroes, they have him
deliver a lengthy speech of lamentation or even have him sing a dirge and 605d
beat his breast; and when we listen to all this, even the best of us, as I'm sure you're aware, feels pleasure. We surrender ourselves, let ourselves be carried along, and share the hero's pain; and then we enthuse about the skill of any poet who makes us feel particularly strong feelings.'

'Yes, I'm aware of this, of course.'

'However, you also appreciate that when we're afflicted by trouble in our own lives, then we take pride in the opposite – in our ability to endure
pain without being upset. We think that this is manly behaviour, and that 605e
only women behave in the way we were sanctioning earlier.'

'I realize that', he said.

'So', I said, 'instead of being repulsed by the sight of the kind of person we'd regret and deplore being ourselves, we enjoy the spectacle and sanction it. Is this a proper way to behave?'

'No, it certainly isn't', he said. 'It's pretty unreasonable, I'd say.'

'I agree', I said, 'and here's even more evidence.' 606a

'What?'

'Consider this. What a poet satisfies and gratifies on these occasions is an aspect of ourselves which we forcibly restrain when tragedy strikes our own lives – an aspect which hungers after tears and the satisfaction of having cried until one can cry no more, since that is what it is in its nature to want to do. When the part of us which is inherently good has been inadequately

trained in habits enjoined by reason, it relaxes its guard over this other
606b part, the part which feels sad. Other people, not ourselves, are feeling these
feelings, we tell ourselves, and it's no disgrace for us to sanction such behaviour and feel sorry for someone who, even while claiming to be good, is
over-indulging in grief; and, we think, we are at least profiting from the
pleasure, and there's no point in throwing away the pleasure by spurning
the whole poem or play. You see, few people have the ability to work out
that we ourselves are bound to store the harvest we reap from others: these
occasions feed the feeling of sadness until it is too strong for us easily to
restrain it when hardship occurs in our own lives.'

606c 'You're absolutely right', he said.

'And doesn't the same go for humour as well? If there are amusing things
which you'd be ashamed to do yourself, but which give you a great deal of
pleasure when you see them in a comic representation or hear about them
in private company – when you don't find them loathsome and repulsive –
then isn't this exactly the same kind of behaviour as we uncovered when
talking about feeling sad? There's a part of you which wants to make people laugh, but your reason restrains it, because you're afraid of being thought
a vulgar clown. Nevertheless, you let it have its way on those other occasions, and you don't realize that the almost inevitable result of giving it
energy in this other context is that you become a comedian in your own
life.'

606d 'Yes, that's very true', he said.

'And the same goes for sex, anger, and all the desires and feelings of
pleasure and distress which, we're saying, accompany everything we do:
poetic representation has the same effect in all these cases too. It irrigates
and tends to these things when they should be left to wither, and it makes
them our rulers when they should be our subjects, because otherwise we
won't live better and happier lives, but quite the opposite.'

'I can't deny the truth of what you're saying', he said.

606e 'Therefore, Glaucon', I went on, 'when you come across people praising
Homer and saying that he is the poet who has educated Greece, that he's a
good source for people to learn how to manage their affairs and gain culture
in their lives, and that one should structure the whole of one's life in accord-
607a ance with his precepts, you ought to be kind and considerate: after all, they're
doing the best they can. You should concede that Homer is a supreme poet
and the original tragedian, but you should also recognize that the only
poems we can admit into our community are hymns to the gods and eulogies of virtuous men. If you admit the entertaining Muse of lyric and epic
poetry, then instead of law and the shared acceptance of reason as the best
guide, the kings of your community will be pleasure and pain.'

'You're quite right', he agreed.

'So,' I said, 'since we've been giving poetry another hearing, there's our 607b
defence: given its nature, we had good grounds for banishing it earlier
from our community. No rational person could have done any different.
However, poetry might accuse us of insensitivity and lack of culture, so
we'd better also tell her that there's an ancient quarrel between poetry and
philosophy. . . . All the same, we ought to point out that if the kinds of 607c
poetry and representation which are designed merely to give pleasure can
come up with a rational argument for their inclusion in a well-governed
community, we'd be delighted – short of compromising the truth as we see
it, which wouldn't be right – to bring them back from exile: after all, we
know from our own experience all about their spell. I mean, haven't *you*
ever fallen under the spell of poetry, Glaucon, especially when the spectacle
is provided by Homer?' 607d

'I certainly have.'

'Under these circumstances, then, if our allegations met a poetic rebuttal in lyric verse or whatever, would we be justified in letting poetry return?'

'Yes.'

'And I suppose we'd also allow people who champion poetry because
they like it, even though they can't compose it, to speak on its behalf in
prose, and to try to prove that there's more to poetry than mere pleasure –
that it also has a beneficial effect on society and on human life in general.
And we won't listen in a hostile frame of mind, because we'll be the win- 607e
ners if poetry turns out to be beneficial as well as enjoyable.'

'Of course we will', he agreed.

'And if it doesn't, Glaucon, then we'll do what a lover does when he
thinks that a love affair he's involved in is no good for him: he reluctantly
detaches himself. Similarly, since we've been conditioned by our wonderful
societies until we have deep-seated love for this kind of poetry, we'll be 608a
delighted if there proves to be nothing better and closer to the truth than
it. As long as it is incapable of rebutting our allegations, however, then
while we listen to poetry we'll be chanting these allegations of ours to
ourselves as a precautionary incantation against being caught once more
by that childish and pervasive love. Our message will be that the commitment appropriate for an important matter with access to the truth shouldn't
be given to this kind of poetry. People should, instead, be worried about
the possible effects, on one's own inner political system, of listening to it
and should tread cautiously; and they should let our arguments guide their 608b
attitude towards poetry.'

'I couldn't agree more', he said.

'You see, my dear Glaucon', I said, 'what's in the balance here is absolutely critical – far more so than people think. It's whether one becomes a good or a bad person, and consequently has the calibre not to be distracted by prestige, wealth, political power, or even poetry from applying oneself to morality and whatever else goodness involves.'

'Looking back over our discussion', he said, 'I can only agree with you. And I think anyone else would do the same as well.'

Note

1 As I pointed out in my introductory remarks, Plato had not in fact arrived at such a swingeing refusal earlier in the book.

Aristotle, *Poetics*, Chapters 1–15

2

From J. L. Ackrill (ed.), *A New Aristotle Reader*, trans. M. E. Hubbard. Oxford: Clarendon Press, 1987, pp. 540–56 [ch. 12 and some passages omitted; words and phrases in square brackets, unless followed by 'Ed.' are the translator's].

People who have only glanced at Aristotle's *Poetics* may be surprised to hear that it is one of the 'most living' of his writings.[1] It is drily written and full of recondite information and critical comments on Greek dramas most of which have been lost. Nevertheless it also contains several, tantalizingly brief, statements which have proved seminal. (This is not to say that all later appeals to Aristotle's authority have been justified: his doctrine of dramatic unity was as badly mangled by Renaissance arbiters of theatrical taste as his concept of *catharsis* ('cleansing') was by Victorian psychiatrists.) As with biology, logic, metaphysics and political science, the legacy to the theory of art of the great Macedonian-born thinker, who lived from 384 to 322 BCE, has decisively shaped Western thought.

Aristotle is the first philosopher on record to appreciate the distinctive functions of art, the manner in which it is encountered or experienced, and the value it can have independent of straightforwardly moral and political goals. In all of this, there is an implicit repudiation of Plato, his teacher. Because the artist *is* an artist, it is irrelevant to accuse him of being inexpert in other matters; because artworks are experienced *as* artworks, it is misguided to condemn their devices as deceptive and to suppose that their impact on the emotions is like that of actual events; and because art has its *own* contribution to make towards the good life, it is wrong to judge it by political criteria.

It is profitable to read the *Poetics* as taking up the challenge in *The Republic* to show that art might bring, not only pleasure, but benefit to human life and have serious value and a claim to truth. For Aristotle is anxious to establish that good art can benefit both the understanding and the emotions – or, better, that in doing either of these, it does both, for Aristotle rejects Plato's Manichaean divide between reason and the passions. Far from the latter

[1] W. D. Ross, *Aristotle*, London: Methuen, 1949, p. 276.

always being a distraction from the life of reason, it will often be *ir*rational not to feel shame or anger, say. Mature understanding and mature emotional sensitivity are inseparable ingredients in the good life of a person. And art can contribute to both.

Art, for Aristotle as for Plato, is indeed *mimesis*, representation or 'imitation', but this does not mean that it is hopelessly removed from the realm of true understanding. The intellect is already engaged in recognizing what is represented (a recognition which is the source of the pleasure yielded by artworks); and in representing the actions of human beings, poetry is able to convey 'general' truths about our condition, ones which accord with the 'probable and necessary', unlike history which merely records particular, contingent events. This is why poetry is 'like philosophy'. (Here Aristotle is taking a swipe at Plato's reference to the 'ancient quarrel' between philosophy and poetry.) Far from having no claim to truth, then, 'what imitation reveals is precisely the real essence of the thing',[2] particularly of human nature and the moral order.

As for the emotions, the point of Aristotle's brief and variously interpreted remark on tragedy's 'effecting through pity and fear the *catharsis* of such emotions' is not, primarily, that art offers psychotherapy through, as it were, providing homeopathic doses of feelings we want to be rid of. Rather, a well-wrought tragedy enables us to 'refine' and educate the emotions by recognizing their appropriateness or otherwise to the structured actions and their outcomes represented on the stage.[3] (In his *Politics*, incidentally, Aristotle refers to a further discussion of *catharsis* in another, now lost, work on poetry.)

It is his attempt to locate the value of art in relation to our intimately associated capacities for understanding and feeling, and not in his recipes for plot construction, character delineation and the like, that readers are likely to discern the abiding importance of Aristotle's *Poetics*.

Chapter 1

1447a The subject I wish to discuss is poetry itself, its species with their respective capabilities, the correct way of constructing plots so that the work turns out well, the number and nature of the constituent elements [of each species], and anything else in the same field of enquiry.

To follow the natural order and take first things first, epic and tragic poetry, comedy and dithyrambic, and most music for the flute or lyre are all, generally considered, varieties of *mimēsis*, differing from each other in

[2] Hans-Georg Gadamer, *The Relevance of the Beautiful and Other Essays*, Cambridge: Cambridge University Press, 1986, p. 99.
[3] See Stephen Halliwell, *Aristotle's* Poetics, London: Duckworth, 1986.

three respects, the media, the objects, and the mode of ***mimēsis***. In some cases where people, whether by technical rules or practised facility, produce various ***mimēseis*** by portraying things, the media are colours and shapes, while in others the medium is the voice; similarly in the arts in question, taken collectively, the media of ***mimēsis*** are rhythm, speech, and harmony, either separately or in combination.

For example, harmony and rhythm are the media of instrumental music, rhythm alone without harmony the medium of dancing, as dancers represent characters, passions, and actions by rhythmic movement and postures.

The art that uses only speech by itself or verse, the verses being homoge- 1447b
neous or of different kinds, has as yet no name; for we have no common term to apply to the [prose] mimes of Sophron and Xenarchus and to the Socratic dialogues, nor any common term for ***mimēseis*** produced in verse, whether iambic trimeters or elegiacs or some other such metre. True, people do attach the making [that is the root of the word *poiētēs*] to the name of a metre and speak of elegiac-makers and hexameter-makers; they think no doubt, that 'makers' is applied to poets not because they make ***mimēseis*** but as a general term meaning 'verse-makers', since they call 'poets' or 'makers' even those who publish a medical or scientific theory in verse. But (1) as Homer and Empedocles have nothing in common except their metre, the latter had better be called a scientific writer, not a poet, if we are to use 'poet' of the former; (2) similarly, if we suppose a man to make his ***mimēsis*** in a medley of all metres, as Chaeremon in fact did in the *Centaur*, a recitation-piece in all the various metres, we still have to call him a poet, a 'maker'.

So much for the simpler kinds. Some use all the media mentioned, rhythm, song, and verse: these are dithyrambic and nomic poetry, tragedy, and comedy. But the two former use them all simultaneously, while the latter use different media in different parts. So much for the differentiae derived from the media.

Chapter 2

The objects of this ***mimēsis*** are people doing things, and these people must 1448a
necessarily be either good or bad, this being, generally speaking, the only line of divergence between characters, since differences of character just are differences in goodness and badness, or else they must be better than are found in the world or worse or just the same, as they are represented by the painters, Polygnotus portraying them as better, Pauson as worse, and Dionysius as they are; clearly therefore each of the varieties of ***mimēsis*** in

question will exhibit these differences, and one will be distinguishable from another in virtue of presenting things as different in this way.

These dissimilarities can in fact be found in dancing and instrumental music, and in the arts using speech and unaccompanied verse: Homer for instance represents people as better and Cleophon as they are, while Hegemon of Thasos, the inventor of parodies, and Nicochares, the author of the *Deiliad*, represent them as worse . . .; this is also the differentia that marks off tragedy from comedy, since the latter aims to represent people as worse, the former as better, than the men of the present day.

Chapter 3

There is still a third difference, the mode in which one represents each of these objects. For one can represent the same objects in the same media

(i) sometimes in narration and sometimes becoming someone else, as Homer does; or
(ii) speaking in one's own person without change, or
(iii) with all the people engaged in the *mimēsis* actually doing things.

These three then, media, objects, and mode, are, as I said at the beginning, the differentiae of poetic *mimēsis*. So, if we use one of them [to separate poets into classes], Sophocles will be in the same class as Homer, since both represent people as good, and if we use another, he will be in the same class as Aristophanes, since they both represent people as actively doing things. . . .

1448b So much for the number and nature of the differentiae of poetic *mimēsis*.

Chapter 4

Poetry, I believe, has two overall causes, both of them natural:

(*a*) *Mimēsis* is innate in human beings from childhood – indeed we differ from the other animals in being most given to *mimēsis* and in making our first steps in learning through it – and pleasure in instances of *mimēsis* is equally general. This we can see from the facts: we enjoy looking at the most exact portrayals of things we do not like to see in real life, the lowest animals, for instance, or corpses. This is because not only philosophers, but all men, enjoy getting to understand something, though it is true that most people feel this pleasure only to a slight degree; therefore they like to see these pictures, because in looking at them they come to understand something and can infer what each thing is, can say, for instance, 'This man in the picture is so-and-so.' If you happen not to have seen the original, the picture will not produce its pleasure *qua* instance of *mimēsis*, but because of its technical finish or colour or for some such other reason.

(*b*) As well as *mimēsis*, harmony and rhythm are natural to us, and verses are obviously definite sections of rhythm. . . .

To enquire whether even tragedy [as distinct from epic] is sufficiently elabo- 1449a
rated in its qualitative elements, judging it in itself and in its relation to the audience, is another story. At any rate, after originating in the improvizations of the leaders of the dithyramb, as comedy did in those of the leaders of the phallic songs still customary in many Greek cities, tragedy gradually grew to maturity, as people developed the capacities they kept discovering in it, and after many changes it stopped altering, since it had attained its full growth. The main changes were:

(i) in the number of actors, raised from one to two by Aeschylus, who made the choral part less important and gave speech the leading role; Sophocles added a third – and also scene-painting;
(ii) in amplitude: as tragedy developed from the satyr-style, its plots were at first slight and its expression comical, and it was a long time before it acquired dignity;
(iii) in metre: the iambic trimeter replaced the trochaic tetrameter, which had been used before as suitable for a satyr-style poetry, that is, for productions involving more dancing; when verbal expression came to the fore, however, nature herself found the right metre, the iambic being the most speakable of all metres; this we can see from the fact that it is the one we most often produce accidentally in conversation, where hexameters are rare and only occur when we depart from conversational tone;
(iv) in the increased number of episodes.

There is no need to say more of this or of the other developments that gave it beauty; it would take too long to go through them in detail.

Chapter 5

Comedy is, as I said, a *mimēsis* of people worse than are found in the world – 'worse' in the particular sense of 'uglier', as the ridiculous is a species of ugliness; for what we find funny is a blunder that does no serious damage or an ugliness that does not imply pain, the funny face, for instance, being one that is ugly and distorted, but not with pain.
[. . .]

Chapter 6

1449b I shall deal later with the art of *mimēsis* in hexameters and with comedy; here I want to talk about tragedy, picking up the definition of its essential nature that results from what I have said.

Well then, a tragedy is a *mimēsis* of a high [serious. Ed.], complete action ('complete' in the sense that applies amplitude), in speech pleasurably enhanced, the different kinds [of enhancement] occurring in separate sections, in dramatic, not narrative form, effecting through pity and fear the *catharsis* of such emotions. By 'speech pleasurably enhanced' I mean that involving rhythm and harmony or song, by 'the different kinds separately' that some parts are in verse alone and others in song.

One can deduce as necessary elements of tragedy (*a*) [from the mode] the designing of the spectacle, since the *mimēsis* is produced by people doing things; (*b*) [from the media] song-writing and verbal expression, the media of tragic *mimēsis*; by 'verbal expression' I mean the composition of the verse-parts, while the meaning of 'song-writing' is obvious to anybody. [Others can be inferred from (*c*) the objects of the *mimēsis*.] A tragedy is a *mimēsis* of an action; action implies people engaged in it; these people must have some definite moral and intellectual qualities, since it is through a
1450a man's qualities that we characterize his actions, and it is of course with reference to their actions that men are said to succeed or fail. We therefore have (i) the *mimēsis* of the action, the plot, by which I mean the ordering of the particular actions; (ii) [the *mimēsis* of] the moral characters of the personages, namely that which makes us say that the agents have certain moral qualities; (iii) [the *mimēsis* of] their intellect, namely those parts in which they demonstrate something in speech or deliver themselves of some general maxim.

So tragedy as a whole will necessarily have six elements, the possession of which makes tragedy qualitatively distinct: they are plot, the *mimēsis* of character, verbal expression, the *mimēsis* of intellect, spectacle, and song-writing. The media of *mimēsis* are two, the mode one, the objects three, and there are no others. Not a few tragedians do in fact use these as qualitative elements; indeed virtually every play has spectacle, the *mimēsis* of character, plot, verbal expression, song, and the *mimēsis* of intellect.

The most important of these elements is the arrangement of the particular actions [as the following arguments show]:

(*a*) A tragedy is [by definition] a *mimēsis* not of people but of their actions and life. Both success and ill success are success and ill success in action – in other words the end and aim of human life is doing something, not just being a certain sort of person; and though we consider people's characters in deciding what sort of person they are, we call them successful or unsuccessful only with reference to their actions. So far therefore from the persons in a play acting as they do in order to represent their characters, the *mimēsis* of their characters is only included along with and because of their actions. So the particular actions, the plot, are what the rest of the tragedy is there for, and what the rest is there for is the most important.

(*b*) A work could not be a tragedy if there were no action. But there could be a tragedy without *mimēsis* of character, and the tragedies of most of the moderns are in fact deficient in it; the same is true of many other poets, and of painters for that matter, of Zeuxis, for instance, in comparison with Polygnotus: the latter is good at depicting character, while Zeuxis' painting has no *mimēsis* of character to speak of.

(*c*) If you put down one after another speeches that depicted character, finely expressed and brilliant in the *mimēsis* of intellect, that would not do the job that, by definition, tragedy does do, while a tragedy with a plot, that is, with an ordered series of particular actions, though deficient in these other points, would do its job much better.

(*d*) The most attractive things in tragedy, *peripeteiai* [reversals. Ed.] and recognition scenes, are parts of the plot.

(*e*) Novices in poetry attain perfection in verbal expression and in the *mimēsis* of character much earlier than in the ordering of the particular actions; this is also true of almost all early poets.

The plot therefore is the principle, or one might say the principle of life [or 'soul'. Ed.], in tragedy, while the *mimēsis* of character comes second in
importance, a relation similar to one we find in painting, where the most 1450b
beautiful colours, if smeared on at random, would give less pleasure than an uncoloured outline that was a picture of something. A tragedy, I repeat, is a *mimēsis* of an action, and it is only because of the action that it is a

mimēsis of the people engaged in it. Third comes the *mimēsis* of their intellect, by which I mean their ability to say what the situation admits and requires; to do this in speeches is the job of political sense and rhetoric, since the older poets made their people speak as the former directs, while the moderns make them observe the rules of rhetoric. Of these two, the *mimēsis* of character is that which makes plain the nature of the moral choices the personages make, so that those speeches in which there is absolutely nothing that the speaker chooses and avoids involve no *mimēsis* of character. By '*mimēsis* of intellect' I mean those passages in which they prove that something is or is not the case or deliver themselves of some general statement. Fourth comes the expression of the spoken parts, by which I mean, as I said before, the expression of thought in words; the meaning is the same whether verse or prose is in question. Of the others, which are there to give pleasure, song-writing is the most important, while spectacle, though attractive, has least to do with art – with the art of poetry, that is; for a work is potentially a tragedy even without public performance and players, and the art of the stage-designer contributes more to the perfection of spectacle than the poet's does.

Chapter 7

Now that these definitions are out of the way, I want to consider what the arrangement of the particular actions should be like, since that is the prime and most important element of tragedy.

Now, we have settled that a tragedy is a *mimēsis* of a complete, that is, of a whole action, 'whole' here implying some amplitude (there can be a whole without amplitude).

By 'whole' I mean 'with a beginning, a middle, and an end'. By 'beginning' I mean 'that which is not necessarily the consequent of something else, but has some state or happening naturally consequent on it'. By 'end' 'a state that is the necessary or usual consequent of something else, but has itself no such consequent', by 'middle' 'that which is consequent and has consequents'. Well-ordered plots, then, will exhibit these characteristics, and will not begin or end just anywhere.

It is not enough for beauty that a thing, whether an animal or anything else composed of parts, should have those parts well ordered; since beauty consists in amplitude as well as in order, the thing must also have amplitude – and not just any amplitude. Though a very small creature could not be beautiful, since our view loses all distinctness when it comes near to taking no perceptible time, an enormously ample one could not be beauti-

ful either, since our view of it is not simultaneous, so that we lose the sense 1451a
of its unity and wholeness as we look it over; imagine, for instance, an animal a thousand miles long. Animate and inanimate bodies, then, must have amplitude, but no more than can be taken in at one view; and similarly a plot must have extension, but no more than can be easily remembered. What is, for the poetic art, the limit of this extension? Certainly not that imposed by the contests and by perception. . . . As the limit imposed by the actual nature of the thing, one may suggest 'the ampler the better, provided it remains clear as a whole', or, to give a rough specification, 'sufficient amplitude to allow a probable or necessary succession of particular actions to produce a change from bad to good or from good to bad fortune'.

Chapter 8

Unity of plot is not, as some think, achieved by writing about one man; for just as the one substance admits innumerable incidental properties, which do not, some of them, make it a such-and-such, so one man's actions are numerous and do not make up any single action. That is why I think the poets mistaken who have produced *Heracleids* or *Theseids* or other poems of the kind, in the belief that the plot would be one just because Heracles was one. Homer especially shows his superiority in taking a right view here – whether by art or nature: in writing a poem on Odysseus he did not introduce everything that was incidentally true of him, being wounded on Parnassus, for instance, or pretending to be mad at the mustering of the fleet, neither of which necessarily or probably implied the other at all; instead he composed the *Odyssey* about an action that is one in the sense I mean, and the same is true of the *Iliad*. On the other mimetic arts a *mimēsis* is one if it is *mimēsis* of one object; and in the same way a plot, being a *mimēsis* of an action, should be a *mimēsis* of one action and that a whole one, with the different sections so arranged that the whole is disturbed by the transposition and destroyed by the removal of any one of them; for if it makes no visible difference whether a thing is there or not, that thing is no part of the whole.

Chapter 9

What I have said also makes plain that the poet's job is saying not what did happen but the sort of thing that would happen, that is, what can happen

in a strictly probable or necessary sequence. The difference between the
1451b historian and the poet is not merely that one writes verse and the other prose – one could turn Herodotus' work into verse and it would be just as much history as before; the essential difference is that the one tells us what happened and the other the sort of thing that would happen. That is why poetry is at once more like philosophy and more worth while than history, since poetry tends to make general statements, while those of history are particular. A 'general statement' means [in this context] one that tells us what sort of man would, probably or necessarily, say or do what sort of things, and this is what poetry aims at, though it attaches proper names; a particular statement on the other hand tells us what Alcibiades, for instance, did or what happened to him.[1]

That poetry does aim at generality has long been obvious in the case of comedy, where the poets make up the plot from a series of probable happenings and then give the persons any names they like, instead of writing about particular people as the lampooners did. In tragedy, however, they still stick to the actual names; this is because it is what is possible that arouses conviction, and while we do not without more ado believe that what never happened is possible, what did happen is clearly possible, since it would not have happened if it were not. Though as a matter of fact, even in some tragedies most names are invented and only one or two well known: in Agathon's *Antheus*, for instance, the names as well as the events are made up, and yet it gives just as much pleasure. So one need not try to stick at any cost to the traditional stories, which are the subject of tragedies; indeed the attempt would be absurd, since even what is well known is well known only to a few, but gives general pleasure for all that.

It is obvious from all this that the poet should be considered a maker of plots, not of verses, since he is a poet *qua* maker of *mimēsis* and the objects of his *mimēsis* are actions. Even if it is incidentally true that the plot he makes actually happened, that does not mean he is not its maker; for there is no reason why some things that actually happen should not be the sort of thing that would probably happen, and it is in virtue of that aspect of them that he is their maker.

Of defective plots or actions the worst are the episodic, those, I mean, in which the succession of the episodes is neither probable nor necessary; bad poets make these on their own account, good ones because of the judges; for in aiming at success in the competition and stretching the plot more
1452a than it can bear they often have to distort the natural order.

Tragedy is a *mimēsis* not only of a complete action, but also of things arousing pity and fear, emotions most likely to be stirred when things happen unexpectedly but because of each other (this arouses more surprise than mere chance events, since even chance events seem more marvellous when they look as if they were meant to happen – take the case of the statue of Mitys in Argos killing Mitys' murderer by falling on him as he looked at it; for we do not think that things like this are merely random); so such plots will necessarily be the best.

Chapter 10

Some plots are simple, some complex, since the actions of which the plots are *mimēsis* fall naturally into the same two classes. By 'simple action' I mean one that is continuous in the sense defined and is a unity and where the change of fortune takes place without *peripeteia* or recognition, by 'complex' one where the change of fortune is accompanied by *peripeteia* or recognition or both. The *peripeteia* and recognition should arise just from the arrangement of the plot, so that it is necessary or probable that they should follow what went before; for there is a great difference between happening next and happening as a result.

Chapter 11

A *peripeteia* occurs when the course of events takes a turn to the opposite in the way described, the change being also probable or necessary in the way I said. For example, in the *Oedipus*, when the man came and it seemed that he would comfort Oedipus and free him from his fear about his mother, by revealing who he was he in fact did the opposite. . . .

Recognition is, as its name indicates, a change from ignorance to knowledge, tending either to affection or to enmity; it determines in the direction of good or ill fortune the fates of the people involved. The best sort of recognition is that accompanied by *peripeteia*, like that in the *Oedipus*. There are of course other kinds of recognition. For a recognition of the sort described can be a recognition of inanimate objects, indeed of quite indifferent ones, and one can also recognize whether someone has committed an act or not. But the one mentioned has most to do with the plot, that is, most to do with the action; for a recognition accompanied by *peripeteia* in this way will involve either pity or fear, and tragedy is by definition a *mimēsis* of actions that rouse these emotions; it is moreover such 1452b
recognitions that lead to good or bad fortune.

Since recognition involves more than one person, in some cases only one person will recognize the other, when it is clear who the former is, and sometimes each has to recognize the other: Orestes, for example, recognized Iphigenia from her sending the letter, but a second recognition was necessary for her to recognize him.

These then are two elements of the plot, and a third is *pathos* [suffering. Ed.]. I have dealt with the first two, *peripeteia* and recognition. A *pathos* is an act involving destruction or pain, for example deaths on stage and physical agonies and woundings and so on.

So much for the parts of tragedy that one ought to use as qualitative elements.

[. . .]

Chapter 13

What ought one to aim at and beware of in composing plots? And what is the source of the tragic effect? These are the questions that naturally follow from what I have now dealt with.

Well, the arrangement of tragedy at its best should be complex, not simple, and it should also present a *mimēsis* of things that arouse fear and pity, as this is what is peculiar to the tragic *mimēsis*.

So it is clear that one should not show virtuous men passing from good to bad fortune, since this does not arouse fear or pity, but only a sense of outrage. Nor should one show bad men passing from bad to good fortune, as this is less tragic than anything, since it has none of the necessary requirements; it neither satisfies our human feeling nor arouses pity and fear. Nor should one show a quite wicked man passing from good to bad for-
1453a tune; it is true that such an arrangement would satisfy our human feeling, but it would not arouse pity or fear, since the one is felt for someone who comes to grief without deserving it, and the other for someone like us (pity, that is, for the man who does not deserve his fate, and fear for someone like us); so this event will not arouse pity or fear. So we have left the man between these. He is one who is not pre-eminent in moral virtue, who passes to bad fortune not through vice or wickedness, but because of some piece of ignorance, and who is of high repute and great good fortune, like Oedipus and Thyestes and the splendid men of such families.

So the good plot must have a single line of development, not a double one as some people say; that line should go from good fortune to bad and not the other way round; the change should be produced not through wickedness, but through some large-scale piece of ignorance; the person ignorant should be the sort of man I have described – certainly not a worse man, though perhaps a better one.

This is borne out by the facts: at first the poets recounted any story that came to hand, but nowadays the best tragedies are about a few families only, for example, Alcmaeon, Oedipus, Orestes, Meleager, Thyestes, Telephus, and others whose lot it was to suffer or commit fearful acts.

Well then, the best tragedy, judged from the standpoint of the tragic art, comes from this sort of arrangement. That is why those who censure Euripides for doing this in his tragedies and making many of them end with disaster are making just the same mistake. For this is correct in the way I said. The greatest proof of this is that on the stage and in the contests such plays are felt to be the most properly tragic, if they are well managed, and Euripides, even if he is a bad manager in the other points, is at any rate the most tragic of the poets.

Second comes the sort of arrangement that some people say is the best: this is the one that has a double arrangement of the action like the *Odyssey*, and ends with opposite fortunes for the good and bad people. It is thought to be the best because of the weakness of the audiences; for the poets follow the lead of the spectators and make plays to their specifications. But this is not the pleasure proper to tragedy, but rather belongs to comedy; for in comedy those who are most bitter enemies throughout the plot, as it might be Orestes and Aegisthus, are reconciled at the end and go off and nobody is killed by anybody.

Chapter 14

Now though pity and fear can be elicited by the spectacle, they can also be 1453b
elicited just by the arrangement of the particular actions, and this is a prior consideration and the sign of a better poet. For the plot ought to be so composed that even without seeing the action, a man who just hears what is going on shudders and feels pity because of what happens; this one would feel on hearing the plot of the *Oedipus*, for instance. But to produce this effect via the spectacle has less to do with the art of tragedy and needs external aids. To go further and use the spectacle to produce something that is merely monstrous, instead of something that rouses fear, is to depart entirely from tragedy. For one should look to tragedy for its own pleasure, not just any pleasure; and since the poet's job is to produce the pleasure springing from pity and fear via ***mimēsis***, this clearly ought to be present in the elements of the action.

What sort of events, then, do seem apt to rouse fear, or [rather] pity? This is my next subject. In such actions, people must do something to those closely connected with them, or to enemies, or to people to whom they are indifferent. Now, if it is a case of two enemies, this arouses no particular pity, whether the one damages the other or only intends to; or at least, pity is felt only at the *pathos* considered in itself. The same is true in the case when people are indifferent to each other. The cases we must look for are those where the *pathos* involves people closely connected, for instance where brother kills brother, son father, mother son, or son mother – or if not kills, then means to kill, or does some other act of the kind.

Well, one cannot interfere with the traditional stories, cannot, for instance, say that Clytaemnestra was not killed by Orestes or Eriphyle by Alcmaeon; what one should do is invent for oneself and use the traditional material well. Let me explain more clearly what I mean by 'well'. One can make the act be committed as the ancient poets did, that is, with the agents knowing and aware [whom they are damaging]; even Euripides has the example of Medea killing her children with full knowledge. [And they can have knowledge and not act.] Or they can commit the deed that rouses terror without knowing to whom they are doing it, and later recognize the connection, like Sophocles' Oedipus; this indeed happens outside the play, but we have examples in the tragedy itself, for example, Astydamas' *Alcmaeon* and Telegonus in the *Wounded Odysseus*. Again, apart from these one might through ignorance intend to do something irreparable, and then recognize the victim-to-be before doing it. These are the only possible ways, as they must either do it or not, and in knowledge or ignorance.

The worst of these is to have the knowledge and the intention and then
1454a not do it; for this is both morally outraging and untragic – 'untragic' because it involves no *pathos*. That is why nobody does behave in this way except very rarely, as Haemon, for example, means to kill Creon in the *Antigone*. The second worst is doing it: the better form of this is when the character does it in ignorance, and recognizes his victim afterwards; for this involves no feeling of outrage and the recognition produces lively surprise. But the best is the last, for example, the case in the *Cresphontes* where Merope means to kill her son and does not, but recognizes him instead. . . .

As I said before, this is why tragedies are about very few families. As it was not art but chance that led the poets in their search to the discovery of how to produce this effect in their plots, they have to go to the families in which such *pathē* occurred.

So much for the arrangement of the particular acts and the qualities required of plots.

Chapter 15

In the representation of character, there are four things that one ought to aim at:

(*a*) First and foremost, the characters represented should be morally good. The speech or action will involve ***mimēsis*** of character if it makes plain, as said before, the nature of the person's moral choice, and the character represented will be good if the choice is good. This is possible in each class: for example, a woman is good and so is a slave, though the one is perhaps inferior, and the other generally speaking low-grade.

(*b*) The characters represented should be suitable: for example, the character represented is brave, but it is not suitable for a woman to be brave or clever in this way.

(*c*) They should be life-like; this is different from the character's being good and suitable in the way I used 'suitable'.

(*d*) They should be consistent: for even if the subject of the ***mimēsis*** is an inconsistent person, and that is the characteristic posited of him, still he ought to be consistently inconsistent.

In the representation of character as well as in the chain of actions one ought always to look for the necessary or probable, so that it is necessary or
probable that a person like this speaks or acts as he does, and necessary or 1454b
probable that this happens after that. Clearly then, the dénouements of plots ought to arise just from the ***mimēsis*** of character, and not from a contrivance, a ***deus ex machina***, as in the ***Medea*** and in the events in the ***Iliad*** about the setting off. The contrivance should be used instead for things outside the play, either all that happened beforehand that a human being could not know, or all that happens later and needs foretelling and reporting; for we attribute omniscience to the gods. In the particular actions themselves there should be nothing irrational, and if there is it should be outside the tragedy, like that of Sophocles' ***Oedipus***.

Since a tragedy is a ***mimēsis*** of people better than are found in the world, one ought to do the same as the good figure-painters; for they too give us the individual form, but though they make people lifelike they represent them as more beautiful than they are. Similarly the poet too in representing people as irascible and lazy and morally deficient in other ways like that, ought nevertheless to make them good, as Homer makes Achilles both good and an example of harsh self-will. . . .

Note

1 In ch. 23 Aristotle makes the further point that tragedy and epic, with their unitary, structured plots, differ from history in that the latter typically tells of events that are disconnected and without direction.

(A) Mo Tzu, 'Against music'
(B) Hsun Tzu, 'A discussion of music'

3

From Basic Writings of Mo Tzu, Hsun Tzu, and Han Fei Tzu, trans. Burton Watson. New York & London: Columbia University Press, 1967, pp. 110–16 of Part I, pp. 112–20 of Part II [footnotes and a few passages omitted].

Although two centuries separate these essays by two famous writers of the classical age of Chinese philosophy, we might imagine them presented at a single symposium, for Hsun Tzu's is a direct response to Mo Tzu's onslaught on music and the arts at large. Their dispute has an echo of one between Plato and Aristotle. The pleasures of music for Mo Tzu, like those of most poetry for Plato, are too trivial to engage the attention of responsible people and a dangerous distraction from the stern demands of civic life. As Aristotle did in the case of drama, Hsun Tzu emphasizes the beneficial impact that music can have upon the emotions and, thereby, upon the conduct of our lives. If the Chinese dispute echoes the Greek one, it is also echoed in modern times. When people voice hostility to government subsidies for 'élitist' arts, they are repeating Mo Tzu's complaint that tax revenues are spent on music for effete entertainments instead of on housing for the poor. Hsun Tzu, one suspects, would not only approve of state support for the arts, but of harnessing the arts in support of the state and its goals, military ones included, in the manner of totalitarian regimes of the twentieth century.

Mo Tzu and Hsun Tzu (or, in the more recent Pinyin spelling, Mozi and Xunzi) were strongly contrasting figures. Mo Tzu (c.479–438 BCE) combined philosophizing with leading a band of soldiers dedicated to austerity and the defence of small, threatened states in this 'Period of the Warring States'. A vitriolic critic of Confucius (sixth to fifth century BCE), he is usually, but not entirely accurately, described as a 'utilitarian'. Certainly, however, his animus against music is based on the conviction that Confucian concern with the performance of rites fails the crucial test of 'bring[ing] benefit to the state and the people'.

Hsun Tzu (c.313–238 BCE) was a less colourful man, his scholarly life only occasionally punctuated, it seems, by work in local administration. He is usually, though again not entirely accurately, portrayed as a 'tough-minded' opponent of his 'tender-minded' fellow-Confucian, Mencius. Broadly, he rejected what he saw as Mencius' rose-tinted view of an innately good human nature, stressing the difficulties in instilling discipline in people all too naturally led astray by desire and passion. This plays an important role in his defence of music, as does his Confucian belief in music as an expression or embodiment of a larger cosmic order, an 'unchanging harmony'.

It is partly due to this metaphysical view of music that 'music is the only art form for which a record of critical consideration exists' in the classical period.[1] Harmony was, perhaps, the central concern of Chinese philosophers – the harmony that is 'the Way of Heaven' and which human beings should emulate in their lives. Interestingly, the leading metaphors for wisdom were auditory rather than visual – 'being in tune' rather than 'seeing the light', for instance. Music, moreover, played a central role in Chinese life of the times: in religious performances, ceremonial rites, the chanting of the Odes, and civic and domestic activity. This means that arguments over the value of music, like that between our two authors, were not only about certain humanly produced sounds, but about whole cultural practices within which those sounds had a role. Indeed, 'music' in the literature of the time was often a metaphor for the arts and culture in general – a metaphor facilitated by the fact that the Chinese character for music (*yue*) was also the character for joy or delight (*yao*), with the result that 'broadly speaking anything that made people happy, that provided sensory enjoyment, could be called *yue*', music.[2] (Hsun Tzu's opening line, 'Music is joy', is therefore a kind of pun in Chinese – rather likes 'Movies are moving (i.e. emotive)' would be in English.)

(A) Mo Tzu, 'Against music'

It is the business of the benevolent man to seek to promote what is beneficial to the world, to eliminate what is harmful, and to provide a model for the world. What benefits men he will carry out; what does not benefit men he will leave alone. Moreover, when the benevolent man plans for the benefit of the world, he does not consider merely what will please the eye, delight the ear, gratify the mouth, and give ease to the body. If in order to

[1] Kenneth DeWoskin, 'Early Chinese music and the origins of aesthetic terminology', in S. Bush & C. Murck (eds), *Theories of the Arts in China*, Princeton: Princeton University Press, 1983, p. 193.

[2] Guo Moruo, quoted in Li Zehou, *The Path of Beauty: a study of Chinese aesthetics*, Hong Kong & Oxford: Oxford University Press, 1994, p. 48. See also John Knoblock, *Xunzi: a translation and study of the complete works*, vol. III, Stanford: Stanford University Press, 1994, pp. 74ff.

gratify the senses he has to deprive the people of the wealth needed for their food and clothing, then the benevolent man will not do so. Therefore Mo Tzu condemns music not because the sound of the great bells and rolling drums, the zithers and pipes, is not delightful; not because the sight of the carvings and ornaments is not beautiful; not because the taste of the fried and broiled meats is not delicious; and not because lofty towers, broad pavilions, and secluded halls are not comfortable to live in. But though the body finds comfort, the mouth gratification, the eye pleasure, and the ear delight, yet if we examine the matter, we will find that such things are not in accordance with the ways of the sage kings, and if we consider the welfare of the world we will find that they bring no benefit to the common people. Therefore Mo Tzu said: Making music is wrong!

Now if the rulers and ministers want musical instruments to use in their government activities, they cannot extract them from the sea water, like salt, or dig them out of the ground, like ore. Inevitably, therefore, they must lay heavy taxes upon the common people before they can enjoy the sound of great bells, rolling drums, zithers, and pipes. In ancient times the sage kings likewise laid heavy taxes on the people, but this was for the purpose of making boats and carts, and when they were completed and people asked, 'What are these for?' the sage kings replied, 'The boats are for use on water, and the carts for use on land, so that gentlemen may rest their feet and laborers spare their shoulders.' So the common people paid their taxes and levies and did not dare to grumble. Why? Because they knew that the taxes would be used for the benefit of the people. Now if musical instruments were also used for the benefit of the people, I would not venture to condemn them. Indeed, if they were as useful as the boats and carts of the sage kings, I would certainly not venture to condemn them.

There are three things the people worry about: that when they are hungry they will have no food, when they are cold they will have no clothing, and when they are weary they will have no rest. These are the three great worries of the people. Now let us try sounding the great bells, striking the rolling drums, strumming the zithers, blowing the pipes, and waving the shields and axes in the war dance. Does this do anything to provide food and clothing for the people? I hardly think so. But let us leave that point for the moment.

Now there are great states that attack small ones, and great families that molest small ones. The strong oppress the weak, the many tyrannize the few, the cunning deceive the stupid, the eminent lord it over the humble, and bandits and thieves rise up on all sides and cannot be suppressed. Now let us try sounding the great bells, striking the rolling drums, strumming the zithers, blowing the pipes, and waving the shields and axes in the war dance. Does this do anything to rescue the world from chaos and restore it to order? I hardly think so. Therefore Mo Tzu said: If you try to promote what is beneficial to the world and eliminate what is harmful by laying heavy taxes on the people for the purpose of making bells, drums, zithers, and pipes, you will get nowhere. So Mo Tzu said: Making music is wrong!

Now the rulers and ministers, seated in their lofty towers and broad pavilions, look about them, and there are the bells, hanging like huge cauldrons. But unless the bells are struck, how can the rulers get any delight out of them? Therefore it is obvious that the rulers must have someone to strike the bells. But they cannot employ old men or young boys, since their eyes and ears are not keen enough and their arms are not strong, and they cannot make the sounds harmonious or see to strike the bells front and back. Therefore the rulers must have young people in their prime, whose eyes and ears are keen and whose arms are so strong that they can make the sounds harmonious and see to strike the bells front and back. If they employ young men, then they will be taking them away from their plowing and planting, and if they employ young women, they will be taking them away from their weaving and spinning. Yet the rulers and ministers will have their music, though their music-making interferes to such an extent with the people's efforts to produce food and clothing! Therefore Mo Tzu said: Making music is wrong!

Now let us suppose that the great bells, rolling drums, zithers, and pipes have all been provided. Still if the rulers and ministers sit quietly all alone and listen to the performance, how can they get any delight out of it? Therefore it is obvious that they must listen in the company of others, either humble men or gentlemen. If they listen in the company of gentlemen, then they will be keeping the gentlemen from attending to affairs of state, while if they listen in the company of humble men, they will be keeping the humble men from pursuing their tasks. Yet the rulers and ministers will have their music, though their music-making interferes to such an extent with the people's efforts to produce food and clothing! Therefore Mo Tzu said: Making music is wrong!

In former times Duke K'ang of Ch'i [404–379 B.C.] loved the music of the Wan dance. The Wan dancers cannot wear robes of cheap cloth or eat coarse food, for it is said that unless they have the finest food and drink, their faces and complexions will not be fit to look at, and unless they have beautiful clothing, their figures and movements will not be worth watching. Therefore the Wan dancers ate only millet and meat, and wore only robes of patterned and embroidered silk. They did nothing to help produce food or clothing, but lived entirely off the efforts of others. Yet the rulers and ministers will have their music, though their music-making interferes to such an extent with the people's efforts to produce food and clothing! Therefore Mo Tzu said: Making music is wrong!

Now man is basically different from the beasts, birds, and insects. The beasts, birds, and insects have feathers and fur for their robes and coats, hoofs and claws for their leggings and shoes, and grass and water for their food and drink. Therefore the male need not plow or plant, the female need not weave or spin, and still they have plenty of food and clothing. But man is different from such creatures. If a man exerts his strength, he may live, but if he does not, he cannot live. If the gentlemen do not diligently attend to affairs of state, the government will fall into disorder, and if humble men do not diligently pursue their tasks, there will not be enough wealth and goods.

If the gentlemen of the world do not believe what I say, then let us try enumerating the various duties of the people of the world and see how music interferes with them. The rulers and ministers must appear at court early and retire late, hearing lawsuits and attending to affairs of government – this is their duty. The gentlemen must exhaust the strength of their limbs and employ to the fullest the wisdom of their minds, directing bureaus within the government and abroad, collecting taxes on the barriers and markets and on the resources of the hills, forests, lakes, and fish weirs, so that the granaries and treasuries will be full – this is their duty. The farmers must leave home early and return late, sowing seed, planting trees, and gathering large crops of vegetables and grain – this is their duty. Women must rise early and go to bed late, spinning, weaving, producing large quantities of hemp, silk, and other fibers, and preparing cloth – this is their duty. Now if those who occupy the position of rulers and ministers are fond of music and spend their time listening to it, then they will not be able to appear at court early and retire late, or hear lawsuits and attend to affairs of government, and as a result the state will fall into disorder and its altars of the soil and grain will be in danger. If those who occupy the position of gentlemen are fond of music and spend their time listening to it, then they will be unable to exhaust the strength of their limbs and employ to the fullest the wisdom of their minds in directing bureaus within the government and abroad, collecting taxes on the barriers and markets and on the resources of the hills, forests, lakes and fish weirs, in order to fill the granaries and treasuries, and as a result the granaries and treasuries will not be filled. If those who occupy the position of farmers are fond of music and spend their time listening to it, then they will be unable to leave home early and return late, sowing seed, planting trees, and gathering large crops of vegetables and grain, and as a result there will be a lack of vegetables and grain. If women are fond of music and spend their time listening to it, then they will be unable to rise early and go to bed late, spinning, weaving, producing large quantities of hemp, silk, and other fibers, and preparing cloth, and as a result there will not be enough cloth. If you ask what it is that has caused the ruler to neglect the affairs of government and the humble man to neglect his tasks, the answer is music. Therefore Mo Tzu said: Making music is wrong!

[. . .]

Therefore Mo Tzu said: If the rulers, ministers, and gentlemen of the world truly desire to promote what is beneficial to the world and eliminate what is harmful, they must prohibit and put a stop to this thing called music!

(B) Hsun Tzu, 'A discussion of music'

Music is joy, an emotion which man cannot help but feel at times. Since man cannot help feeling joy, his joy must find an outlet in voice and an expression in movement. The outcries and movements, and the inner emotional changes which occasion them, must be given full expression in accordance with the way of man. Man must have his joy, and joy must have its expression, but if that expression is not guided by the principles of the Way, then it will inevitably become disordered. The former kings hated such disorder, and therefore they created the musical forms of the odes and hymns in order to guide it. In this way they made certain that the voice would fully express the feelings of joy without becoming wild and abandoned, that the form would be well ordered but not unduly restrictive, that the directness, complexity, intensity, and tempo of the musical performance would be of the proper degree to arouse the best in man's nature, and that evil and improper sentiments would find no opening to enter by. It was on this basis that the former kings created their music. And yet Mo Tzu criticizes it. Why?

When music is performed in the ancestral temple of the ruler, and the ruler and his ministers, superiors and inferiors, listen to it together, there are none who are not filled with a spirit of harmonious reverence. When it is performed within the household, and father and sons, elder and younger brothers listen to it together, there are none who are not filled with a spirit of harmonious kinship. And when it is performed in the community, and old people and young together listen to it, there are none who are not filled with a spirit of harmonious obedience. Hence music brings about complete unity and induces harmony. It arranges its accoutrements to comprise an adornment to moderation; it blends its performance to achieve the completion of form. It is sufficient to lead men the single Way or to bring order to ten thousand changes. This is the manner in which the former kings created their music. And yet Mo Tzu criticizes it. Why?

When one listens to the singing of the odes and hymns, his mind and will are broadened; when he takes up the shield and battle-ax and learns the postures of the war dance, his bearing acquires vigor and majesty; when he learns to observe the proper positions and boundaries of the dance stage and to match his movements with the accompaniments, he can move correctly in rank and his advancings and retirings achieve order. Music teaches men how to march abroad to punish offenders and how to behave at home with courtesy and humility. Punishing offenders and behaving with courtesy and humility are based upon the same principle. If one marches abroad to punish offenders in accordance with the way learned through music, then there will be no one who will not obey and submit; if one behaves at home with courtesy and humility, then there will be no one who will not obey and be submissive. Hence music is the great arbiter of the world, the key to central harmony, and a necessary requirement of human emotion. This is the manner in which the former kings created their music. And yet Mo Tzu criticizes it. Why?

Moreover, music was used by the former kings to give expression to their delight, and armies and weapons were used to give expression to their anger. The former kings were careful to show delight or anger only upon the correct occasions. Therefore, when they showed delight, the world joined with them in harmony, and when they showed anger, the violent and unruly shook with fear. The way of the former kings was to encourage and perfect rites and music, and yet Mo Tzu criticizes such music. Therefore, I say that Mo Tzu's attempts to teach the Way may be compared to a blind man trying to distinguish black from white [or] a deaf man trying to tell a clear tone from a muddy one. . . .

Music enters deeply into men and transforms them rapidly. Therefore, the former kings were careful to give it the proper form. When music is moderate and tranquil, the people become harmonious and shun excess. When music is stern and majestic, the people become well behaved and shun disorder. When the people are harmonious and well behaved, then the troops will be keen in striking power and the cities well guarded, and enemy states will not dare to launch an attack. In such a case, the common people will dwell in safety, take delight in their communities, and look up to their superiors with complete satisfaction. Then the fame of the state will become known abroad, its glory will shine forth greatly, and all people within the four seas will long to become its subjects. Then at last a true king may be said to have arisen.

But if music is seductive and depraved, then the people will become abandoned and mean-mannered. Those who are abandoned will fall into disorder; those who are mean-mannered will fall to quarreling; and where there is disorder and quarreling, the troops will be weak, the cities will revolt, and the state will be menaced by foreign enemies. In such a case, the common people will find no safety in their dwellings and no delight in their communities, and they will feel only dissatisfaction towards their superiors. Hence, to turn away from the proper rites and music and to allow evil music to spread is the source of danger and disgrace. For this reason the former kings honored the proper rites and music and despised evil music. As I have said before, it is the duty of the chief director of music to enforce the ordinances and commands, to examine songs and writings, and to abolish licentious music, attending to all matters at the appropriate time, so that strange and barbaric music is not allowed to confuse the elegant classical modes.

Mo Tzu claims that the sage kings rejected music and that the Confucians are wrong to encourage it. But a gentleman will understand that this is not so. Music is something which the sage kings found joy in, for it has the power to make good the hearts of the people, to influence men deeply, and to reform their ways and customs with facility. Therefore, the former kings guided the people with rites and music, and the people became harmonious. If the people have emotions of love and hatred, but no ways in which to express their joy or anger, then they will become disordered. Because the former kings hated such disorder, they reformed the actions of the people and created proper music for them, and as a result the world became obedient. The fasting and mourning garments and the sound of lamenting and weeping cause the heart to be sad. The buckling on of armor and helmet, the songs sung as men march in rank cause the heart to be stirred to valor. Seductive looks and the songs of Cheng and Wei [two regions. Ed.] cause the heart to grow licentious, while the donning of court robes, sashes, and formal caps, the Shao dance, and the Wu song, cause the heart to feel brave and majestic. Therefore the gentleman does not allow his ears to listen to licentious sounds, his eyes to look at seductive beauty, or his mouth to speak evil words. These three things the gentleman is careful about. When depraved sounds move a man, they cause a spirit of rebellion to rise in him, and when such a spirit has taken shape, then disorder results. But when correct sounds move a man, they cause a spirit of obedience to rise, and when such a spirit has arisen, good order results. As singers blend their voices with that of the leader, so good or evil arise in response to the force that calls them forth. Therefore, the gentleman is careful to choose his environment.

The gentleman utilizes bells and drums to guide his will, and lutes and zithers to gladden his heart. In the movements of the war dance he uses shields and battle-axes; as decorations in the peace dance he uses feather ornaments and yak tails; and he sets the rhythm with sounding stones and woodwinds. Therefore, the purity of his music is modeled after Heaven, its breadth is modeled after the earth, and is posturings and turnings imitate the four seasons. Hence, through the performance of music the will is made pure, and through the practice or rites the conduct is brought to perfection, the eyes and ears become keen, the temper becomes harmonious and calm, and customs and manners are easily reformed. All the world becomes peaceful and joins together in the joy of beauty and goodness. Therefore I say that music is joy. The gentleman takes joy in carrying out the Way; the petty man takes joy in gratifying his desires. He who curbs his desires in accordance with the Way will be joyful and free from disorder, but he who forgets the Way in the pursuit of desire will fall into delusion and joylessness. Therefore, music is the means of guiding joy, and the metal, stone, stringed, and bamboo instruments are the means of guiding virtue. When music is performed, the people will set their faces toward the true direction. Hence music is the most effective means to govern men. And yet Mo Tzu criticizes it!

Music embodies an unchanging harmony, while rites represent unalterable reason. Music unites that which is the same; rites distinguish that which is different; and through the combination of rites and music the human heart is governed. To seek out the beginning and exhaust all change – this is the emotional nature of music; to illuminate the truth and do away with what is false – this is the essence of ritual. Because he criticized music, one would expect Mo Tzu to have met with some punishment. And yet in his time the enlightened kings had all passed away and there was no one to correct his errors, so that stupid men continue to study his doctrines and bring jeopardy to themselves. The gentleman makes clear the nature of music – this is his virtue. But an age of disorder hates goodness and will not listen to the teachings of the gentleman, and alas, alas, they are left unfulfilled. Study the matter well, my students, and do not let yourselves be deluded!

This is the symbolism of music: the drum represents a vast pervasiveness; the bells represent fullness; the sounding stones represent restrained order; the mouth organs represent austere harmony; the flutes represent a spirited outburst; the ocarina and bamboo whistle represent breadth of tone; the zither represents gentleness; the lute represents grace; the songs represent purity and fulfillment; and the spirit of the dance joins with the Way of Heaven. The drum is surely the lord of music, is it not? Hence, it resembles

Heaven, while the bells resemble earth, the sounding stones resemble water, the mouth organs and lutes resemble the sun, and the scrapers resemble the myriad beings of creation. How can one understand the spirit of the dance? The eyes cannot see it; the ears cannot hear it. And yet, when all the posturings and movements, all the steps and changes of pace are ordered and none are lacking in the proper restraint, when all the power of muscle and bone are brought into play, when all is matched exactly to the rhythm of the drums and bells and there is not the slightest awkwardness or discord – there is the spirit of the dance in all its manifold fullness and intensity! . . .

Plotinus, *Enneads*, I.6

4

From Plotinus: Enneads vol. I, trans. A. H. Armstrong, Cambridge, Mass.: Harvard University Press, 1966, pp. 229–63 [words and phrases in square brackets, unless followed by 'Ed.', are the translator's].

Plato, as I noted earlier (p. 11), discusses aesthetic issues outside *The Republic*, most famously in 'Diotima's speech' in the *Symposium*. The topic of this dialogue is erotic love, and Diotima (a seeress of Socrates' former acquaintance), having proposed that the object of love is beauty, sets out to explain the significance of this love. Her (and Plato's) answer, crudely, is that love of mundane beauty – of a boy's body, say – is only explicable as a stage towards love of something higher: nothing less, in fact, than that ultimate object of true knowledge, the Form of the Good, which is also the Form of Beauty. (The Greek *kalon* can mean both 'good' and 'beautiful'.) In the claim that a person ascends from 'physical beauty to moral beauty, and from moral beauty to the beauty of knowledge' one detects the inspiration for Keats' line, 'Beauty is truth, truth beauty', and more generally for the immensely influential idea – found in John Ruskin, for example – that mundane beauty is a reflection of a divine order.

Certainly it was the inspiration for the chapter on beauty by the Egyptian-born neo-Platonist philosopher, Plotinus (*c*.204–70 CE), a thinker whose stock has risen in recent years to the point of being hailed, by one writer, as the 'greatest of Greek philosophers'.[1] As in Plato's *Symposium*, the remarks on beauty in the *Enneads* ('The Nines', so-called because of the arrangement into six books of nine chapters each) are set against a complex metaphysical system. The mundane world of 'souls', which include plants and animals as well as human minds, 'emanates' from the realm of Forms (and the 'intellect' in which these exist), which in turn 'emanates' from the ineffable One or Good that is 'above being' and available only to mystical insight. At the other end of the scale, 'below being', is formless matter, totally indeterminate stuff which requires the imposition of form to produce the things and creatures of the

[1] S. R. L. Clark, *Limits and Renewals*, vol. 3, Oxford: Clarendon Press, 1991, p. 205.

everyday world. (Substitute 'God' for 'the One' and you have something like the philosophical vision of St Augustine, who was deeply impressed by Plotinus.)

Informed by this quasi-Platonic system, the chapter on beauty – Plotinus' 'best-known and most influential work'[2] – also follows Plato in insisting that beauty is not confined to perceptual objects, though it is with these that the discussion begins. People's characters, for example, can be beautiful, just as their faces can. Having rejected the Stoics' view that beauty is a matter of proportion, Plotinus argues that it is due, rather, to the presence of form. Since form is present through the participation of the immaterial Forms, it follows that something is the more beautiful the more removed it is from 'shapeless' matter. And since this distance from the material is also what makes for moral goodness – a courageous person, for instance, is indifferent to his physical welfare – there is an intimate connection between the beautiful and the good. (One can see why, according to a disciple and biographer, Plotinus 'seemed ashamed of being in [a] body'.[3]) On the nature of this intimate connection, Plotinus is uncertain, sometimes speaking of it as an identity, sometimes not. (He is equally hesitant over whether the One is itself beautiful or the source of all beauty.)

In *Enneads* I.6, Plotinus does not discuss the arts, but one can guess what he might say – a guess confirmed by his later remark that the best artists 'do not simply imitate the visible, but go beyond, to the principles [and Forms] which produce nature', thereby being 'in possession of beauty' (V.8). Thus it is Plotinus, not Plato (for whom artists *do* 'simply imitate the visible'), who inspired the Renaissance's (and Schopenhauer's (chapter 10)) elevated conception of art as a medium for communicating an invisible and intelligible world to us. And it is Plotinus who stands behind the still powerful tradition of locating aesthetic value in the form of artworks or natural objects, not in their matter or content. (See the extracts from Kant and Bell in this volume.) Finally, it is to Plotinus that those people should look for whom the experience of beauty purifies and edifies, educating the understanding of our moral being and of the intelligible order upon which we depend.

1. Beauty is mostly in sight, but it is to be found too in things we hear, in combinations of words and also in music, and in all music [not only in songs]; for tunes and rhythms are certainly beautiful: and for those who are advancing upwards from sense-perception ways of life and actions and characters and intellectual activities are beautiful, and there is the beauty of

[2] Dominic O'Meara, *Plotinus: an introduction to the* Enneads, Oxford: Clarendon Press, 1995, p. 95.

[3] Porphyry, *On the Life of Plotinus*, in *Plotinus: Enneads*, vol. 1, trans. A. H. Armstrong, Cambridge, Mass.: Harvard University Press, 1966, p. 3.

virtue. If there is any beauty prior to these, this discussion will reveal it.

Very well then, what is it which makes us imagine that bodies are beautiful and attracts our hearing to sounds because of their beauty? And how are all the things which depend on soul beautiful? Are they all made beautiful by one and the same beauty or is there one beautifulness in bodies and a different one in other things? And what are they, or what is it? Some things, bodies for instance, are not beautiful from the nature of the objects themselves, but by participation, others are beauties themselves, like the nature of virtue. The same bodies appear sometimes beautiful, sometimes not beautiful, so that their being bodies is one thing, their being beautiful another. What is this principle, then, which is present in bodies? We ought to consider this first. What is it that attracts the gaze of those who look at something, and turns and draws them to it makes them enjoy the sight? If we find this perhaps we can use it as a stepping-stone and get a sight of the rest.

Nearly everyone says that it is good proportion of the parts to each other and to the whole, with the addition of good colour, which produces visible beauty, and that with the objects of sight and generally with everything else, being beautiful is being well-proportioned and measured. On this theory nothing single and simple but only a composite thing will have any beauty. It will be the whole which is beautiful, and the parts will not have the property of beauty by themselves, but will contribute to the beauty of the whole. But if the whole is beautiful the parts must be beautiful too; a beautiful whole can certainly not be composed of ugly parts; all the parts must have beauty. For these people, too, beautiful colours, and the light of the sun as well, since they are simple and do not derive their beautifulness from good proportion, will be excluded from beauty. And how do they think gold manages to be beautiful? And what makes lightning in the night and stars beautiful to see? And in sounds in the same way the simple will be banished, though often in a composition which is beautiful as a whole each separate sound is beautiful. And when, though the same good proportion is there all the time, the same face sometimes appears beautiful and sometimes does not, surely we must say that being beautiful is something else over and above good proportion, and good proportion is beautiful because of something else?

But if when these people pass on to ways of life and beautiful expressions of thought they allege good proportion as the cause of beauty in these too, what can be meant by good proportion in beautiful ways of life or laws or studies or branches of knowledge? How can speculations be well-proportioned in relation to each other? If it is because they agree, there can be concord and agreement between bad ideas. The statement that 'righteousness is a fine sort of silliness' agrees with and is in tune with the saying that 'morality is stupidity'; the two fit perfectly. Again, every sort of virtue is a beauty of the soul, a truer beauty than those mentioned before; and how is virtue well-proportioned? Not like magnitudes or a number. We grant that the soul has several parts, but what is the formula for the composition or mixture in the soul of parts or speculations? And what [on this theory] will the beauty of the intellect alone by itself be?

2. So let us go back to the beginning and state what the primary beauty in bodies really is. It is something which we become aware of even at the first glance; the soul speaks of it as if it understood it, recognizes and welcomes it and as it were adapts itself to it. But when it encounters the ugly it shrinks back and rejects it and turns away from it and is out of tune and alienated from it. Our explanation of this is that the soul, since it is by nature what it is and is related to the higher kind of reality in the realm of being, when it sees something akin to it or a trace of its kindred reality, is delighted and thrilled and returns to itself and remembers itself and its own possessions.

What likeness, then, is there between beautiful things here and There? If there is a likeness, let us agree that they are alike. But how are both the things in that world and the things in this beautiful? We maintain that the things in this world are beautiful by participating in form; for every shapeless thing which is naturally capable of receiving shape and form is ugly and outside the divine formative power as long as it has no share in formative power and form. This is absolute ugliness. But a thing is also ugly when it is not completely dominated by shape and formative power, since its matter has not submitted to be completely shaped according to the form. The form, then, approaches and composes that which is to come into being from many parts into a single ordered whole; it brings it into a completed unity and makes it one by agreement of its parts; for since it is one itself, that which is shaped by it must also be one as far as a thing can be which is composed of many parts.

So beauty rests upon the material thing when it has been brought into unity, and gives itself to parts and wholes alike. When it comes upon something that is one and composed of like parts it gives the same gift to the whole; as sometimes art gives beauty to a whole house with its parts, and sometimes a nature gives beauty to a single stone. So then the beautiful body comes into being by sharing in a formative power which comes from the divine forms.

3. The power ordained for the purpose recognizes this, and there is nothing more effective for judging its own subject-matter, when the rest of the soul judges along with it; or perhaps the rest of the soul too pronounces

the judgement by fitting the beautiful body to the form in itself and using this for judging beauty as we use a ruler for judging straightness. But how does the bodily agree with that which is before body? How does the architect declare the house outside beautiful by fitting it to the form of house within him? The reason is that the house outside, apart from the stones, is the inner form divided by the external mass of matter, without parts but appearing in many parts. When sense-perception, then, sees the form in bodies binding and mastering the nature opposed to it, which is shapeless, and shape riding gloriously upon other shapes, it gathers into one that which appears dispersed and brings it back and takes it in, now without parts, to the soul's interior and presents it to that which is within as something in tune with it and fitting it and dear to it; just as when a good man sees a trace of virtue in the young, which is in tune with his own inner truth, the sight delights him.

And the simple beauty of colour comes about by shape and the mastery of the darkness in matter by the presence of light which is incorporeal and formative power and form. This is why fire itself is more beautiful than all other bodies, because it has the rank of form in relation to the other elements; it is above them in place and is the finest and subtlest of all bodies, being close to the incorporeal. It alone does not admit the others; but the others admit it: for it warms them but is not cooled itself; it has colour primarily and all other things take the form of colour from it. So it shines and glitters as if it was a form. The inferior thing which becomes faint and dull by the fire's light, is not beautiful any more, as not participating in the whole form of colour. The melodies in sounds, too, the imperceptible ones which make the perceptible ones, make the soul conscious of beauty in the same way, showing the same thing in another medium. It is proper to sensible melodies to be measured by numbers not according to any and every sort of formula but one which serves for the production of form so that it may dominate.

So much, then, for the beauties in the realm of sense, images and shadows which, so to speak, sally out and come into matter and adorn it and excite us when they appear.

4. But about the beauties beyond, which it is no more the part of sense to see, but the soul sees them and speaks of them without instruments – we must go up to them and contemplate them and leave sense to stay down below. Just as in the case of the beauties of sense it is impossible for those who have not seen them or grasped their beauty – those born blind, for instance, – to speak about them, in the same way only those can speak about the beauty of ways of life who have accepted the beauty of ways of life and kinds of knowledge and everything else of the sort; and people

cannot speak about the splendour of virtue who have never even imagined how fair is the face of justice and moral order; 'neither the evening nor the morning star are as fair'. [Aristotle, *Nicomachean Ethics*, 1129b. Ed.] But there must be those who see this beauty by that with which the soul sees things of this sort, and when they see it they must be delighted and overwhelmed and excited much more than by those beauties we spoke of before, since now it is true beauty they are grasping. These experiences must occur whenever there is contact with any sort of beautiful thing, wonder and a shock of delight and longing and passion and a happy excitement. One can have these experiences by contact with invisible beauties, and souls do have them, practically all, but particularly those who are more passionately in love with the invisible, just as with bodies all see them, but all are not stung as sharply, but some, who are called lovers, are most of all.

5. Then we must ask the lovers of that which is outside sense 'What do you feel about beautiful ways of life, as we call them, and beautiful habits and well-ordered characters and in general about virtuous activities and dispositions and the beauty of souls? What do you feel when you see your own inward beauty? How are you stirred to wild exultation, and long to be with yourselves, gathering your selves together away from your bodies?' For this is what true lovers feel.

But what is it which makes them feel like this? Not shape or colour or any size, but soul, without colour itself and possessing a moral order without colour and possessing all the other light of the virtues; you feel like this when you see, in yourself or in someone else, greatness of soul, a righteous life, a pure morality, courage with its noble look, and dignity and modesty advancing in a fearless, calm and unperturbed disposition, and the godlike light of intellect shining upon all this. We love and delight in these qualities, but why do we call them beautiful? They exist and appear to us and he who sees them cannot possibly say anything else except that they are what really exists. What does 'really exists' mean? That they exist as beauties.

But the argument still requires us to explain why real beings make the soul lovable. What is this kind of glorifying light on all the virtues? Would you like to take the opposites, the uglinesses in soul, and contrast them with the beauties? Perhaps a consideration of what ugliness is and why it appears so will help us to find what we are looking for. Suppose, then, an ugly soul, dissolute and unjust, full of all lusts, and all disturbance, sunk in fears by its cowardice and jealousies by its pettiness, thinking mean and mortal thoughts as far as it thinks at all, altogether distorted, loving impure pleasures, living a life which consists of bodily sensations and finding delight in its ugliness. Shall we not say that its ugliness came to it as a [falsely perceived. Ed.] 'beauty' brought in from outside, injuring it and making it impure and 'mixed with a great deal of evil', [Plato, *Phaedo*, 66b5. Ed.] with its life and perceptions no longer pure, but by the admixture of evil living a dim life and diluted with a great deal of death, no longer seeing what a soul ought to see, no longer left in peace in itself because it keeps on being dragged out, and down, and to the dark? Impure, I think, and dragged in every direction towards the objects of sense, with a great deal of bodily stuff mixed into it, consorting much with matter and receiving a form other than its own it has changed by a mixture which makes it worse; just as if anyone gets into mud or filth he does not show any more the beauty which he had: what is seen is what he wiped off on himself from the mud and filth; his ugliness has come from an addition of alien matter, and his business, if he is to be beautiful again, is to wash and clean himself and so be again what he was before.

So we shall be right in saying that the soul becomes ugly by mixture and dilution and inclination towards the body and matter. This is the soul's ugliness, not being pure and unmixed, like gold, but full of earthiness; if anyone takes the earthy stuff away the gold is left, and is beautiful, when it is singled out from other things and is alone by itself. In the same way the soul too, when it is separated from the lusts which it has through the body with which it consorted too much, and freed from its other affections, purged of what it gets from being embodied, when it abides alone has put away all the ugliness which came from the other nature.

6. For, as was said in old times, self-control, and courage and every virtue, is a purification, and so is even wisdom itself. This is why the mysteries are right when they say riddlingly that the man who has not been purified will lie in mud when he goes to Hades, because the impure is fond of mud by reason of its badness; just as pigs, with their unclean bodies, like that sort of thing. For what can true self-control be except not keeping company with bodily pleasures, but avoiding them as impure and belonging to something impure? Courage, too, is not being afraid of death. And death is the separation of body and soul; and a man does not fear this if he welcomes the prospect of being alone. Again, greatness of soul is despising the things here: and wisdom is an intellectual activity which turns away from the things below and leads the soul to those above.

So the soul when it is purified becomes form and formative power, altogether bodiless and intellectual and entirely belonging to the divine, whence beauty springs and all that is akin to it. Soul, then, when it is raised to the level of intellect increases in beauty. Intellect and the things of intellect are its beauty, its own beauty and not another's, since only then [when it is perfectly conformed to intellect] is it truly soul. For this reason it is right to say that the soul's becoming something good and beautiful is its being made like to God, because from Him come beauty and all else which falls to the lot of real beings. Or rather, beautifulness is reality, and the other kind of thing is the ugly, and this same is the primary evil; so for God the qualities of goodness and beauty are the same, or the realities, the good and beauty.*

So we must follow the same line of enquiry to discover beauty and goodness, and ugliness and evil. And first we must posit beauty which is also the good: from this immediately comes intellect, which is beauty; and soul is given beauty by intellect. Everything else is beautiful by the shaping of soul, the beauties in actions and in ways of life. And soul makes beautiful the bodies which are spoken of as beautiful; for since it is a divine thing and a kind of part of beauty, it makes everything it grasps and masters beautiful, as far as they are capable of participation.

7. So we must ascend again to the good, which every soul desires. Anyone who has seen it knows what I mean when I say that it is beautiful. It is desired as good, and the desire for it is directed to good, and the attainment of it is for those who go up to the higher world and are converted and strip off what we put on in our descent (just as for those who go up to the celebrations of sacred rites there are purifications, and strippings off of the clothes they wore before, and going up naked) until, passing in the ascent all that is alien to the God, one sees with one's self alone. That alone, simple, single and pure, from which all depends and to which all look and are and live and think: for it is cause of life and mind and being.

If anyone sees it, what passion will he feel, what longing in his desire to be united with it, what a shock of delight! The man who has not seen it may desire it as good, but he who has seen it glories in its beauty and is full of wonder and delight, enduring a shock which causes no hurt, loving with true passion and piercing longing; he laughs at all other loves and despises what he thought beautiful before; it is like the experience of those who have met appearances of gods or spirits and do not any more appreciate as they did the beauty of other bodies.

'What then are we to think if anyone contemplates the absolute beauty which exists pure by itself, uncontaminated by flesh or body, not in earth or heaven, that it may keep its purity?' All these other things are external additions and mixtures and not primary, but derived from it. If then one sees That which provides for all and remains by itself and gives to all but receives nothing into itself, if he abides in the contemplation of this kind of beauty and rejoices in being made like it, how can he need any other

* God, the First Principle of reality, has no qualities, but is absolutely single and simple, at once Absolute Good and Absolute Beauty [Tr.].

beauty? For this, since it is beauty most of all, and primary beauty, makes its lovers beautiful and lovable. Here the greatest, the ultimate contest is set before our souls; all our toil and trouble is for this, not to be left without a share in the best of visions. The man who attains this is blessed in seeing that 'blessed sight', and he who fails to attain it has failed utterly. A man has not failed if he fails to win beauty of colours or bodies, or power or office or kingship even, but if he fails to win this and only this. For this he should give up the attainment of kingship and of rule over all earth and sea and sky, if only by leaving and overlooking them he can turn to That and see.

8. But how shall we find the way? What method can we devise? How can one see the 'inconceivable beauty' [Plato, *Symposium*, 218e2. Ed.] which stays within in the holy sanctuary and does not come out where the profane may see it? Let him who can, follow and come within, and leave outside the sight of his eyes and not turn back to the bodily splendours which he saw before. When he sees the beauty in bodies he must not run after them; we must know that they are images, traces, shadows, and hurry away to that which they image. For if a man runs to the image and wants to seize it as if it was the reality (like a beautiful reflection playing on the water, which some story somewhere, I think, said riddlingly a man wanted to catch and sank down into the stream and disappeared) then this man who clings to beautiful bodies and will not let them go, will, like the man in the story, but in soul, not in body, sink down into the dark depths where intellect has no delight, and stay blind in Hades, consorting with shadows there and here.

This would be truer advice 'Let us fly to our dear country.' [Homer, *Iliad*, 2.140. Ed.] What then is our way of escape, and how are we to find it? We shall put out to sea, as Odysseus did, from the witch Circe or Calypso – as the poet says (I think with a hidden meaning) – and was not content to stay though he had delights of the eyes and lived among much beauty of sense [Homer, *Odyssey*, 9–10. Ed.]. Our country from which we came is there, our Father is there. How shall we travel to it, where is our way of escape? We cannot get there on foot; for our feet only carry us everywhere in this world, from one country to another. You must not get ready a carriage, either, or a boat. Let all these things go, and do not look. Shut your eyes, and change to and wake another way of seeing, which everyone has but few use.

9. And what does this inner sight see? When it is just awakened it is not at all able to look at the brilliance before it. So that the soul must be trained, first of all to look at beautiful ways of life: then at beautiful works, not those which the arts produce, but the works of men who have a name of

goodness: then look at the souls of the people who produce the beautiful works.

How then can you see the sort of beauty a good soul has? Go back into yourself and look; and if you do not yet see yourself beautiful, then, just as someone making a statue which has to be beautiful cuts away here and polishes there and makes one part smooth and clears another till he has given his statue a beautiful face, so you too must cut away excess and straighten the crooked and clear the dark and make it bright, and never stop 'working on your statue' till the divine glory of virtue shines out on you, till you see 'self-mastery enthroned upon its holy seat'. [Plato, *Phaedrus*, 254b7. Ed.] If you have become this, and see it, and are at home with yourself in purity, with nothing hindering you from becoming in this way one, with no inward mixture of anything else, but wholly yourself, nothing but true light, not measured by dimensions, or bounded by shape into littleness, or expanded to size by unboundedness, but everywhere unmeasured, because greater than all measure and superior to all quantity; when you see that you have become this, then you have become sight; you can trust yourself then; you have already ascended and need no one to show you; concentrate your gaze and see. This alone is the eye that sees the great beauty.

But if anyone comes to the sight blear-eyed with wickedness, and unpurified, or weak and by his cowardice unable to look at what is very bright, he sees nothing, even if someone shows him what is there and possible to see. For one must come to the sight with a seeing power made akin and like to what is seen. No eye ever saw the sun without becoming sun-like [Plato, *The Republic*, 508b3. Ed.], nor can a soul see beauty without becoming beautiful. You must become first all godlike and all beautiful if you intend to see God and beauty. First the soul will come in its ascent to intellect and there will know the Forms, all beautiful, and will affirm that these, the Ideas, are beauty; for all things are beautiful by these, by the products and essence of intellect. That which is beyond this we call the nature of the Good, which holds beauty as a screen before it.

So in a loose and general way of speaking the Good is the primary beauty; but if one distinguishes the intelligibles [from the Good] one will say that the place of the Forms is the intelligible beauty, but the Good is That which is beyond, the 'spring and origin' of beauty; or one will place the Good and the primal beauty on the same level: in any case, however, beauty is in the intelligible world.

Shih-t'ao, *Quotes on Painting* 5

From Lin Yutang, *The Chinese Theory of Art: translations from the Masters of Chinese art*. London: Heinemann, 1967, pp. 140–56 [footnotes and §§ 9–14 omitted; words and phrases in square brackets are the translator's].

The author of this remarkable little seventeenth century book – 'perhaps the standard work on aesthetics' among Chinese writings on the visual arts[1] – is, regrettably, the only practising visual artist of note represented in this reader. A leading member of the 'individualist' school which flourished during the early days of the Ch'ing (or Manchu) dynasty after 1644, Shih-t'ao (or Tao Chi or, in Pinyin transliteration, Dao Ji) remains one of the most influential of all Chinese painters, his 'unusual compositions' marked by a 'self-assured spontaneity, a contemplative appreciation of the moods of landscape . . . and . . . bold and even eccentric brushwork'.[2] Hardly less influential is this essay, written in protest against the academic style of his predecessors and the contemporary obsession with copying the work of the ancient Masters. Both his paintings and words anticipate anti-academic European artists of the nineteenth century and may remind some people of Van Gogh. The title his translator gives to these *Quotes on Painting (Hua Yulu)*, 'An Expressionist credo', is not entirely inappropriate. Indeed, Shih-t'ao's more abstract paintings (notably, *10,000 Ugly Ink Dots*) might, at a cursory glance, appear to be by a disciple of the 'Abstract expressionist', Jackson Pollock.[3]

Shih-t'ao (*c*.1642–1718), a scion of the imperial Ming family born in Kwangsi, became a Buddhist monk, although he seems to have spent most of his life on the road rather than in a monastery, and his views reflect the influences of Confucianism and Taoism as much as that of Ch'an (or Zen) Buddhism. There are several references in his essay to the Confucian 'Heaven' which is the prototype of order and harmony on earth, to primal unity of the Tao (Way) with

[1] Li Zehou, *The Path of Beauty: a study of Chinese aesthetics*, Hong Kong & Oxford: Oxford University Press, 1994, p. 231.

[2] Harold Osborne (ed.), *Oxford Companion to Art*, Oxford: Clarendon Press, 1979, p. 1121.

[3] For a discussion and some plates of Shih-t'ao's paintings, see Max Loehr, *The Great Painters of China*, Oxford: Phaidon, 1980, pp. 302ff.

which things do or should accord, and to the Taoist ideal of 'non-action' (*wu wei*), of effortless, receptive 'affable impassivity', as Chuang Tzu had put it.

This eclectic heritage should give pause before attaching labels like 'expressionist' and 'individualist' to Shih-t'ao's position. While the painter should indeed express something, rather than faithfully copy things, it is less his emotions or personality than the 'inner law' – the 'life and movement' – of the cosmos which the artist of genius incorporates. Again, the painter should be 'an individual', removing the 'whiskers of the ancients' from his face, in the sense of rejecting ossified 'methods' and of remaining free from convention. But this is in order that he may recover that 'pure mind' which enables uncontaminated insight into the forms of the cosmos and of the essential unity of the One or the Tao. Such views, despite their Taoist and Buddhist flavourings, anticipate some of the great credos of European romanticism, Wordsworth's, Turner's and Hölderlin's, for example.

A pivotal role in the essay is played by Shih-t'ao's term 'one-stroke', as when he talks admiringly of the 'one-stroke method'. This does not refer, as one might be forgiven for thinking, to some minimalist technique – completing a drawing in a single movement of the brush, say (although Shih-t'ao did often follow the *alla prima* precept of not retouching one's original brushwork). This is shown by the fact that 'the gods' and 'Heaven' also employ the 'one-stroke method'. What Shih-t'ao seems to mean is a single, in the sense of continuous, creative process, whereby forms are produced out of chaos. It is this process, through which the world itself comes to be, that the artist implicitly grasps when, with his strokes, he lends 'definition' to chaotic 'clouds' of ink, making hills and woods 'come alive'. In Shih-t'ao's essay, we find one of the most robust and earliest statements in modern times of the ancient conviction that the artist works in emulation of the divine.

▶▶▶ 1. *The One-Stroke Method.* In the primeval past there was no method. The primeval chaos was not differentiated. When the primeval chaos was differentiated, method (law) was born. How was this method born? It was born of one-stroke. This one-stroke is that out of which all phenomena are born, applied by the gods and to be applied by man. People of the world do not know this. Therefore this one stroke (*i-hua*) method is established by me. The establishment of this one-stroke method creates a method out of no-method, and a method which covers all methods.

All painting comes from the understanding mind. If, then, the artist fails to understand the inner law and catch the outward gestures of the delicate complexities of hills and streams and human figures, or the nature of birds and animals and vegetation, or the dimensions of ponds and pavilions and towers, it is because he has not grasped the underlying principle of the one-stroke. Even as one makes a distant journey by starting with a first step, so this one-stroke contains in itself the universe and beyond; thousands and myriads of strokes and ink all begin here and end here, waiting only for one to take advantage of it. A man should be able to show the universe in one stroke, his idea clearly expressed, the execution well done. If the wrist is not fully responsive, then the picture is not good; if the picture is not good, it is because the wrist fails to respond. Give it life and lustre by circular movement and bends, and by stopping movement give it spaciousness. It shoots out, pulls in; it can be square or round, go straight or twist along, upwards or downwards, to the right and to the left. Thus it lifts and dips in sudden turns, breaks loose or cuts across, like the gravitation of water, or the shooting up of a flame, naturally and without the least straining of effect. In this way it penetrates all inner nature of things, gives form to all expressions, never away from the method, and gives life to all. With a casual stroke, hills and streams, all life and vegetation and human habitations take their form and gesture, the scene and the feeling connected with it caught hidden or exposed. People do not see how such a painting is created, but the act of drawing never departs from the understanding mind.

For since the primeval chaos became differentiated, the one-stroke method was born. Since the one-stroke method was born, all objects of the universe appeared. Therefore I say, 'This one principle covers all.'

2. *From Method Freed.* The T-square and compasses are the perfect norms of squares and circles, and the universe is the revolving movement of squares and circles. People know that there are such squares and circles, but do not know the revolving movement of heaven and earth. Thus heaven and earth bind man to a 'method', and through ignorance man becomes enslaved by it. Despite all natural and acquired intelligence, one never understands the inner law of things. Thus one is not freed by the method, but on the contrary is obstructed by it. In ancient as well as modern times, the obstructions due to method remain because the nature of one-stroke is not understood. Once it is understood, the obstacles fall away from man's vision and he can paint freely according to his will; painting according to his will automatically removes the obstacles. For painting is depicting the forms of the universe. How can it be done except by brush and ink? Ink comes by itself in heavy and light shades, in wet and dry. The brush is held by man, and from it come contours and texture lines and dry and wet ink-washes. Of course there was a method among the ancients for without the method [of squares and circles] they would be without formal limits. Thus it is seen that the one-stroke is not just to establish formal limits to the limitless, nor does it establish the limits by a 'method'. Method and

obstructions do not coexist. Method is created of the painting and obstructions fall away during the creation. When method and obstructions do not interfere, the nature of the revolutions of heaven and earth is understood. Thus the principle of painting is revealed and the principle of the single-stroke is fully comprehended.

3. *Development.* The ancients furnish the means for insight, recognition. To 'develop' means to know such means and spurn them. I seldom see people who inherit the bequest of the past and can further develop it. Those who inherit but do not develop fail because of their limited insight. If the insight or recognition is limited to being like the past, then it is not a broad insight. Therefore the gentleman [or 'superior person'. Ed.] takes the past merely as a means of modern development.

Again it is said, 'The perfect man has no method.' It is not that he has no method, but rather the best of methods, which is the method of no-method. For there is expediency besides the principle, and flexible development besides the 'method'. One should know the principle and its flexible adaptation in expediency, as one should know the method and apply it flexibly. For what is painting but the great method of changes and developments in the universe? The spirit and essence of hills and streams, the development and growth of the creation, the action of the forces of the *yin* and the *yang*,[1] all are revealed by the brush and ink for the depiction of this universe and for our enjoyment. People nowadays do not understand this. They always say, 'The texture strokes of such-and-such an artist can be the foundation of art. One's art will not have permanent appeal unless it is like the landscape of such-and-such an artist. The calm and detached atmosphere of such-and-such an artist can establish one's moral tone. Without such skill, art will be merely an amusement.' Thus the painter becomes a slave to a certain known artist and not his master. Even if he succeeds in imitating the model well, he is only eating the left-overs of his home. Of what value is that to the artist himself? Or some say to me. 'A certain artist broadens me. Another artist deepens me. To what school shall I belong? What class shall I choose? To whom shall I want to be compared? What should be the influence? What kinds of dots and washes? What kinds of contour and texture lines? What kind of structure and disposition will enable me to come near to the ancients and the ancients to come near to me?'

People who talk like this forget they have a self ('me') too, besides the ancient models. I am as I am; I exist. I cannot stick the whiskers of the ancients on my face, nor put their entrails in my belly. I have my own entrails and chest, and I prefer to twitch my own whiskers. If sometimes by chance I happen to resemble someone, it is he who happens to come to me, and not I who try to be his death. This is the way it is. Why should I model myself upon the ancients and not develop my own forte?

4. *Respect Your Gift.* As between natural gift and insight, the natural gift comes first. For if insight comes before the gift, it is not an [inborn] gift. The wisest of the ancients developed their inborn gifts from what they learned, and developed what they learned fully aware of what their inborn gift was. But it could concern knowledge of some special thing: this would be a minor talent, for minor ability. They were not able to recognize the power of the one-stroke and fully develop it. For the one-stroke is contained in all things. A painting receives the ink, ink receives from the brush, the brush from the artist's wrist, and the artist's wrist from his directing mind. This receiving is like the way life is created by heaven and forms are made by the earth.

The important thing is that a man should respect his natural gift and not neglect it. To know or conceive a painting and not develop it is to shackle oneself. One who receives the gift of painting must respect it and keep it, strengthen it, not dissipate it abroad, not let it go to sleep inside. The *I Ching* [*Book of Changes*] says, 'The forces of heaven are strong. A gentleman constantly strengthens himself without cease.' This is the way to respect your gift.

5. *On Brush and Ink.* Among the ancients, some have brush [-power] but no ink [-power]. Others have ink [-power] but no brush [-power]. The difference lies not in external nature but in the man's natural talent itself. The ink splashes on to the brush by soul and the brush controls the ink by spirit. Without nourishment and culture the ink lacks soul; without vitality the brush lacks spirit. Those who receive the well-nourished ink but have not the vital spirit have ink-power but no brush-power. Those who have the vital spirit but do not transform the cultured soul have brush-power, but no ink-power. Life in nature consists in the ink-wash expressing the concrete forms of hills and rivers and things, seen from the front or the back, from the side and on a slant, scattered or clustered together, distant or near, external or internal, solid or empty, continuous or broken; they have layers and sections and falling aspects; they have charm and elusive expanse. Thus all nature presents its soul to man and man has the power to control its vitality and culture. If it were not so, how could the brush and ink create the embryonic form and skeletal structure, the opening up and closing in [of spaces], the bodies and functions, the forms and gestures, and picture those that are bending in ceremony or standing erect, those that crouch and leap and hide and soar, and all those that are rugged,

expansive, stiff and tall, all those that are awe-inspiring and overpowering and strange – how else could all this soul and spirit of things be captured and given their full effect on paper?

6. *Control of the Wrist.* Some may object, saying, 'There are instructions on art, in chapter and verse, and detailed instructions on the use of the brush and ink. We have never heard of one talking in vague, general terms about the life and movement of hills and streams and trying to communicate it to others. Perhaps Shih-t'ao thinks highly of himself and wants to establish some kind of esoteric art. So he spurns the lowly details.'

It is certainly not so. What is born in us may be from unknown depths, but its expression is here and now. What can be put into the distance comes from the recognition of some object close at hand. The one-stroke is something elementary in calligraphy and painting; the modified line is a common elementary way of controlling the brush and ink. The mountains and seas are but copies of swellings and hollows of things near by. Life and movement are the elementary principles of contour and texture lines. If one knows, for instance, objects confined to a particular locality, that is the original for a locality. If, then, that particular locality has a certain hill and a certain group of peaks and the artist confines himself to drawing that hill and those peaks, without change, then these become laborious restrictions on the artist's talent. Would that do?

Besides, without change in the life and movement, attention is given to the superficial contour and texture strokes. Without change in method, the life and movement become stereotyped. Without knowledge of light and shadow, one sees only a row of hills and connections of waterways. Without the provision of woods and hills, one feels the emptiness of the scene. To avoid these four errors, one must begin with wrist control. For if the wrist is infinitely flexible and responsive, then the drawing goes in different ways. If the brush is quick and sure, then the forms take definite shape. When the wrist is firm, the drawing is sure and expressive, and when it is flexible, it darts and dances and soars. Or with a perpendicular position, the strokes strike the paper squarely without showing the tip of the brush. Or it may incline and make possible many graceful dragging lines. When it moves fast, it gathers force; when it moves slowly, there is a meaningful dip and turn. When the wrist moves, unconsciously inspired, the result is true to nature, and when it changes, the result can be weird and fantastic. When the wrist is gifted with genius, the painting is beyond the work of human minds, and when the wrist moves with the spirit, the hills and streams yield up their souls.

7. *Cloudy Forms.* Where the brush and ink blend, cloudy forms are produced. Undifferentiated, such cloudy forms represent chaos, and to bring definition out of chaos, there is inevitably the single-stroke. For with the stroke, the hills come alive, the water moves, the woods grow and prosper and the men are given that carefree atmosphere. To be able to control the mixture of brush and ink (stroke and wash), disperse the cloudy forms and create the universe and thus become a good artist on one's own and be known to posterity – this comes from intelligence. One must avoid laborious details, flatness, or falling into a set pattern, being woolly, lacking coherence or going against the inner nature of things. Stand firm in the sea of ink, seek life in the movement of the brush-tip; create a new surface and texture on the foot-long material, and give forth light from the unformed darkness. Then, even if the brush and ink and the drawings are all wrong, the 'me', the 'self', remains there. For one controls the ink and is not controlled by it, handles the brush and is not handled by it. One gives form to the embryo, the embryo does not assume its own form. From one, it divides into tens of thousands, and from the ten thousand shapes of things, one attends to the One, transforming the One into the primeval cloudy forms – this is the height of artistic ability.

8. *Hills and Streams.* The substance of hills and streams embodies the inner law of the universe. But by the method of brush and ink one catches their appearance. One cannot attend to the appearance without regard to the inner law, or attend to the substance alone without regard to the method, for thus the inner law would be violated and the method become futile. To avoid the violation of inner law and the degeneration of method, the ancients tried to reach out to the One. For if the One was not understood, all phenomena would become obstacles; on the other hand, with the understanding of the One, all things have their place. The inner law of painting and the method of the painting brush are but [to catch] the substance and appearance of the universe. The hills and streams are the life and movement of the universe. The changes of light and darkness and rain and clear days are the expression of the hills and streams; the distances and distribution, their layout; the crossing and recrossing and meeting and merging, their rhythm; the light and shade, the *yin* and *yang*, their demeanour. The gathering and distribution of water and clouds express the continuity of hills and streams; the gestures of crouching and leaping up and turning of directions express their movements. That which is high and clear constitutes the standard of heaven; that which is thick and heavy forms the norm of earth. Heaven binds the hills and streams by means of winds and clouds; the earth awakens them to movement by means of water and rocks.

Without these powers of heaven and earth, there would be no natural disasters. Yet heaven cannot bind up the hills and streams to make them conform to one shape, nor can the movement of the surf striking upon rocks serve to point out the differences in live, moving landscapes.

Besides, the mountains and waters are immense, and cloud formations spread across peaks for ten thousand miles. From a narrow point of view, even genii cannot cover the entire expanse. But with the one-stroke, man takes part in the creation of the universe. The artist surveys the layout of hills and streams, estimates the width and length of the land, examines the distribution of mountain peaks and observes the airy forlornness of clouds and mists. He looks at the earth spread out before him and takes a swift glance at the distant ranges, and knows that they are all under the overlordship of heaven and earth. Heaven has the standard to transform the spirit of hills and streams, earth has this norm to activate their pulse beat, and I have this one-stroke to penetrate into their very body and spirit.

Well, then, fifty years ago I was not yet born out of the hills and streams. Nor do I intend to neglect them and let them hide away their secrets. The hills and streams have appointed me to speak for them. They are in me and I am in them. I search out the extraordinary peaks and put them on paper. We meet and comprehend one another in spirit.

[. . .]

15. *Keep Away from the Hustle-Bustle.* A materialist attends to the affairs of the world. A man enslaved by the material world lives in a state of tension. He who is tense labours over his paintings and destroys himself. He who moves among the hustle and bustle of the world handles his brush and ink with caution and restraint. Thus the environment impinges upon a man, can only do him harm and in the end make him unhappy. I meet the world as it comes, yield superficially to the hustlers, and thus achieve peace of mind. With peace of mind comes a painting. People know about paintings, but do not understand paintings of one-stroke. For the important thing in art work is contemplation. When one contemplates the One (unity of all things), one sees it and that makes one happy. Then one's paintings have a mysterious depth which is unfathomable. I believe nobody has said this before, and therefore touch upon it again.

16. *Nonconformism.* The intelligence of the ignorant and the conventional people is about the same. The conventional people follow the ignorant and the ignorant have a mind completely veiled. Remove the veil and the ignorant become wise; leave the conventional man uncontaminated

and his mind remains pure. Therefore the perfect man has to think his way through, has to have a perspective. With a perspective, he becomes transformed; by thinking his way through, he merges into nature. He responds to the affairs of the world without signs and deals with them without visible traces. His ink seems to be there by itself, and his brush moves as if not doing anything. Thus the little scroll controls all objects of creation. One who keeps his mind calm will find that ignorance is replaced by wisdom and conventionality by purity of mind.

17. *Calligraphy Included.* Ink can build up the forms of hills and streams, and the brush can threaten and overthrow their foundations. They are not to be treated lightly. After knowing well all human history, one must have a sea of ink controlled by a mountain of brushes to have a wide range of subjects. Let go and it encompasses the eight extremities and the nine continents, the four sacred mountains and the four oceans; gather it up and they are conveniently tucked away in your breast. There is no limitation to methods or skills, and the skills can be shown in calligraphy as well as in paintings. For these are twin arts with the same function. The single-stroke is the origin of all calligraphy and painting, which are, as it were, the material application of the first principle. To know the applications and forget the first principle of the one-stroke is like children who forget their ancestry. One might forget the God-given while entangled with material objects, and so know that the universe is eternal and yet ascribe the work to man. Heaven can give man his method, but not his skill, inspire him with a painting, but the change and development are up to the man himself. When a man, however, strives after skill apart from the method, or makes changes apart from the [concept of the] painting, he is forsaken by heaven, and his work will not last. For heaven grants unto man according to his ability: to the great he grants great wisdom; to the small, petty wisdom.

Therefore all painting and calligraphy are based on heaven and perfected by man. A man acting according to his greater or lesser talent given by heaven will have the [true] method of calligraphy and painting, and develop it further. . . .

18. *Maintaining Function.* The ancients were able to express forms through brush and ink and by means of hills and streams, the actions without action and transformations of things without [visible means of] transformation. They left a name for posterity without being well known in their lifetime, for they had gone through the awakening and growth and life, recorded in the work they left behind, and had thus incorporated into themselves the substance of hills and streams. With regard to ink, the artist

has received the function of awakening and growth; with regard to the brush, the function of life; with regard to mountains and rivers, the function of understructure; with regard to contour and surface lines, the function of spontaneity. With regard to the seas and oceans, he has received the function of the universe; with regard to the low backyards, the function of the moment; with regard to no-action that of action; with regard to the one-stroke, that of all strokes; with regard to the responsive wrist, that of the tip of the brush.

The artist who takes these functions upon himself must maintain such functions and know what the several functions are before he commits them to paper. If not, his mind is limited and superficial and cannot carry out the functions he undertakes.

For heaven has invested the mountains with many functions. The body of the mountain comes from its location; its spirituality from its spirit; its changes of mood from growth and change; its first awakening and growth from its clarity; its stretching across vast areas from movement; its hidden potentialities come from silence; its bowing and curtsying features from courtesy; its rambling manner comes from a peaceful disposition; its grouping together from caution; its airiness from wisdom; its beauty from delicacy of spirit; its leaping and crouching from the military spirit; its awe-inspiring aspect from its dangerous shapes; its reaching out to heaven from its height; its massiveness from its generosity; and its superficialities come from what is small in it. These are the functions of the nature of the mountain itself, not what it receives from others to thrust upon Nature. Man can take these functions from Nature and maintain them and not because the mountain thrusts them upon man. Thus it is seen that the mountain takes up these functions and maintains them and they cannot be changed or substituted. Therefore the true man (*jen*) never leaves his true manhood and enjoys the mountains.

It is the same with water. Water does many things. These are things that water does. It reaches out in vast rivers and lakes to spread its benefits – such is its virtue. It seeks the lowly humble places – such is its sense of courtesy. Its tides ebb and flow ceaselessly – such is its strength. It swirls about and seeks its level – such is its law. It reaches out to all places – such is its far-reaching power. Its essence is clear and pure – such is its goodness. It turns about and reaches towards the [East China Sea] – such is its goal. For water carries out these functions from the primeval damp chaos. Unless it were able to carry out these functions, it would not be able to circulate to all parts and be the arteries of the world. To know the functions of the mountain without knowing the functions of water is like a man sinking in a sea without knowledge of its shores or standing upon its shores without knowledge of the vast expanse beyond. Therefore the wise man knows the shores and watches the water passing by and his spirit is pleased.

For the immensity of the world is revealed only by the function of water, and water encircles and embraces it through the pressure of mountains. If the mountains and water do not come together and function, there will be nothing to circulate with or about, nothing to embrace. And if there is no circulation and embracing, there will be no means of life and growth. When the means of life and growth are under control, then there is the wherewithal of circulation and embracing, and with circulation and embracing open and possible, the functions of mountains and water are fulfilled.

As for the painter, the value lies not in the vastness of mountains and water, but in their controllability, not in their number and quantity, but in their flexibility in change. Only flexibility in change enables one to paint like a great master, and only control can manage their vastness. The function of the brush is not in the brush, but in something of value created – the function of ink is not in the ink but in its receptivity and response. Likewise the functions in mountains and water lie not in themselves, but in their respective silence and mobility. The proper functions of the ancients and the moderns are not in themselves but in their respective primitiveness and freedom. Thus each has its proper function clearly defined, and the ink and brush-work last for ever, for their functions are adequately fulfilled.

So in speaking of these functions, one sees that they are laws of growth and life. The One controls All, and All are controlled by One – not by mountains, not by waters, not by brush and ink, not by the ancients, nor by the moderns, nor by the sages. Such are the functions when they are properly maintained.

Note

1 The two interacting polarities of ancient Chinese cosmology – the 'dark', 'feminine' and 'hidden' (*yin*) versus the 'bright', 'masculine' and 'open' (*yang*).

6 David Hume, 'Of the standard of taste'

From David Hume, *Essays: moral, political and literary*. Oxford: Oxford University Press, 1965, pp. 231–55 [archaic spellings of proper names modernized].

1,500 years divide Plotinus' chapter on beauty from Hume's essay on taste (1757), but it might as well be 15,000, so different are the contexts assumed and the problems addressed. Although the Greek thinkers represented in this volume were centrally concerned with the value of art and beauty as contributing to human life, they were not similarly taxed by the status of judgements of aesthetic value, such as 'This design is beautiful.' By the eighteenth century, however, the status of such judgements had become a salient problem. First, the 'modern' philosophy inspired by Galileo and Descartes seemed to suggest that the only objective features of the world were those, like shape, which figured in the natural sciences' conception of the world. Among the features thus banished from objective reality were moral and aesthetic ones, which implied that judgements in these areas could only be subjective ones – expressions of feelings, say. A second important development, inspired by Newton's success in identifying general laws of nature, was the Enlightenment ambition to identify similarly general laws of *human* nature, ones as much at work in the moral and aesthetic arenas as in any other. We cannot, wrote the Earl of Shaftesbury in 1711, 'deny the common and natural sense of a sublime and beautiful'.[1] But if there is such a 'common and natural' aesthetic sense, how can manifest disagreements between people's aesthetic appreciations be explained, or explained away?

These two developments seemed to pull in opposite directions. If aesthetic judgements are merely subjective – something apparently confirmed by large-scale disagreement in taste – what substance is there to talking of a common or universal aesthetic sense? The Scottish philosopher and historian David Hume (1711–76) – 'the greatest of all British philosophers', according to A. J. Ayer[2] –

[1] *Characteristics*, Indianapolis: Bobbs-Merrill, 1964, p. 252.

[2] *Hume*, in *The British Empiricists*, Oxford: Oxford University Press, 1992, p. 185.

attempts to show in his essay that the tension here is illusory. Judgements of beauty are indeed subjective in the sense that beauty is not a feature belonging to reality independent of human feeling or sentiment. (Hume, however, vacillates over where, as it were, to locate beauty, sometimes speaking of it as a feature of sentiment itself, sometimes (and more usually) as a 'power of producing . . . pleasure' which things have in virtue of their 'order and construction'.[3]) This in no way implies, however, that aesthetic judgements are subjective in the quite different sense of being merely personal. Someone who judges the seventeenth century Scottish translator, John Ogilby, to be the equal of Milton is as mistaken as one who judges a mole-hill to be as high as a mountain.

Even very widespread disagreement in taste is no threat to the existence of 'universal principles of taste', grounded in natural, common sentiment. This is because people very often 'labour under some defect', such as prejudice, which prevents their responding to poems or paintings in accordance with natural sentiment. Among a community of 'true judges' immune to such defects there would be agreement in judgements of beauty – except, Hume concedes, where these judgements reflect the particular 'humours' of individuals or the particular 'manners' of an age or culture. Much of the essay is devoted to establishing criteria for recognizing these 'true judges' or ideal art critics.

As with his parallel approach to moral judgement, Hume's account of aesthetic judgements has been enormously influential. Santayana, Herbert Read and many other writers have concurred in the view that beauty and other aesthetic qualities are essentially powers which things have to affect us in certain ways. Even those, like Kant (chapter 7), who reject his solution follow Hume in identifying the central question of aesthetics to be that of reconciling our sense that 'beauty is in the eye of the beholder' with the conviction that there can be better and worse, true and false, judgements.

Doubtless, if Hume is to sound convincing to the modern ear, his account needs 'up-dating' in certain respects. The relentless concentration on *beauty* as the essential aesthetic value belongs to an earlier age than our own, as does the sanguine deflation of what are surely deep and significant cultural divides in appreciation to differences in the 'manners of countries'. The notion of the 'true judge', arguably, is plausible only where one is considering aesthetic judgements *within* a cultural tradition and *over* a limited genre of artworks. It is one thing to look for 'true judges' of the respective merits of Ogilby and Milton; another to look for ones to arbitrate between Beethoven and the Beatles, let alone between Beethoven and raga composers.

▶▶▶ The great variety of Taste, as well as of opinion, which prevails in the world, is too obvious not to have fallen under every one's observation. Men of the

[3] Hume, *A Treatise of Human Nature*, Oxford: Clarendon Press, 1960, p. 299.

most confined knowledge are able to remark a difference of taste in the narrow circle of their acquaintance, even where the persons have been educated under the same government, and have early imbibed the same prejudices. But those who can enlarge their view to contemplate distant nations and remote ages, are still more surprised at the great inconsistence and contrariety. We are apt to call *barbarous* whatever departs widely from our own taste and apprehension; but soon find the epithet of reproach retorted on us. And the highest arrogance and self-conceit is at last startled, on observing an equal assurance on all sides, and scruples, amidst such a contest of sentiment, to pronounce positively in its own favour.

As this variety of taste is obvious to the most careless enquirer, so will it be found, on examination, to be still greater in reality than in appearance. The sentiments of men often differ with regard to beauty and deformity of all kinds, even while their general discourse is the same. There are certain terms in every language which import blame, and others praise; and all men who use the same tongue must agree in their application of them. Every voice is united in applauding elegance, propriety, simplicity, spirit in writing; and in blaming fustian, affectation, coldness, and a false brilliancy. But when critics come to particulars, this seeming unanimity vanishes; and it is found, that they had affixed a very different meaning to their expressions. In all matters of opinion and science, the case is opposite; the difference among men is there oftener found to lie in generals than in particulars, and to be less in reality than in appearance. An explanation of the terms commonly ends the controversy: and the disputants are surprised to find that they had been quarrelling, while at bottom they agreed in their judgement.

Those who found morality on sentiment, more than on reason, are inclined to comprehend ethics under the former observation, and to maintain, that, in all questions which regard conduct and manners, the difference among men is really greater than at first sight it appears. It is indeed obvious, that writers of all nations and all ages concur in applauding justice, humanity, magnanimity, prudence, veracity; and in blaming the opposite qualities. Even poets and other authors, whose compositions are chiefly calculated to please the imagination, are yet found, from Homer down to Fénelon [1651–1715, French theologian. Ed.], to inculcate the same moral precepts, and to bestow their applause and blame on the same virtues and vices. This great unanimity is usually ascribed to the influence of plain reason, which, in all these cases, maintains similar sentiments in all men, and prevents those controversies to which the abstract sciences are so much exposed. So far as the unanimity is real, this account may be admitted as satisfactory. But we must also allow, that some part of the seeming harmony in morals may be accounted for from the very nature of language. The word *virtue*, with its equivalent in every tongue, implies praise, as that of *vice* does blame; and no one, without the most obvious and grossest impropriety, could affix reproach to a term, which in general acceptation is understood in a good sense: or bestow applause, where the idiom requires disapprobation. Homer's general precepts, where he delivers any such, will never be controverted; but it is obvious, that, when he draws particular pictures of manners and represents heroism in Achilles, and prudence in Ulysses, he intermixes a much greater degree of ferocity in the former, and of cunning and fraud in the latter, than Fénelon would admit of. The sage Ulysses, in the Greek poet, seems to delight in lies and fictions, and often employs them without any necessity, or even advantage. But his more scrupulous son, in the French epic writer, exposes himself to the most imminent perils, rather than depart from the most exact line of truth and veracity.

The admirers and followers of the Koran insist on the excellent moral precepts interspersed throughout that wild and absurd performance. But it is to be supposed, that the Arabic words, which correspond to the English, equity, justice, temperance, meekness, charity, were such as, from the constant use of that tongue, must always be taken in a good sense: and it would have argued the greatest ignorance, not of morals, but of language, to have mentioned them with any epithets, besides those of applause and approbation. But would we know, whether the pretended prophet had really attained a just sentiment of morals, let us attend to his narration, and we shall soon find, that he bestows praise on such instances of treachery, inhumanity, cruelty, revenge, bigotry, as are utterly incompatible with civilized society. No steady rule of right seems there to be attended to; and every action is blamed or praised, so far only as it is beneficial or hurtful to the true believers.

The merit of delivering true general precepts in ethics is indeed very small. Whoever recommends any moral virtues, really does no more than is implied in the terms themselves. That people who invented the word *charity*, and used it in a good sense, inculcated more clearly, and much more efficaciously, the precept, *Be charitable*, than any pretended legislator or prophet, who should insert such a *maxim* in his writings. Of all expressions, those which, together with their other meaning, imply a degree either of blame or approbation, are the least liable to be perverted or mistaken.

It is natural for us to seek a *Standard of Taste*; a rule by which the various sentiments of men may be reconciled; at least a decision afforded confirming one sentiment, and condemning another.

There is a species of philosophy, which cuts off all hopes of success in such an attempt, and represents the impossibility of ever attaining any standard of taste. The difference, it is said, is very wide between judgement and sentiment. All sentiment is right; because sentiment has a reference to nothing beyond itself, and is always real, wherever a man is conscious of it. But all determinations of the understanding are not right; because they have a reference to something beyond themselves, to wit, real matter of fact; and are not always conformable to that standard. Among a thousand different opinions which different men may entertain of the same subject, there is one, and but one, that is just and true: and the only difficulty is to fix and ascertain it. On the contrary, a thousand different sentiments, excited by the same object, are all right; because no sentiment represents what is really in the object. It only marks a certain conformity or relation between the object and the organs or faculties of the mind; and if that conformity did not really exist, the sentiment could never possibly have being. Beauty is no quality in things themselves: it exists merely in the mind which contemplates them; and each mind perceives a different beauty. One person may even perceive deformity, where another is sensible of beauty; and every individual ought to acquiesce in his own sentiment, without pretending to regulate those of others. To seek the real beauty, or real deformity, is as fruitless an enquiry, as to pretend to ascertain the real sweet or real bitter. According to the disposition of the organs, the same object may be both sweet and bitter; and the proverb has justly determined it to be fruitless to dispute concerning tastes. It is very natural, and even quite necessary, to extend this axiom to mental, as well as bodily taste; and thus common sense, which is so often at variance with philosophy, especially with the sceptical kind, is found, in one instance at least, to agree in pronouncing the same decision.

But though this axiom, by passing into a proverb, seems to have attained the sanction of common sense; there is certainly a species of common sense, which opposes it, at least serves to modify and restrain it. Whoever would assert an equality of genius and elegance between Ogilby and Milton, or Bunyan and Addison, would be thought to defend no less an extravagance, than if he had maintained a mole-hill to be as high as Tenerife, or a pond as extensive as the ocean. Though there may be found persons, who give the preference to the former authors; no one pays attention to such a taste; and we pronounce, without scruple, the sentiment of these pretended critics to be absurd and ridiculous. The principle of the natural equality of tastes is then totally forgot, and while we admit it on some occasions, where the objects seem near an equality, it appears an extravagant paradox, or rather a palpable absurdity, where objects so disproportioned are compared together.

It is evident that none of the rules of composition are fixed by reasonings *a priori*, or can be esteemed abstract conclusions of the understanding, from comparing those habitudes and relations of ideas, which are eternal and immutable. Their foundation is the same with that of all the practical sciences, experience; nor are they any thing but general observations, concerning what has been universally found to please in all countries and in all ages. Many of the beauties of poetry, and even of eloquence, are founded on falsehood and fiction, on hyperboles, metaphors, and an abuse or perversion of terms from their natural meaning. To check the sallies of the imagination, and to reduce every expression to geometrical truth and exactness, would be the most contrary to the laws of criticism; because it would produce a work, which, by universal experience, has been found the most insipid and disagreeable. But though poetry can never submit to exact truth, it must be confined by rules of art, discovered to the author either by genius or observation. If some negligent or irregular writers have pleased, they have not pleased by their transgressions of rule or order, but in spite of these transgressions: they have possessed other beauties, which were conformable to just criticism; and the force of these beauties has been able to overpower censure, and give the mind a satisfaction superior to the disgust arising from the blemishes. Ariosto [1474–1535, Italian epic poet. Ed.] pleases; but not by his monstrous and improbable fictions, by his bizarre mixture of the serious and comic styles, by the want of coherence in his stories, or by the continual interruptions of his narration. He charms by the force and clearness of his expression, by the readiness and variety of his inventions, and by his natural pictures of the passions, especially those of the gay and amorous kind: and, however his faults may diminish our satisfaction, they are not able entirely to destroy it. Did our pleasure really arise from those parts of his poem, which we denominate faults, this would be no objection to criticism in general: it would only be an objection to those particular rules of criticism, which would establish such circumstances to be faults, and would represent them as universally blamable. If they are found to please, they cannot be faults, let the pleasure which they produce be ever so unexpected and unaccountable.

But though all the general rules of art are founded only on experience, and on the observation of the common sentiments of human nature, we must not imagine, that, on every occasion, the feelings of men will be conformable to these rules. Those finer emotions of the mind are of a very tender and delicate nature, and require the concurrence of many favourable circumstances to make them play with facility and exactness, according to their general and established principles. The least exterior hindrance to such small springs, or the least internal disorder, disturbs their motion, and confounds the operations of the whole machine. When we would make an experiment of this nature, and would try the force of any beauty or deformity, we must choose with care a proper time and place, and bring the fancy to a suitable situation and disposition. A perfect serenity of mind, a recollection of thought, a due attention to the object; if any of these circumstances be wanting, our experiment will be fallacious, and we shall be unable to judge of the catholic and universal beauty. The relation, which nature has placed between the form and the sentiment, will at least be more obscure; and it will require greater accuracy to trace and discern it. We shall be able to ascertain its influence, not so much from the operation of each particular beauty, as from the durable admiration which attends those works that have survived all the caprices of mode and fashion, all the mistakes of ignorance and envy.

The same Homer who pleased at Athens and Rome two thousand years ago, is still admired at Paris and at London. All the changes of climate, government, religion, and language, have not been able to obscure his glory. Authority or prejudice may give a temporary vogue to a bad poet or orator; but his reputation will never be durable or general. When his compositions are examined by posterity or by foreigners, the enchantment is dissipated, and his faults appear in their true colours. On the contrary, a real genius, the longer his works endure, and the more wide they are spread, the more sincere is the admiration which he meets with. Envy and jealousy have too much place in a narrow circle; and even familiar acquaintance with his person may diminish the applause due to his performances: but when these obstructions are removed, the beauties, which are naturally fitted to excite agreeable sentiments, immediately display their energy; and while the world endures, they maintain their authority over the minds of men.

It appears, then, that amidst all the variety and caprice of taste, there are certain general principles of approbation or blame, whose influence a careful eye may trace in all operations of the mind. Some particular forms or qualities, from the original structure of the internal fabric are calculated to please, and others to displease; and if they fail of their effect in any particular instance, it is from some apparent defect or imperfection in the organ. A man in a fever would not insist on his palate as able to decide concerning flavours; nor would one affected with the jaundice pretend to give a verdict with regard to colours. In each creature there is a sound and a defective state; and the former alone can be supposed to afford us a true standard of taste and sentiment. If, in the sound state of the organ, there be an entire or a considerable uniformity of sentiment among men, we may thence derive an idea of the perfect beauty; in like manner as the appearance of objects in daylight, to the eye of a man in health, is denominated their true and real colour, even while colour is allowed to be merely a phantasm of the senses.

Many and frequent are the defects in the internal organs, which prevent or weaken the influence of those general principles, on which depends our sentiment of beauty or deformity. Though some objects, by the structure of the mind, be naturally calculated to give pleasure, it is not to be expected that in every individual the pleasure will be equally felt. Particular incidents and situations occur, which either throw a false light on the objects, or hinder the true from conveying to the imagination the proper sentiment and perception.

One obvious cause why many feel not the proper sentiment of beauty, is the want of that *delicacy* of imagination which is requisite to convey a sensibility of those finer emotions. This delicacy every one pretends to: every one talks of it; and would reduce every kind of taste or sentiment to its standard. But as our intention in this Essay is to mingle some light of the understanding with the feelings of sentiment, it will be proper to give a more accurate definition of delicacy than has hitherto been attempted. And not to draw our philosophy from too profound a source, we shall have recourse to a noted story in [Cervantes'] *Don Quixote* [pt. 2, ch. 13. Ed.].

It is with good reason, says Sancho to the squire with the great nose, that I pretend to have a judgement in wine: this is a quality hereditary in our family. Two of my kinsmen were once called to give their opinion of a hogshead, which was supposed to be excellent, being old and of a good vintage. One of them tastes it, considers it; and, after mature reflection, pronounces the wine to be good, were it not for a small taste of leather which he perceived in it. The other, after using the same precautions, gives also his verdict in favour of the wine; but with the reserve of a taste of iron, which he could easily distinguish. You cannot imagine how much they were both ridiculed for their judgement. But who laughed in the end? On emptying the hogshead, there was found at the bottom an old key with a leathern thong tied to it.

The great resemblance between mental and bodily taste will easily teach us to apply this story. Though it be certain that beauty and deformity, more than sweet and bitter, are not qualities in objects, but belong entirely to the sentiment, internal or external, it must be allowed, that there are certain qualities in objects which are fitted by nature to produce those particular feelings. Now, as these qualities may be found in a small degree, or may be mixed and confounded with each other, it often happens that the taste is not affected with such minute qualities, or is not able to distinguish all the particular flavours, amidst the disorder in which they are presented. Where the organs are so fine as to allow nothing to escape them, and at the same time so exact as to perceive every ingredient in the composition, this we call delicacy of taste, whether we employ these terms in the literal or metaphorical sense. Here then the general rules of beauty are of use, being drawn from established models, and from the observation of what pleases or displeases, when presented singly and in a high degree; and if the same qualities, in a continued composition, and in a smaller degree, affect not the organs with a sensible delight or uneasiness, we exclude the person from all pretensions to this delicacy. To produce these general rules or avowed patterns of composition, is like finding the key with the leathern thong, which justified the verdict of Sancho's kinsmen, and confounded those pretended judges who had condemned them. Though the hogshead had never been emptied, the taste of the one was still equally delicate, and that of the other equally dull and languid; but it would have been more difficult to have proved the superiority of the former, to the conviction of every bystander. In like manner, though the beauties of writing had never been methodized, or reduced to general principles; though no excellent models had ever been acknowledged, the different degrees of taste would still have subsisted, and the judgement of one man been preferable to that of another; but it would not have been so easy to silence the bad critic, who might always insist upon his particular sentiment, and refuse to submit to his antagonist. But when we show him an avowed principle of art; when we illustrate this principle by examples, whose operation, from his own particular taste, he acknowledges to be conformable to the principle; when we prove that the same principle may be applied to the present case, where he did not perceive or feel its influence: he must conclude, upon the whole, that the fault lies in himself, and that he wants the delicacy which is requisite to make him sensible of every beauty and every blemish in any composition or discourse.

It is acknowledged to be the perfection of every sense or faculty, to perceive with exactness its most minute objects, and allow nothing to escape its notice and observation. The smaller the objects are which become sensible to the eye, the finer is that organ, and the more elaborate its make and composition. A good palate is not tried by strong flavours, but by a mixture of small ingredients, where we are still sensible of each part, notwithstanding its minuteness and its confusion with the rest. In like manner, a quick and acute perception of beauty and deformity must be the perfection of our mental taste; nor can a man be satisfied with himself while he suspects that any excellence or blemish in a discourse has passed him unobserved. In this case, the perfection of the man, and the perfection of the sense of feeling, are found to be united. A very delicate palate, on many occasions, may be a great inconvenience both to a man himself and to his friends. But a delicate taste of wit or beauty must always be a desirable quality, because it is the source of all the finest and most innocent enjoyments of which human nature is susceptible. In this decision the sentiments of all mankind are agreed. Wherever you can ascertain a delicacy of taste, it is sure to meet with approbation; and the best way of ascertaining it is, to appeal to those models and principles which have been established by the uniform consent and experience of nations and ages.

But though there be naturally a wide difference, in point of delicacy, between one person and another, nothing tends further to increase and improve this talent, than *practice* in a particular art, and the frequent survey or contemplation of a particular species of beauty. When objects of any kind are first presented to the eye or imagination, the sentiment which attends them is obscure and confused; and the mind is, in a great measure, incapable of pronouncing concerning their merits or defects. The taste cannot perceive the several excellences of the performance, much less distinguish the particular character of each excellency, and ascertain its quality and degree. If it pronounce the whole in general to be beautiful or deformed, it is the utmost that can be expected; and even this judgement, a person so unpractised will be apt to deliver with great hesitation and reserve. But allow him to acquire experience in those objects, his feeling becomes more exact and nice: he not only perceives the beauties and defects of each part, but marks the distinguishing species of each quality, and assigns it suitable praise or blame. A clear and distinct sentiment attends him through the whole survey of the objects; and he discerns that very degree and kind of approbation or displeasure which each part is naturally fitted to produce. The mist dissipates which seemed formerly to hang over the object; the organ acquires greater perfection in its operations, and can pronounce, without danger of mistake, concerning the merits of every performance. In a word, the same address and dexterity which practice gives to the execution of any work, is also acquired by the same means in the judging of it.

So advantageous is practice to the discernment of beauty, that, before we can give judgement on any work of importance, it will even be requisite that that very individual performance be more than once perused by us, and be surveyed in different lights with attention and deliberation. There is a flutter or hurry of thought which attends the first perusal of any piece, and which confounds the genuine sentiment of beauty. The relation of the parts is not discerned: the true characters of style are little distinguished. The several perfections and defects seem wrapped up in a species of confusion, and present themselves indistinctly to the imagination. Not to mention, that there is a species of beauty, which, as it is florid and superficial, pleases at first; but being found incompatible with a just expression either of reason or passion, soon palls upon the taste, and is then rejected with disdain, at least rated at a much lower value.

It is impossible to continue in the practice of contemplating any order of beauty, without being frequently obliged to form *comparisons* between the several species and degrees of excellence, and estimating their proportion to each other. A man who has had no opportunity of comparing the different kinds of beauty, is indeed totally unqualified to pronounce an opinion with regard to any object presented to him. By comparison alone we fix the epithets of praise or blame, and learn how to assign the due degree of each. The coarsest daubing contains a certain lustre of colours and exactness of imitation, which are so far beauties, and would affect the mind of a peasant or Indian with the highest admiration. The most vulgar ballads are not entirely destitute of harmony or nature; and none but a person familiarized to superior beauties would pronounce their members harsh, or narration uninteresting. A great inferiority of beauty gives pain to a person conversant in the highest excellence of the kind, and is for that reason pronounced a deformity; as the most finished object with which we are acquainted is naturally supposed to have reached the pinnacle of perfection, and to be entitled to the highest applause. One accustomed to see, and examine, and weigh the several performances, admired in different ages and nations, can alone rate the merits of a work exhibited to his view, and assign its proper rank among the productions of his genius.

But to enable a critic the more fully to execute this undertaking, he must preserve his mind free from all *prejudice*, and allow nothing to enter into his consideration, but the very object which is submitted to his examination. We may observe, that every work of art, in order to produce its due effect on the mind, must be surveyed in a certain point of view, and cannot be fully relished by persons whose situation, real or imaginary, is not conformable to that which is required by the performance. An orator addresses himself to a particular audience, and must have a regard to their particular genius, interests, opinions, passions, and prejudices; otherwise he hopes in vain to govern their resolutions, and inflame their affections. Should they even have entertained some prepossessions against him, however unreasonable, he must not overlook this disadvantage: but, before he enters upon the subject, must endeavour to conciliate their affection, and acquire their good graces. A critic of a different age or nation, who should peruse this discourse, must have all these circumstances in his eye, and must place himself in the same situation as the audience, in order to form a true judgement of the oration. In like manner, when any work is addressed to the public, though I should have a friendship or enmity with the author, I must depart from this situation, and, considering myself as a man in general, forget, if possible, my individual being, and my peculiar circumstances. A person influenced by prejudice complies not with this condition, but obstinately maintains his natural position, without placing himself in that point of view which the performance supposes. If the work be addressed to persons of a different age or nation, he makes no allowance for their peculiar views and prejudices; but, full of the manners of his own age and country, rashly condemns what seemed admirable in the eyes of those for whom alone the discourse was calculated. If the work be executed for the public, he never sufficiently enlarges his comprehension, or forgets his interest as a friend or enemy, as a rival or commentator. By this means his sentiments are perverted; nor have the same beauties and blemishes the same influence upon him, as if he had imposed a proper violence on his imagination, and had forgotten himself for a moment. So far his taste evidently departs from the true standard, and of consequence loses all credit and authority.

It is well known, that, in all questions submitted to the understanding, prejudice is destructive of sound judgement, and perverts all operations of the intellectual faculties: it is no less contrary to good taste; nor has it less influence to corrupt our sentiment of beauty. It belongs to *good sense* to check its influence in both cases; and in this respect, as well as in many others, reason, if not an essential part of taste, is at least requisite to the operations of this latter faculty. In all the nobler productions of genius, there is a mutual relation and correspondence of parts; nor can either the beauties or blemishes be perceived by him whose thought is not capacious enough to comprehend all those parts, and compare them with each other, in order to perceive the consistence and uniformity of the whole. Every work of art has also a certain end or purpose for which it is calculated; and is to be deemed more or less perfect, as it is more or less fitted to attain this end. The object of eloquence is to persuade, of history to instruct, of poetry to please, by means of the passions and the imagination. These ends we must carry constantly in our view when we peruse any performance; and we must be able to judge how far the means employed are adapted to their respective purposes. Besides, every kind of composition, even the most poetical, is nothing but a chain of propositions and reasonings; not always, indeed, the justest and most exact, but still plausible and specious, however disguised by the colouring of the imagination. The persons introduced in tragedy and epic poetry must be represented as reasoning, and thinking, and concluding, and acting, suitably to their character and circumstances; and without judgement, as well as taste and invention, a poet can never hope to succeed in so delicate an undertaking. Not to mention, that the same excellence of faculties which contributes to the improvement of reason, the same clearness of conception, the same exactness of distinction, the same vivacity of apprehension, are essential to the operations of true taste, and are its infallible concomitants. It seldom or never happens, that a man of sense, who has experience in any art, cannot judge of its beauty; and it is no less rare to meet with a man who has a just taste without a sound understanding.

Thus, though the principles of taste be universal, and nearly, if not entirely, the same in all men; yet few are qualified to give judgement on any work of art, or establish their own sentiment as the standard of beauty. The organs of internal sensation are seldom so perfect as to allow the general principles their full play, and produce a feeling correspondent to those principles. They either labour under some defect, or are vitiated by some disorder; and by that means excite a sentiment, which may be pronounced erroneous. When the critic has no delicacy, he judges without any distinction, and is only affected by the grosser and more palpable qualities of the object: the finer touches pass unnoticed and disregarded. Where he is not aided by practice, his verdict is attended with confusion and hesitation. Where no comparison has been employed, the most frivolous beauties, such as rather merit the name of defects, are the object of his admiration. Where he lies under the influence of prejudice, all his natural sentiments are perverted. Where good sense is wanting, he is not qualified to discern the beauties of design and reasoning, which are the highest and most excellent. Under some or other of these imperfections, the generality of men labour, and hence a true judge in the finer arts is observed, even during the most polished ages, to be so rare a character: strong sense, united to delicate sentiment, improved by practice, perfected by comparison, and cleared of all prejudice, can alone entitle critics to this valuable character; and the joint verdict of such, wherever they are to be found, is the true standard of taste and beauty.

But where are such critics to be found? By what marks are they to be known? How distinguish them from pretenders? These questions are embarrassing; and seem to throw us back into the same uncertainty from which, during the course of this Essay, we have endeavoured to extricate ourselves.

But if we consider the matter aright, these are questions of fact, not of sentiment. Whether any particular person be endowed with good sense and a delicate imagination, free from prejudice, may often be the subject of dispute, and be liable to great discussion and enquiry: but that such a character is valuable and estimable, will be agreed in by all mankind. Where these doubts occur, men can do no more than in other disputable questions which are submitted to the understanding: they must produce the best arguments that their invention suggests to them; they must acknowledge a true and decisive standard to exist somewhere, to wit, real existence and matter of fact; and they must have indulgence to such as differ from them in their appeals to this standard. It is sufficient for our present purpose, if we have proved, that the taste of all individuals is not upon an equal footing, and that some men in general, however difficult to be particularly pitched upon, will be acknowledged by universal sentiment to have a preference above others.

But, in reality, the difficulty of finding, even in particulars, the standard of taste, is not so great as it is represented. Though in speculation we may readily avow a certain criterion in science, and deny it is sentiment, the matter is found in practice to be much more hard to ascertain in the former case than in the latter. Theories of abstract philosophy, systems of profound theology, have prevailed during one age: in a successive period these have been universally exploded: their absurdity has been detected: other theories and systems have supplied their place, which again gave place to their successors: and nothing has been experienced more liable to the revolutions of chance and fashion than these pretended decisions of science. The case is not the same with the beauties of eloquence and poetry. Just expressions of passion and nature are sure, after a little time, to gain public applause, which they maintain for ever. Aristotle, and Plato, and Epicurus, and Descartes, may successively yield to each other: but Terence and Virgil maintain an universal, undisputed empire over the minds of men. The abstract philosophy of Cicero has lost its credit: the vehemence of his oratory is still the object of our admiration.

Though men of delicate taste be rare, they are easily to be distinguished in society by the soundness of their understanding, and the superiority of their faculties above the rest of mankind. The ascendant, which they acquire, gives a prevalence to that lively approbation with which they receive any productions of genius, and renders it generally predominant. Many men, when left to themselves, have but a faint and dubious perception of beauty, who yet are capable of relishing any fine stroke which is pointed out to them. Every convert to the admiration of the real poet or orator, is the cause of some new conversion. And though prejudices may prevail for a time, they never unite in celebrating any rival to the true genius, but yield at last to the force of nature and just sentiment. Thus, though a civilized nation may easily be mistaken in the choice of their admired philosopher, they never have been found long to err, in their affection for a favourite epic or tragic author.

But notwithstanding all our endeavours to fix a standard of taste, and reconcile the discordant apprehensions of men, there still remain two sources of variation, which are not sufficient indeed to confound all the boundaries of beauty and deformity, but will often serve to produce a difference in the degrees of our approbation or blame. The one is the different humours of particular men; the other, the particular manners and opinions of our age and country. The general principles of taste are uniform in human nature: where men vary in their judgements, some defect or perversion in the faculties may commonly be remarked; proceeding either from prejudice, from want of practice, or want of delicacy: and there is just reason for approving one taste, and condemning another. But where there is such a diversity in the internal frame or external situation as is entirely blameless on both sides, and leaves no room to give one the preference above the other; in that case a certain degree of diversity in judgement is unavoidable, and we seek in vain for a standard, by which we can reconcile the contrary sentiments.

A young man, whose passions are warm, will be more sensibly touched with amorous and tender images, than a man more advanced in years, who takes pleasure in wise, philosophical reflections, concerning the conduct of life, and moderation of the passions. At twenty, Ovid may be the favourite author, Horace at forty, and perhaps Tacitus at fifty. Vainly would we, in such cases, endeavour to enter into the sentiments of others, and divest ourselves of those propensities which are natural to us. We choose our favourite author as we do our friend, from a conformity of humour and disposition. Mirth or passion, sentiment or reflection; whichever of these most predominates in our temper, it gives us a peculiar sympathy with the writer who resembles us.

One person is more pleased with the sublime, another with the tender, a third with raillery. One has a strong sensibility to blemishes, and is extremely studious of correctness; another has a more lively feeling of beauties, and pardons twenty absurdities and defects for one elevated or pathetic stroke. The ear of this man is entirely turned towards conciseness and energy; that man is delighted with a copious, rich, and harmonious expression. Simplicity is affected by one; ornament by another. Comedy, tragedy, satire, odes, have each its partisans, who prefer that particular species of writing to all others. It is plainly an error in a critic, to confine his approbation to one species or style of writing, and condemn all the rest. But it is almost impossible not to feel a predilection for that which suits our particular turn and disposition. Such performances are innocent and unavoidable, and can never reasonably be the object of dispute, because there is no standard by which they can be decided.

For a like reason, we are more pleased, in the course of our reading, with pictures and characters that resemble objects which are found in our own age and country, than with those which describe a different set of customs. It is not without some effort that we reconcile ourselves to the simplicity of ancient manners, and behold princesses carrying water from the spring, and kings and heroes dressing their own victuals. We may allow in general, that the representation of such manners is not fault in the author, nor deformity in the piece; but we are not so sensibly touched with them. For this reason, comedy is not easily transferred from one age or nation to another. A Frenchman or Englishman is not pleased with the *Andria* of Terence, or *Clitia* of Machiavelli; where the fine lady, upon whom all the play turns, never once appears to the spectators, but is always kept behind the scenes, suitably to the reserved humour of the ancient Greeks and modern Italians. A man of learning and reflection can make allowance for these peculiarities of manners; but a common audience can never divest themselves so far of their usual ideas and sentiments, as to relish pictures which nowise resemble them.

But here there occurs a reflection, which may, perhaps, be useful in examining the celebrated controversy concerning ancient and modern learning; where we often find the one side excusing any seeming absurdity in the ancients from the manners of the age, and the other refusing to admit this excuse, or at least admitting it only as an apology for the author, not for the performance. In my opinion, the proper boundaries in this subject have seldom been fixed between the contending parties. Where any innocent peculiarities of manners are represented, such as those above mentioned, they ought certainly to be admitted; and a man who is shocked with them, gives an evident proof of false delicacy and refinement. The poet's *monument more durable than brass* [Horace, *Odes*. 3.30.1. Ed.], must fall to the ground like common brick or clay, were men to make no allowance for the continual revolutions of manners and customs, and would admit of nothing but what was suitable to the prevailing fashion. Must we throw aside the pictures of our ancestors, because of their ruffs and farthingales? But where the ideas of morality and decency alter from one age to another, and where vicious manners are described, without being marked with the proper characters of blame and disapprobation, this must be allowed to disfigure the poem, and to be a real deformity. I cannot, nor is it proper I should, enter into such sentiments; and however I may excuse the poet, on account of the manners of his age, I can never relish the composition. The want of humanity and of decency, so conspicuous in the characters drawn by several of the ancient poets, even sometimes by Homer and the Greek tragedians, diminishes considerably the merit of their noble performances, and gives modern authors an advantage over them. We are not interested in the fortunes and sentiments of such rough heroes; we are displeased to find the limits of vice and virtue so much confounded; and whatever indulgence we may give to the writer on account of his prejudices, we cannot prevail on ourselves to enter into his sentiments, or bear an affection to characters which we plainly discover to be blamable.

The case is not the same with moral principles as with speculative opinions of any kind. These are in continual flux and revolution. The son embraces a different system from the father. Nay, there scarcely is any man, who can boast of great constancy and uniformity in this particular. Whatever speculative errors may be found in the polite writings of any age or country, they detract but little from the value of those compositions. There needs but a certain turn of thought or imagination to make us enter into all the opinions which then prevailed, and relish the sentiments or conclusions derived from them. But a very violent effort is requisite to change our judgement of manners, and excite sentiments of approbation or blame, love or hatred, different from those to which the mind, from long custom, has been familiarized. And where a man is confident of the rectitude of that moral standard by which he judges, he is justly jealous of it, and will not pervert the sentiments of his heart for a moment, in complaisance to any writer whatsoever.

Of all speculative errors, those which regard religion are the most excusable in compositions of genius; nor is it ever permitted to judge of the civility or wisdom of any people, or even of single persons, by the grossness or refinement of their theological principles. The same good sense that directs men in the ordinary occurrences of life, is not hearkened to in religious matters, which are supposed to be placed altogether above the cognizance of human reason. On this account, all the absurdities of the Pagan system of theology must be overlooked by every critic, who would pretend to form a just notion of ancient poetry; and our posterity, in their turn, must have the same indulgence to their forefathers. No religious principles can ever be imputed as a fault to any poet, while they remain merely principles, and take not such strong possession of his heart as to lay him under the imputation of *bigotry or superstition*. Where that happens, they confound the sentiments of morality, and alter the natural boundaries of vice and virtue. They are therefore eternal blemishes, according to the principle above mentioned; nor are the prejudices and false opinions of the age sufficient to justify them.

It is essential to the Roman Catholic religion to inspire a violent hatred of every other worship, and to represent all Pagans, Mahometans, and heretics, as the objects of divine wrath and vengeance. Such sentiments, though they are in reality very blamable, are considered as virtues by the zealots of that communion, and are represented in their tragedies and epic poems as a kind of divine heroism. This bigotry has disfigured two very fine tragedies of the French theatre, [Corneille's] *Polieucte* and [Racine's] *Athalia*; where an intemperate zeal for particular modes of worship is set off with all the pomp imaginable, and forms the predominant character of the heroes. 'What is this', says the sublime Joad to Josabet, finding her in discourse with Mathan the priest of Baal, 'Does the daughter of David speak to this traitor? Are you not afraid lest the earth should open, and pour forth flames to devour you both? Or lest these holy walls should fall and crush you together? What is his purpose? Why comes that enemy of God hither to poison the air, which we breathe, with his horrid presence?' Such sentiments are received with great applause on the theatre of Paris; but at London the spectators would be full as much pleased to hear Achilles tell Agamemnon, that he was a dog in his forehead, and a deer in his heart; or Jupiter threaten Juno with a sound drubbing, if she will not be quiet.

Religious principles are also a blemish in any polite composition, when they rise up to superstition, and intrude themselves into every sentiment, however remote from any connection with religion. It is no excuse for the poet, that the customs of his country had burdened life with so many religious ceremonies and observances, that no part of it was exempt from that yoke. It must for ever be ridiculous in Petrarch to compare his mistress, Laura, to Jesus Christ. Nor is it less ridiculous in that agreeable libertine, Boccaccio, very seriously to give thanks to God Almighty and the ladies, for their assistance in defending him against his enemies.

7 Immanuel Kant, 'Critique of aesthetic judgement', Sections 1–14, 16, 23–4, 28

From Immanuel Kant, *The Critique of Judgement*, trans. J. C. Meredith. Oxford: Clarendon Press, 1952 [some passages omitted; footnotes are Kant's].

A problem with Hume's characterization of beauty (as a power in things to afford us pleasure) is its breadth. For that power is possessed by such agreeable items as warm baths and dry martinis as well as by things which, as we see it, invite more authentically aesthetic judgements. It is Kant, more than anyone, who is responsible for pressing the distinction suggested here, and indeed for the terminology I have just used. This is one reason he is spoken of as 'the father of modern aesthetics' and his 'Critique of aesthetic judgement' described as a work without which 'aesthetics would not exist in its modern form'.[1] In aesthetics, as elsewhere, Immanuel Kant (1724–1804), although he barely ventured from his native Königsberg, has had the largest influence, certainly since Descartes, upon philosophy in modern times.

The work just mentioned forms the First Part of *The Critique of Judgement* (1790), and at first glance has little connection with the Second Part, 'Critique of teleological judgement', beyond a brief discussion of 'purposiveness' or 'finality'. Kant, however, regarded the book as a unity and indeed as his crowning achievement, in which the doctrines of his two earlier critiques – of pure and practical reason – were combined or 'bridged'. The relation between the two parts, and between them and his earlier books, is a matter for students of Kant. In the present context, 'Critique of aesthetic judgement' is presented as a free-standing contribution to aesthetics.

I have selected sections on judgements of taste and on the sublime in nature, for it is in these, I believe, that Kant's most enduring contributions reside. But these constitute only one-fifth of the work, so that much of interest is being omitted, including most of his remarks on art. This may seem to be an

Reprinted by permission of Oxford University Press.

[1] Eva Schaper, 'Taste, sublimity, and genius: the aesthetics of nature and art', in P. Guyer (ed.), *The Cambridge Companion to Kant*, Cambridge: Cambridge University Press, 1992, p. 368; Roger Scruton, *Kant*, Oxford: Oxford University Press, 1982, p. 79.

odd omission but, ironically, it is not these remarks which have been most influential, not even in the philosophy of art. Many readers, however, will certainly want to look up Kant's comments on the 'genius' and the ineffable 'aesthetic ideas' which he communicates (§§ 46–50), which inspired early nineteenth century romantics. Kant, I like to think, would approve of my selection since, for reasons of both personal taste and philosophical import, it was judgements of natural beauty which most concerned him. He states, indeed, that 'art can only be termed beautiful' when it has 'the appearance of nature' (§ 45).

The problem or 'antinomy' addressed in the sections on taste is similar to Hume's: how can judgements which are aesthetic and hence subjective, in that they 'denote the feeling' of the perceiver, nevertheless demand universal assent? Kant's strategy is a radicalization of Hume's pruning of the 'defects' under which most perceivers usually labour. For Kant, a judgement is only a purely aesthetic one when it is 'disinterested', free of any desires or needs, including an interest in the actual existence of the object perceived, which might distort a person's appreciation. When so freed, there is nothing left to account for one person's judgement differing from another's, which is why I can and must insist that my pleasure in an object is 'universally communicable'. After all, this pleasure is a function, according to Kant, of a certain 'free play' between the faculties of imagination and understanding common to all human beings, which some objects, by virtue of their 'form' and appearance of 'finality' or 'design', are suited to encourage. The four 'moments' in Kant's analytic of the beautiful' spell these claims out: the first and third identify the nature of the pleasure – 'disinterested' and owing to an impression of 'finality' – announced by judgements of taste; the second and last identify crucial aspects of such judgements – that they demand universal assent, and necessarily so – which distinguish them from mere judgements of 'agreeableness'.

In 1712, Joseph Addison had referred to the 'agreeable horror' induced by the Alps, vast deserts and other awe-inspiring natural phenomena. The implication, developed in Edmund Burke's essay on *Our Ideas of the Sublime and the Beautiful* (1757), was that aesthetic appreciation is not confined to beauty and does not always consist in unalloyed pleasure. For Kant, who holds that appreciation of beauty is tied to recognition of form and apparent design, it is especially important to distinguish and explain a different mode of appreciation appropriate to the 'mathematical' vastness of the unlimited heavens and the 'dynamic', formless might of oceans and volcanoes. Following Addison and Burke, he calls the object of such appreciation 'the sublime'.[2] His proposal is that the source of such appreciation resides at once in the intimations of a 'supersensuous' realm of being beyond the grasp of our understanding and in

[2] On the sublime in eighteenth century philosophy, see Mary Mothersill, 'Sublime', in D. E. Cooper (ed.), *A Companion to Aesthetics*, Oxford: Blackwell, 1992.

the sense of our own 'pre-eminence above nature' in being able, so to speak, not to succumb in helpless confusion or terror before the immeasurable. The proposal was, predictably, attractive to the romantics and 'nature-mystics' of the next generation and is currently receiving renewed attention within that flourishing branch of environmental philosophy called 'environmental aesthetics'.[3]

It is, nevertheless, kant's doctrines of the 'analytic of the beautiful' which invite the label 'the father of modern aesthetics'. The idea that it is the formal features of a thing or artwork, considered independently of any 'content' it may have, which are the proper objects of aesthetic appraisal has had immense influence – for example, on the early champions of 'abstract' art. Above all, the idea that aesthetic appraisal is distinguished from any other kind – such as moral and pragmatic – by a contemplative 'disinterestedness' is the thesis which every proponent of an alternative account has felt compelled to combat first since Kant articulated it two centuries ago.

First Book
Analytic of the Beautiful

First Moment
Of the judgement of Taste: Moment of Quality*

§ 1

The judgement of taste is aesthetic.

If we wish to discern whether anything is beautiful or not, we do not refer the representation of it to the Object by means of understanding with a view to cognition, but by means of the imagination (acting perhaps in conjunction with understanding) we refer the representation to the Subject and its feeling of pleasure or displeasure. The judgement of taste, therefore, is not a cognitive judgement, and so not logical, but is aesthetic – which means that it is one whose determining ground *cannot be other than subjective.* Every reference of representations is capable of being objective, even that of sensations (in which case it signifies the real in an empirical representation). The one exception to this is the feeling of pleasure or displeasure. This denotes

[3] See Barry Sadler & Allen Carlson (eds), *Environmental Aesthetics: essays in interpretation*, Victoria: University of Victoria, 1982.

* The definition of taste here relied upon is that it is the faculty of estimating the beautiful. But the discovery of what is required for calling an object beautiful must be reserved for the analysis of judgements of taste. . . .

nothing in the Object, but is a feeling which the Subject has of itself and of the manner in which it is affected by the representation.

To apprehend a regular and appropriate building with one's cognitive faculties, be the mode of representation clear or confused, is quite a different thing from being conscious of this representation with an accompanying sensation of delight. Here the representation is referred wholly to the Subject, and what is more to its feeling of life – under the name of the feeling of pleasure or displeasure – and this forms the basis of a quite separate faculty of discriminating and estimating, that contributes nothing to knowledge. All it does is to compare the given representation in the Subject with the entire faculty of representations of which the mind is conscious in the feeling of its state. Given representations in a judgement may be empirical, and so aesthetic; but the judgement which is pronounced by their means is logical, provided it refers them to the Object. Conversely, be the given representations even rational, but referred in a judgement solely to the Subject (to its feeling), they are always to that extent aesthetic.

§ 2

The delight which determines the judgement of taste is independent of all interest.

The delight which we connect with the representation of the real existence of an object is called interest. Such a delight, therefore, always involves a reference to the faculty of desire, either as its determining ground, or else as necessarily implicated with its determining ground. Now, where the question is whether something is beautiful, we do not want to know, whether we, or any one else, are, or even could be, concerned in the real existence of the thing, but rather what estimate we form of it on mere contemplation (intuition or reflection). If any one asks me whether I consider that the palace I see before me is beautiful, I may, perhaps, reply that I do not care for things of that sort that are merely made to be gaped at. Or I may reply in the same strain as that Iroquois *sachem* [chief. Ed.] who said that nothing in Paris pleased him better than the eating-houses. I may even go a step further and inveigh with the vigour of a *Rousseau* against the vanity of the great who spend the sweat of the people on such superfluous things. Or, in fine, I may quite easily persuade myself that if I found myself on an uninhabited island, without hope of ever again coming among men, and could conjure such a palace into existence by a mere wish, I should still not trouble to do so, so long as I had a hut there that was comfortable enough for me. All this may be admitted and approved; only it is not the point now at issue. All one wants to know is whether the mere representation of the object is to my liking, no matter how indifferent I may be to the real existence of the object of this representation. It is quite plain that in order to say that the object *is beautiful*, and to show that I have taste, everything turns on the meaning which I can give to this representation, and not on any factor which makes me dependent on the real existence of the object. Every one must allow that a judgement on the beautiful which is tinged with the slightest interest, is very partial and not a pure judgement of taste. One must not be in the least prepossessed in favour of the real existence of the thing, but must preserve complete indifference in this respect, in order to play the part of judge in matters of taste.

This proposition, which is of the utmost importance, cannot be better explained than by contrasting the pure disinterested* delight which appears in the judgement of taste with that allied to an interest – especially if we can also assure ourselves that there are no other kinds of interest beyond those presently to be mentioned.

§ 3

Delight in the agreeable *is coupled with interest.*

That is *agreeable* which the senses find pleasing in sensation. This at once affords a convenient opportunity for condemning and directing particular attention to a prevalent confusion of the double meaning of which the word 'sensation' is capable. All delight (as is said or thought) is itself sensation (of a pleasure). Consequently everything that pleases, and for the very reason that it pleases, is agreeable – and according to its different degrees, or its relations to other agreeable sensations, is attractive, charming, delicious, enjoyable, &c. But if this is conceded, then impressions of sense, which determine inclination, or principles of reason, which determine the will, or mere contemplated forms of intuition, which determine judgement, are all on a par in everything relevant to their effect upon the feeling of pleasure, for this would be agreeableness in the sensation of one's state; and since, in the last resort, all the elaborate work of our faculties must issue in and unite in the practical as its goal, we could credit our faculties with no other appreciation of things and the worth of things, than that

* A judgement upon an object of our delight may be wholly *disinterested* but withal very *interesting*, i.e. it relies on no interest, but it produces one. Of this kind are all pure moral judgements. But, of themselves, judgements of taste do not even set up any interest whatsoever. Only in society is it *interesting* to have taste – a point which will be explained in the sequel.

consisting in the gratification which they promise. How this is attained is in the end immaterial; and, as the choice of the means is here the only thing that can make a difference, men might indeed blame one another for folly or imprudence, but never for baseness or wickedness; for they are all, each according to his own way of looking at things, pursuing one goal, which for each is the gratification in question.

When a modification of the feeling of pleasure or displeasure is termed sensation, this expression is given quite a different meaning to that which it bears when I call the representation of a thing (through sense as a receptivity pertaining to the faculty of knowledge) sensation. For in the latter case the representation is referred to the Object, but in the former it is referred solely to the Subject and is not available for any cognition, not even for that by which the Subject *cognizes* itself.

Now in the above definition the word 'sensation' is used to denote an objective representation of sense; and, to avoid continually running the risk of misinterpretation, we shall call that which must always remain purely subjective, and is absolutely incapable of forming a representation of an object, by the familiar name of feeling. The green colour of the meadows belongs to *objective* sensation, as the perception of an object of sense; but its agreeableness to *subjective* sensation, by which no object is represented: i.e. to feeling, through which the object is regarded as an Object of delight (which involves no cognition of the object).

Now, that a judgement on an object by which its agreeableness is affirmed, expresses an interest in it, is evident from the fact that through sensation it provokes a desire for similar objects, consequently the delight presupposes, not the simple judgement about it, but the bearing its real existence has upon my state so far as affected by such an Object. Hence we do not merely say of the agreeable that it *pleases*, but that it *gratifies*. I do not accord it a simple approval, but inclination is aroused by it, and where agreeableness is of the liveliest type a judgement on the character of the Object is so entirely out of place, that those who are always intent only on enjoyment (for that is the word used to denote intensity of gratification) would fain dispense with all judgement.

§ 4

Delight in the good *is coupled with interest.*

That is *good* which by means of reason commends itself by its mere concept. We call that *good for something* (useful) which only pleases as a means; but that which pleases on its own account we call *good in itself*. In both cases the concept of an end is implied, and consequently the relation of reason to (at least possible) willing, and thus a delight in the *existence* of an Object or action, i.e. some interest or other.

To deem something good, I must always know what sort of a thing the object is intended to be, i.e. I must have a concept of it. That is not necessary to enable me to see beauty in a thing. Flowers, free patterns, lines aimlessly intertwining – technically termed foliage, – have no signification, depend upon no definite concept, and yet please. Delight in the beautiful must depend upon the reflection on an object precursory to some (not definitely determined) concept. It is thus also differentiated from the agreeable, which rests entirely upon sensation.

In many cases, no doubt, the agreeable and the good seem convertible terms. Thus it is commonly said that all (especially lasting) gratification is of itself good; which is almost equivalent to saying that to be permanently agreeable and to be good are identical. But it is readily apparent that this is merely a vicious confusion of words, for the concepts appropriate to these expressions are far from interchangeable. The agreeable, which, as such, represents the object solely in relation to sense, must in the first instance be brought under principles of reason through the concept of an end, to be, as an object of will, called good. But that the reference to delight is wholly different where what gratifies is at the same time called *good*, is evident from the fact that with the good the question always is whether it is mediately or immediately good, i.e. useful or good in itself; whereas with the agreeable this point can never arise, since the word always means what pleases immediately – and it is just the same with what I call beautiful.

Even in everyday parlance a distinction is drawn between the agreeable and the good. We do not scruple to say of a dish that stimulates the palate with spices and other condiments that it is agreeable – owning all the while that it is not good: because, while it immediately *satisfies* the senses, it is mediately displeasing, i.e. in the eye of reason that looks ahead to the consequences. Even in our estimate of health this same distinction may be traced. To all that possess it, it is immediately agreeable – at least negatively, i.e. as remoteness of all bodily pains. But, if we are to say that it is good, we must further apply to reason to direct it to ends, that is, we must regard it as a state that puts us in a congenial mood for all we have to do. Finally, in respect of happiness every one believes that the greatest aggregate of the pleasures of life, taking duration as well as number into account, merits the name of a true, nay even of the highest, good. But reason sets its face against this too. Agreeableness is enjoyment. But if this is all that we are bent on, it would be foolish to be scrupulous about the means that procure it for us – whether it be obtained passively by the bounty of nature or actively and by the work of our own hands. But that there is any intrinsic worth in the real existence of a man who merely lives for *enjoyment*, however busy he may be in this respect, even when in so doing he serves others – all equally with himself intent only on enjoyment – as an excellent means to that one end, and does so, moreover, because through sympathy he shares all their gratifications, – this is a view to which reason will never let itself be brought round. Only by what a man does heedless of enjoyment, in complete freedom and independently of what he can procure passively from the hand of nature, does he give to his existence, as the real existence of a person, an absolute worth. Happiness, with all its plethora of pleasures, is far from being an unconditioned good.*

But, despite all this difference between the agreeable and the good, they both agree in being invariably coupled with an interest in their object. This is true, not alone of the agreeable, § 3, and of the mediately good, i.e. the useful, which pleases as a means to some pleasure, but also of that which is good absolutely and from every point of view, namely the moral good which carries with it the highest interest. For the good is the Object of will, i.e. of a rationally determined faculty of desire. But to will something, and to take a delight in its existence, i.e. to take an interest in it, are identical.

§ 5

Comparison of the three specifically different kinds of delight.

Both the Agreeable and the Good involve a reference to the faculty of desire, and are thus attended, the former with a delight pathologically conditioned (by stimuli), the latter with a pure practical delight. Such delight is determined not merely by the representation of the object, but also by the represented bond of connection between the Subject and the real existence of the object. It is not merely the object, but also its real existence, that pleases. On the other hand the judgement of taste is simply *contemplative*, i.e. it is a judgement which is indifferent as to the existence of an object, and only decides how its character stands with the feeling of pleasure and displeasure. But not even is this contemplation itself directed to concepts; for the judgement of taste is not a cognitive judgement (neither a theoretical one nor a practical), and hence, also, is not *grounded* on concepts, nor yet *intentionally directed* to them.

* An obligation to enjoyment is a patent absurdity. And the same, then, must also be said of a supposed obligation to actions that have merely enjoyment for their aim, no matter how spiritually this enjoyment may be refined in thought (or embellished), and even if it be a mystical, so-called heavenly, enjoyment.

The agreeable, the beautiful, and the good thus denote three different relations of representations to the feeling of pleasure and displeasure, as a feeling in respect of which we distinguish different objects or modes of representation. Also, the corresponding expressions which indicate our satisfaction in them are different. The *agreeable* is what GRATIFIES a man; the *beautiful* what simply PLEASES him; the *good* what is ESTEEMED (*approved*), i.e. that on which he sets an objective worth. Agreeableness is a significant factor even with irrational animals; beauty has purport and significance only for human beings, i.e. for beings at once animal and rational (but not merely for them as rational – intelligent beings – but only for them as at once animal and rational); whereas the good is good for every rational being in general; – a proposition which can only receive its complete justification and explanation in the sequel. Of all these three kinds of delight, that of taste in the beautiful may be said to be the one and only disinterested and *free* delight; for, with it, no interest, whether of sense or reason, extorts approval. And so we may say that delight, in the three cases mentioned, is related to *inclination*, to *favour*, or to *respect*. For FAVOUR is the only free liking. An object of inclination, and one which a law of reason imposes upon our desire, leaves us no freedom to turn anything into an object of pleasure. All interest presupposes a want, or calls one forth; and, being a ground determining approval, deprives the judgement on the object of its freedom.

So far as the interest of inclination in the case of the agreeable goes, every one says: Hunger is the best sauce; and people with a healthy appetite relish everything, so long as it is something they can eat. Such delight, consequently, gives no indication of taste having anything to say to the choice. Only when men have got all they want can we tell who among the crowd has taste or not. Similarly there may be correct habits (conduct) without virtue, politeness without good-will, propriety without honour, &c. For where the moral law dictates, there is, objectively, no room left for free choice as to what one has to do; and to show taste in the way one carries out these dictates, or in estimating the way others do so, is a totally different matter from displaying the moral frame of one's mind. For the latter involves a command and produces a need of something, whereas moral taste only plays with the objects of delight without devoting itself sincerely to any.

Definition of the Beautiful Derived from the First Moment

Taste is the faculty of estimating an object or a mode of representation by means of a delight or aversion ***apart from any interest.*** The object of such a delight is called ***beautiful.***

Second Moment
Of the Judgement of Taste: Moment of Quantity

§ 6

The beautiful is that which, apart from concepts, is represented as the Object of a universal *delight.*

This definition of the beautiful is deducible from the foregoing definition of it as an object of delight apart from any interest. For where any one is conscious that his delight in an object is with him independent of interest, it is inevitable that he should look on the object as one containing a ground of delight for all men. For, since the delight is not based on any inclination of the Subject (or on any other deliberate interest), but the Subject feels himself completely *free* in respect of the liking which he accords to the object, he can find as reason for his delight no personal conditions to which his own subjective self might alone be party. Hence he must regard it as resting on what he may also presuppose in every other person; and therefore he must believe that he has reason for demanding a similar delight from every one. Accordingly he will speak of the beautiful as if beauty were a quality of the object and the judgement logical (forming a cognition of the Object by concepts of it); although it is only aesthetic, and contains merely a reference of the representation of the Object to the Subject; – because it still bears this resemblance to the logical judgement, that it may be presupposed to be valid for all men. But this universality cannot spring from concepts. For from concepts there is no transition to the feeling of pleasure or displeasure (save in the case of pure practical laws, which, however, carry an interest with them; and such an interest does not attach to the pure judgement of taste). The result is that the judgement of taste, with its attendant consciousness of detachment from all interest, must involve a claim to validity for all men, and must do so apart from universality attached to Objects, i.e. there must be coupled with it a claim to subjective universality.

§ 7

Comparison of the beautiful with the agreeable and the good by means of the above characteristic.

As regards the *agreeable* every one concedes that his judgement, which he bases on a private feeling, and in which he declares that an object pleases him, is restricted merely to himself personally. Thus he does not take it amiss if, when he says that Canary-wine is agreeable, another corrects the expression and reminds him that he ought to say: It is agreeable *to me*. This applies not only to the taste of the tongue, the palate, and the throat, but to what may with any one be agreeable to eye or ear. A violet colour is to one soft and lovely: to another dull and faded. One man likes the tone of wind instruments, another prefers that of string instruments. To quarrel over such points with the idea of condemning another's judgement as incorrect when it differs from our own, as if the opposition between the two judgements were logical, would be folly. With the agreeable, therefore, the axiom holds good: *Every one has his own taste* (that of sense).

The beautiful stands on quite a different footing. It would, on the contrary, be ridiculous if any one who plumed himself on his taste were to think of justifying himself by saying: This object (the building we see, the dress that person has on, the concert we hear, the poem submitted to our criticism) is beautiful *for me*. For if it merely pleases *him*, he must not call it *beautiful*. Many things may for him possess charm and agreeableness – no one cares about that; but when he puts a thing on a pedestal and calls it beautiful, he demands the same delight from others. He judges not merely for himself, but for all men, and then speaks of beauty as if it were a property of things. Thus he says the *thing* is beautiful; and it is not as if he counted on others agreeing in his judgement of liking owing to his having found them in such agreement on a number of occasions, but he *demands* this agreement of them. He blames them if they judge differently, and denies them taste, which he still requires of them as something they ought to have; and to this extent it is not open to men to say: Every one has his own taste. This would be equivalent to saying that there is no such thing at all as taste, i.e. no aesthetic judgement capable of making a rightful claim upon the assent of all men.

Yet even in the case of the agreeable we find that the estimates men form do betray a prevalent agreement among them, which leads to our crediting some with taste and denying it to others, and that, too, not as an organic sense but as a critical faculty in respect of the agreeable generally. So of one who knows how to entertain his guests with pleasures (of enjoyment through all the senses) in such a way that one and all are pleased, we say that he has taste. But the universality here is only understood in a comparative sense; and the rules that apply are, like all empirical rules, *general* only, not *universal*, – the latter being what the judgement of taste upon the beautiful deals or claims to deal in. It is a judgement in respect of sociability so far as resting on empirical rules. In respect of the good it is true that judgements also rightly assert a claim to validity for every one; but the good is only represented as an Object of universal delight *by means of a concept*, which is the case neither with the agreeable nor the beautiful.

§ 8

In a judgement of taste the universality of delight is only represented as subjective.

This particular form of the universality of an aesthetic judgement, which is to be met with in a judgement of taste, is a significant feature, not for the logician certainly, but for the transcendental philosopher. It calls for no small effort on his part to discover its origin, but in return it brings to light a property of our cognitive faculty which, without this analysis, would have remained unknown.

First, one must get firmly into one's mind that by the judgement of taste (upon the beautiful) the delight in an object is imputed to *every one*, yet without being founded on a concept (for then it would be the good), and that this claim to universality is such an essential factor of a judgement by which we describe anything as *beautiful*, that were it not for its being present to the mind it would never enter into any one's head to use this expression, but everything that pleased without a concept would be ranked as agreeable. For in respect of the agreeable every one is allowed to have his own opinion, and no one insists upon others agreeing with his judgement of taste, which is what is invariably done in the judgement of taste about beauty. The first of these I may call the taste of sense, the second, the taste of reflection: the first laying down judgements merely private, the second, on the other hand, judgements ostensibly of general validity (public), but both alike being aesthetic (not practical) judgements about an object merely in respect of the bearings of its representation on the feeling of pleasure or displeasure. Now it does seem strange that while with the taste of sense it is not alone experience that shows that its judgement (of pleasure or displeasure in something) is not universally valid, but every one willingly refrains from imputing this agreement to others (despite the frequent actual prevalence of a considerable consensus of general opinion even in these judgements), the taste of reflection, which, as experience teaches, has often enough to put up with a rude dismissal of its claims to universal validity of its judgement (upon the beautiful), can (as it actually does) find it possible for all that, to formulate judgements capable of demanding this agreement in its universality. Such agreement it does in fact require from every one for each of its judgements of taste, – the persons who pass these judgements not quarreling over the possibility of such a claim, but only failing in particular cases to come to terms as to the correct application of this faculty.

First of all we have here to note that a universality which does not rest upon concepts of the Object (even though these are only empirical) is in no way logical, but aesthetic, i.e. does not involve any objective quantity of the judgement, but only one that is subjective. For this universality I use the expression *general validity*, which denotes the validity of the reference of a representation, not to the cognitive faculties, but to the feeling of pleasure or displeasure for every Subject. (The same expression, however, may also be employed for the logical quantity of the judgement, provided we add *objective* universal validity, to distinguish it from the merely subjective validity which is always aesthetic.)

Now a judgement that has *objective universal validity* has always got the subjective also, i.e. if the judgement is valid for everything which is contained under a given concept, it is valid also for all who represent an object by means of this concept. But from a *subjective universal validity*, i.e. the aesthetic, that does not rest on any concept, no conclusion can be drawn to the logical; because judgements of that kind have no bearing upon the Object. But for this very reason the aesthetic universality attributed to a judgement must also be of a special kind, seeing that it does not join the predicate of beauty to the concept of the *Object* taken in its entire logical sphere, and yet does extend this predicate over the whole sphere of *judging Subjects.*

In their logical quantity all judgements of taste are *singular* judgements. For, since I must present the object immediately to my feeling of pleasure or displeasure, and that, too, without the aid of concepts, such judgements cannot have the quantity of judgements with objective general validity. Yet by taking the singular representation of the Object of the judgement of taste, and by comparison coverting it into a concept according to the conditions determining that judgement, we can arrive at a logically universal judgement. For instance, by a judgement of taste I describe the rose at which I am looking as beautiful. The judgement, on the other hand, resulting from the comparison of a number of singular representations: Roses in general are beautiful, is no longer pronounced as a purely aesthetic judgement, but as a logical judgement founded on one that is aesthetic. Now the judgement, 'The rose is agreeable' (to smell) is also, no doubt, an aesthetic and singular judgement, but then it is not one of taste but of sense. For it has this point of difference from a judgement of taste, that the latter imports an *aesthetic quantity* of universality, i.e. of validity for every one which is not to be met with in a judgement upon the agreeable. It is only judgements upon the good which, while also determining the delight in an object, possess logical and not mere aesthetic universality; for it is as involving a cognition of the Object that they are valid of it, and on that account valid for every one.

In forming an estimate of Objects merely from concepts, all representation of beauty goes by the board. There can, therefore, be no rule according to which any one is to be compelled to recognize anything as beautiful. Whether a dress, a house, or a flower is beautiful is a matter upon which one declines to allow one's judgement to be swayed by any reasons or principles. We want to get a look at the Object with our own eyes, just as if our delight depended on sensation. And yet, if upon so doing, we call the object beautiful, we believe ourselves to be speaking with a universal voice, and lay claim to the concurrence of every one, whereas no private sensation would be decisive except for the observer alone and *his* liking.

Here, now, we may perceive that nothing is postulated in the judgement of taste but such a *universal voice* in respect of delight that is not mediated by concepts; consequently, only the *possibility* of an aesthetic judgement capable of being at the same time deemed valid for every one. The judgement of taste itself does not *postulate* the agreement of every one (for it is only competent for a logically universal judgement to do this, in that it is able to bring forward reasons); it only *imputes* this agreement to every one, as an instance of the rule in respect of which it looks for confirmation, not from concepts, but from the concurrence of others. The universal voice is, therefore, only an idea – resting upon grounds the investigation of which is here postponed. It may be a matter of uncertainty whether a person who thinks he is laying down a judgement of taste is, in fact, judging in conformity with that idea; but that this idea is what is contemplated in his judgement, and that, consequently, it is meant to be a judgement of taste, is proclaimed claimed by his use of the expression 'beauty'. For himself he can be certain on the point from his mere consciousness of the separation of everything belonging to the agreeable and the good from the delight remaining to him; and this is all for which he promises himself the agreement of every one – a claim which, under these conditions, he would also be warranted in making, were it not that he frequently sinned against them, and thus passed an erroneous judgement of taste.

§ 9

Investigation of the question of the relative priority in a judgement of taste of the feeling of pleasure and the estimating of the object.

The solution of this problem is the key to the Critique of taste, and so is worthy of all attention.

Were the pleasure in a given object to be the antecedent, and were the universal communicability of this pleasure to be all that the judgement of taste is meant to allow to the representation of the object, such a sequence would be self-contradictory. For a pleasure of that kind would be nothing but the feeling of mere agreeableness to the senses, and so, from its very nature, would possess no more than private validity, seeing that it would be immediately dependent on the representation through which the object *is given*.

Hence it is the universal capacity for being communicated incident to the mental state in the given representation which, as the subjective condition of the judgement of taste, must be fundamental, with the pleasure in the object as its consequent. Nothing, however, is capable of being universally communicated but cognition and representation so far as appurtenant to cognition. For it is only as thus appurtenant that the representation is objective, and it is this alone that gives it a universal point of reference with which the power of representation of every one is obliged to harmonize. If, then, the determining ground of the judgement as to this universal communicability of the representation is to be merely subjective, that is to say, is to be conceived independently of any concept of the object, it can be nothing else than the mental state that presents itself in the mutual relation of the powers of representation so far as they refer a given representation *to cognition in general.*

The cognitive powers brought into play by this representation are here engaged in a free play, since no definite concept restricts them to a particular rule of cognition. Hence the mental state in this representation must be one of a feeling of the free play of the powers of representation in a given representation for a cognition in general. Now a representation, whereby an object is given, involves, in order that it may become a source of cognition at all, *imagination* for bringing together the manifold of intuition [perception, roughly. Ed.], and *understanding* for the unity of the concept uniting the representations. This state of *free play* of the cognitive faculties attending a representation by which an object is given must admit of universal communication: because cognition, as a definition of the Object with which given representations (in any Subject whatever) are to accord, is the one and only representation which is valid for every one.

As the subjective universal communicability of the mode of representation in a judgement of taste is to subsist apart from the presupposition of any definite concept, it can be nothing else than the mental state present in the free play of imagination and understanding (so far as these are in mutual accord, as is requisite for ***cognition in general***): for we are conscious that this subjective relation suitable for a cognition in general must be just as valid for every one, and consequently as universally communicable, as is any determinate cognition, which always rests upon that relation as its subjective condition.

Now this purely subjective (aesthetic) estimating of the object, or of the representation through which it is given, is antecedent to the pleasure in it, and is the basis of this pleasure in the harmony of the cognitive faculties. Again, the above-described universality of the subjective conditions of estimating objects forms the sole foundation of this universal subjective validity of the delight which we connect with the representation of the object that we call beautiful.

That an ability to communicate one's mental state, even though it be only in respect of our cognitive faculties, is attended with a pleasure, is a fact which might easily be demonstrated from the natural propensity of mankind to social life, i.e. empirically and psychologically. But what we have here in view calls for something more than this. In a judgement of taste the pleasure felt by us is exacted from every one else as necessary, just as if, when we call something beautiful, beauty was to be regarded as a quality of the object forming part of its inherent determination according to concepts; although beauty is for itself, apart from any reference to the feeling of the Subject, nothing. But the discussion of this question must be reserved until we have answered the further one of whether, and how, aesthetic judgements are possible ***a priori***.

At present we are exercised with the lesser question of the way in which we become conscious, in a judgement of taste, of a reciprocal subjective common accord of the powers of cognition. Is it aesthetically by sensation and our mere internal sense? Or is it intellectually by consciousness of our intentional activity in bringing these powers into play?

Now if the given representation occasioning the judgement of taste were a concept which united understanding and imagination in the estimate of the object so as to give a cognition of the Object, the consciousness of this relation would be intellectual (as in the objective schematism of judgement dealt with in the Critique). But, then, in that case the judgement would not be laid down with respect to pleasure and displeasure, and so would not be a judgement of taste. But, now, the judgement of taste determines the Object, independently of concepts, in respect of delight and of the predicate of beauty. There is, therefore, no other way for the subjective unity of the relation in question to make itself known than by sensation. The quickening of both faculties (imagination and understanding) to an indefinite, but yet, thanks to the given representation, harmonious activity, such as belongs to cognition generally, is the sensation whose universal communicability is postulated by the judgement of taste. An objective relation can, of course, only be thought, yet in so far as, in respect of its conditions, it is subjective, it may be felt in its effect upon the mind, and, in the case of a relation (like that of the powers of representation to a faculty of cognition generally) which does not rest on any concept, no other consciousness of it is possible beyond that through sensation of its effect upon the mind – an effect consisting in the more facile play of both mental powers (imagination and understanding) as quickened by their mutual accord. A representation which is singular and independent of comparison with other representations, and, being such, yet accords with the conditions of the universality that is the general concern of understanding, is one that brings the cognitive faculties into that proportionate accord which we require for all cognition and which we therefore deem valid for every one who is so constituted as to judge by means of understanding and sense conjointly (i.e. for every man).

Definition of the Beautiful Drawn from the Second Moment

The *beautiful* is that which, apart from a concept, pleases universally.

Third Moment
Of Judgements of Taste: Moment of the Relation *of the Ends Brought under Review in Such Judgements*

§ 10

Finality in general.

Let us define the meaning of 'an end' in transcendental terms (i.e. without presupposing anything empirical, such as the feeling of pleasure). An end is the object of a concept so far as this concept is regarded as the cause of the object (the real ground of its possibility); and the causality of a *concept* in respect of its *Object* is finality (*forma finalis*). Where, then, not the cognition of an object merely, but the object itself (its form or real existence) as an effect, is thought to be possible only through a concept of it, there we imagine an end. The representation of the effect is here the determining ground of its cause and takes the lead of it. The consciousness of the causality of a representation in respect of the state of the Subject as one tending *to preserve a continuance* of that state, may here be said to denote in a general way what is called pleasure; whereas displeasure is that representation which contains the ground for converting the state of the representations into their opposite (for hindering or removing them).

The faculty of desire, so far as determinable only through concepts, i.e. so as to act in conformity with the representation of an end, would be the will. But an Object, or state of mind, or even an action may, although its possibility does not necessarily presuppose the representation of an end, be called final simply on account of its possibility being only explicable and intelligible for us by virtue of an assumption on our part of a fundamental causality according to ends, i.e. a will that would have so ordained it according to a certain represented rule. Finality, therefore, may exist apart from an end, in so far as we do not locate the causes of this form in a will, but yet are able to render the explanation of its possibility intelligible to ourselves only by deriving it from a will. Now we are not always obliged to look with the eye of reason into what we observe (i.e. to consider it in its possibility). So we may at least observe a finality of form, and trace it in objects – though by reflection only – without resting it on an end (as the material of the *nexus finalis*).

§ 11

The sole foundation of the judgement of taste is the form of finality *of an object (or mode of representing it).*

Whenever an end is regarded as a source of delight it always imports an interest as determining ground of the judgement on the object of pleasure. Hence the judgement of taste cannot rest on any subjective end as its ground. But neither can any representation of an objective end, i.e. of the possibility of the object itself on principles of final connection, determine the judgement of taste, and, consequently, neither can any concept of the good. For the judgement of taste is an aesthetic and not a cognitive judgement, and so does not deal with any *concept* of the nature or of the internal or external possibility, by this or that cause, of the object, but simply with the relative bearing of the representative powers so far as determined by a representation.

Now this relation, present when an object is characterized as beautiful, is coupled with the feeling of pleasure. This pleasure is by the judgement of taste pronounced valid for every one; hence an agreeableness attending the representation is just as incapable of containing the determining ground of the judgement as the representation of the perfection of the object or the concept of the good. We are thus left with the subjective finality in the representation of an object, exclusive of any end (objective or subjective) – consequently the bare form of finality in the representation whereby an object is *given* to us, so far as we are conscious of it – as that which is alone capable of constituting the delight which, apart from any concept, we estimate as universally communicable, and so of forming the determining ground of the judgement of taste.

§ 12

The judgement of taste rests upon a priori *grounds.*

[. . .]

The pleasure in aesthetic judgements . . . is merely contemplative and does not bring about an interest in the Object; whereas in the moral judgement it is practical. The consciousness of mere formal finality in the play of the cognitive faculties of the Subject attending a representation whereby an object is given, is the pleasure itself, because it involves a determining ground of the Subject's activity in respect of the quickening of its cognitive powers, and thus an internal causality (which is final) in respect of cognition generally, but without being limited to a definite cognition, and consequently a mere form of the subjective finality of a representation in an aesthetic judgement. This pleasure is also in no way practical, neither resembling that from the pathological ground of agreeableness nor that from the intellectual ground of the represented good. But still it involves an inherent causality, that, namely, of *preserving a continuance* of the state of the representation itself and the active engagement of the cognitive powers without ulterior aim. We *dwell* on the contemplation of the beautiful because this contemplation strengthens and reproduces itself. The case is analogous (but analogous only) to the way we linger on a charm in the representation of an object which keeps arresting the attention, the mind all the while remaining passive.

§ 13

The pure judgement of taste is independent of charm and emotion.

Every interest vitiates the judgement of taste and robs it of its impartiality. This is especially so where instead of, like the interest of reason, making finality take the lead of the feeling of pleasure, it grounds it upon this feeling – which is what always happens in aesthetic judgements upon anything so far as it gratifies or pains. Hence judgements so influenced can either lay no claim at all to a universally valid delight, or else must abate their claim in proportion as sensations of the kind in question enter into the determining grounds of taste. Taste that requires an added element of *charm* and *emotion* for its delight, not to speak of adopting this as the measure of its approval, has not yet emerged from barbarism.

And yet charms are frequently not alone ranked with beauty (which ought properly to be a question merely of the form) as supplementary to the aesthetic universal delight, but they have been accredited as intrinsic beauties, and consequently the matter of delight passed off for the form. This is a misconception which, like many others that have still an underlying element of truth, may be removed by a careful definition of these concepts.

A judgement of taste which is uninfluenced by charm or emotion (though these may be associated with the delight in the beautiful), and whose determining ground, therefore, is simply finality of form, is a *pure judgement of taste*.

§ 14

Exemplification.

Aesthetic, just like theoretical (logical) judgements, are divisible into empirical and pure. The first are those by which agreeableness or disagreeableness, the second those by which beauty, is predicated of an object or its mode of representation. The former are judgements of sense (material aesthetic judgements), the latter (as formal) alone judgements of taste proper.

A judgement of taste, therefore, is only pure so far as its determining ground is tainted with no merely empirical delight. But such a taint is always present where charm or emotion have a share in the judgement by which something is to be described as beautiful.

[. . .]

Nevertheless charms may be added to beauty to lend to the mind, beyond a bare delight, an adventitious interest in the representation of the object, and thus to advocate taste and its cultivation. This applies especially where taste is as yet crude and untrained. But they are positively subversive of the judgement of taste, if allowed to obtrude themselves as grounds of estimating beauty. For so far are they from contributing to beauty, that it is only where taste is still weak and untrained, that, like aliens, they are admitted as a favour, and only on terms that they do not violate that beautiful form.

In painting, sculpture, and in fact in all the formative arts, in architecture and horticulture, so far as fine arts, the ***design*** is what is essential. Here it is not what gratifies in sensation but merely what pleases by its form, that is the fundamental prerequisite for taste. The colours which give brilliancy to the sketch are part of the charm. They may no doubt, in their own way, enliven the object for sensation, but make it really worth looking at and beautiful they cannot. Indeed, more often than not the requirements of the beautiful form restrict them to a very narrow compass, and, even where charm is admitted, it is only this form that gives them a place of honour.

All form of objects of sense (both of external and also, mediately, of internal sense) is either ***figure*** or ***play.*** In the latter case it is either play of figures (in space: mimic and dance), or mere play of sensations (in time). The ***charm*** of colours, or of the agreeable tones of instruments, may be added: but the ***design*** in the former and the ***composition*** in the latter constitute the proper object of the pure judgement of taste. To say that the purity alike of colours and of tones, or their variety and contrast, seem to contribute to beauty, is by no means to imply that, because in themselves agreeable, they therefore yield an addition to the delight in the form and one on a par with it. The real meaning rather is that they make this form more clearly, definitely, and completely intuitable, and besides stimulate the representation by their charm, as they excite and sustain the attention directed to the object itself.

[. . .]

Emotion – a sensation where an agreeable feeling is produced merely by means of a momentary check followed by a more powerful outpouring of the vital force – is quite foreign to beauty. Sublimity (with which the feeling of emotion is connected) requires, however, a different standard of estimation from that relied upon by taste. [see § 23ff. Ed.] A pure judgement of taste has, then, for its determining ground neither charm nor emotion, in a word, no sensation as matter of the aesthetic judgement.

[. . .]

§ 16

A judgement of taste by which an object is described as beautiful under the condition of a definite concept is not pure.

There are two kinds of beauty: free beauty (*pulchritudo vaga*), or beauty which is merely dependent (*pulchritudo adhaerens*). The first presupposes no concept of what the object should be; the second does presuppose such a concept and, with it, an answering perfection of the object. Those of the first kind are said to be (self-subsisting) beauties of this thing or that thing; the other kind of beauty, being attached to a concept (conditioned beauty), is ascribed to Objects which come under the concept of a particular end.

Flowers are free beauties of nature. Hardly any one but a botanist knows the true nature of a flower, and even he, while recognizing in the flower the reproductive organ of the plant, pays no attention to this natural end when using his taste to judge of its beauty. Hence no perfection of any kind – no internal finality, as something to which the arrangement of the manifold is related – underlies this judgement. Many birds (the parrot, the humming-bird, the bird of paradise), and a number of crustacea, are self-subsisting beauties which are not appurtenant to any object defined with respect to its end, but please freely and on their own account. So designs *à la grecque*, foliage for framework or on wall-papers, &c., have no intrinsic meaning; they represent nothing – no Object under a definite concept – and are free beauties. We may also rank in the same class what in music are called fantasias (without a theme), and, indeed, all music that is not set to words.

In the estimate of a free beauty (according to mere form) we have the pure judgement of taste. No concept is here presupposed of any end for which the manifold should serve the given Object, and which the latter, therefore, should represent – an incumbrance which would only restrict the freedom of the imagination that, as it were, is at play in the contemplation of the outward form.

But the beauty of man (including under this head that of a man, woman, or child), the beauty of a horse, or of a building (such as a church, palace, arsenal, or summer-house), presupposes a concept of the end that defines what the thing has to be, and consequently a concept of its perfection; and is therefore merely appendant beauty. Now, just as it is a clog on the purity of the judgement of taste to have the agreeable (of sensation) joined with beauty to which properly only the form is relevant, so to combine the good with beauty (the good, namely, of the manifold to the thing itself according to its end) mars its purity.

Much might be added to a building that would immediately please the eye, were it not intended for a church. A figure might be beautified with all manner of flourishes and light but regular lines, as is done by the New Zealanders with their tattooing, were we dealing with anything but the figure of a human being. And here is one whose rugged features might be softened and given a more pleasing aspect, only he has got to be a man, or is, perhaps, a warrior that has to have a warlike appearance.

Now the delight in the manifold of a thing, in reference to the internal end that determines its possibility, is a delight based on a concept, whereas delight in the beautiful is such as does not presuppose any concept, but is immediately coupled with the representation through which the object is given (not through which it is thought). If, now, the judgement of taste in respect of the latter delight is made dependent upon the end involved in the former delight as a judgement of reason, and is thus placed under a restriction, then it is no longer a free and pure judgement of taste.

Taste, it is true, stands to gain by this combination of intellectual delight with the aesthetic. For it becomes fixed, and, while not universal, it enables rules to be prescribed for it in respect of certain definite final Objects. But these rules are then not rules of taste, but merely rules for establishing a union of taste with reason, i.e. of the beautiful with the good – rules by which the former becomes available as an intentional instrument in respect of the latter, for the purpose of bringing that temper of the mind which is self-sustaining and of subjective universal validity to the support and maintenance of that mode of thought which, while possessing objective universal validity, can only be preserved by a resolute effort. But, strictly speaking, perfection neither gains by beauty, nor beauty by perfection. The truth is rather this, when we compare the representation through which an object is given to us with the Object (in respect of what it is meant to be) by means of a concept, we cannot help reviewing it also in respect of the sensation in the Subject. Hence there results a gain to the *entire faculty* of our representative power when harmony prevails between both states of mind.

In respect of an object with a definite internal end, a judgement of taste would only be pure where the person judging either has no concept of this end, or else makes abstraction from it in his judgement. But in cases like this, although such a person should lay down a correct judgement of taste, since he would be estimating the object as a free beauty, he would still be found fault with by another who saw nothing in its beauty but a dependent quality (i.e. who looked to the end of the object) and would be accused by him of false taste, though both would, in their own way, be judging

correctly: the one according to what he had present to his senses, the other according to what was present in his thoughts. This distinction enables us to settle many disputes about beauty on the part of critics; for we may show them how one side is dealing with free beauty and the other with that which is dependent: the former passing a pure judgement of taste, the latter one that is applied intentionally.
[. . .]

Definition of the Beautiful Derived from this Third Moment

Beauty *is the form of* finality *in an object, so far as perceived in it* apart from the representation of an end.
[. . .]

Second Book
Analytic of the Sublime

§ 23

Transition from the faculty of estimating the beautiful to that of estimating the sublime.

The beautiful and the sublime agree on the point of pleasing on their own account. Further they agree in not presupposing either a judgement of sense or one logically determinant, but one of reflection. Hence it follows that the delight does not depend upon a sensation, as with the agreeable, nor upon a definite concept, as does the delight in the good, although it has, for all that, an indeterminate reference to concepts. Consequently the delight is connected with the mere presentation or faculty of presentation, and is thus taken to express the accord, in a given intuition, of the faculty of presentation, or the imagination, with the *faculty of concepts* that belongs to understanding or reason, in the sense of the former assisting the latter. Hence both kinds of judgements are *singular*, and yet such as profess to be universally valid in respect of every Subject, despite the fact that their claims are directed merely to the feeling of pleasure and not to any knowledge of the object.

There are, however, also important and striking differences between the two. The beautiful in nature is a question of the form of the object, and this consists in limitation, whereas the sublime is to be found in an object even devoid of form, so far as it immediately involves, or else by its presence provokes, a representation of *limitlessness*, yet with a super-added thought of its totality. Accordingly the beautiful seems to be regarded as a presentation of an indeterminate concept of understanding, the sublime as a presentation of an indeterminate concept of reason. Hence the delight is in the former case coupled with the representation of *Quality*, but in this case with that of *Quantity*. Moreover, the former delight is very different from the latter in kind. For the beautiful is directly attended with a feeling of the furtherance of life, and is thus compatible with charms and a playful imagination. On the other hand, the feeling of the sublime is a pleasure that only arises indirectly, being brought about by the feeling of a momentary check to the vital forces followed at once by a discharge all the more powerful, and so it is an emotion that seems to be no sport, but dead earnest in the affairs of the imagination. Hence charms are repugnant to it; and, since the mind is not simply attracted by the object, but is also alternately repelled thereby, the delight in the sublime does not so much involve positive pleasure as admiration or respect, i.e. merits the name of a negative pleasure.[1]

But the most important and vital distinction between the sublime and the beautiful is certainly this: that if, as is allowable, we here confine our attention in the first instance to the sublime in Objects of nature (that of art being always restricted by the conditions of an agreement with nature) we observe that whereas natural beauty (such as is self-subsisting) conveys a finality in its form making the object appear, as it were, preadapted to our power of judgement, so that it thus forms of itself an object of our delight, that which, without our indulging in any refinements of thought, but, simply in our apprehension of it, excites the feeling of the sublime, may appear, indeed, in point of form to contravene the ends of our power of judgement, to be ill-adapted to our faculty of presentation, and to be, as it were, an outrage on the imagination, and yet it is judged all the more sublime on that account.

From this it may be seen at once that we express ourselves on the whole inaccurately if we term any *Object of nature* sublime, although we may with perfect propriety call many such objects beautiful. For how can that which is apprehended as inherently contra-final be noted with an expression of approval? All that we can say is that the object lends itself to the presentation of a sublimity discoverable in the mind. For the sublime, in the strict sense of the word, cannot be contained in any sensuous form, but rather concerns ideas of reason, which, although no adequate presentation of them is possible, may be excited and called into the mind by that very inadequacy itself which does admit of sensuous presentation. Thus the broad ocean agitated by storms cannot be called sublime. Its aspect is horrible, and one must have stored one's mind in advance with a rich stock of ideas, if such an intuition is to raise it to the pitch of a feeling which is itself sublime – sublime because the mind has been incited to abandon sensibility, and employ itself upon ideas involving higher finality.

Self-subsisting natural beauty reveals to us a technic of nature which shows it in the light of a system ordered in accordance with laws the principle of which is not to be found within the range of our entire faculty of understanding. This principle is that of a finality relative to the employment of judgement in respect of phenomena which have thus to be assigned, not merely to nature regarded as aimless mechanism, but also to nature regarded after the analogy of art. Hence it gives a veritable extension, not, of course, to our knowledge of Objects of nature, but to our conception of nature itself – nature as mere mechanism being enlarged to the conception of nature as art – an extension inviting profound enquiries as to the possibility of such a form. But in what we are wont to call sublime in nature there is such an absence of anything leading to particular objective principles and corresponding forms of nature, that it is rather in its chaos, or in its wildest and most irregular disorder and desolation, provided it gives signs of magnitude and power, that nature chiefly excites the ideas of the sublime. Hence we see that the concept of the sublime in nature is far less important and rich in consequences than that of its beauty. It gives on the whole no indication of anything final in nature itself, but only in the possible *employment* of our intuitions of it in inducing a feeling in our own selves of a finality quite independent of nature. For the beautiful in nature we must seek a ground external to ourselves, but for the sublime one merely in ourselves and the attitude of mind that introduces sublimity into the representation of nature. This is a very needful preliminary remark. It entirely separates the ideas of the sublime from that of a finality of *nature*, and makes the theory of the sublime a mere appendage to the aesthetic estimate of the finality of nature, because it does not give a representation of any particular form in nature, but involves no more than the development of a final employment by the imagination of its own representation.

§ 24

Subdivision of an investigation of the feeling of the sublime.

[. . .]

But the analysis of the sublime obliges a division not required by that of the beautiful, namely one into the *mathematically* and the *dynamically* sublime.

For the feeling of the sublime involves as its characteristic feature a mental *movement* combined with the estimate of the object, whereas taste in respect of the beautiful presupposes that the mind is in *restful* contemplation, and preserves it in this state. But this movement has to be estimated as subjectively final (since the sublime pleases). Hence it is referred through the imagination either to the *faculty of cognition* or to that of *desire*; but to whichever faculty the reference is made the finality of the given representation is estimated only in respect of these faculties (apart from end or interest). Accordingly the first is attributed to the Object as a *mathematical*, the second as a *dynamical*, affection of the imagination. Hence we get the above double mode of representing an Object as sublime.

B. The Dynamically Sublime in Nature

§ 28

Nature as Might.

Might is a power which is superior to great hindrances. It is termed *dominion* if it is also superior to the resistance of that which itself possesses might. Nature considered in an aesthetic judgement as might that has no dominion over us, is *dynamically sublime*.

If we are to estimate nature as dynamically sublime, it must be represented as a source of fear (though the converse, that every object that is a source of fear is, in our aesthetic judgement, sublime, does not hold). For in forming an aesthetic estimate (no concept being present) the superiority to hindrances can only be estimated according to the greatness of the resistance. Now that which we strive to resist is an evil, and, if we do not find our powers commensurate to the task, an object of fear. Hence the aesthetic judgement can only deem nature a might, and so dynamically sublime, in so far as it is looked upon as an object of fear.

But we may look upon an object as *fearful*, and yet not be afraid *of* it, if, that is, our estimate takes the form of our simply *picturing to ourselves* the case of our wishing to offer some resistance to it, and recognizing that all such resistance would be quite futile. So the righteous man fears God without being afraid of Him, because he regards the case of his wishing to resist God and His commandments as one which need cause *him* no anxiety. But in every such case, regarded by him as not intrinsically impossible, he cognizes Him as One to be feared.

One who is in a state of fear can no more play the part of a judge of the sublime of nature than one captivated by inclination and appetite can of the beautiful. He flees from the sight of an object filling him with dread; and it is impossible to take delight in terror that is seriously entertained.

Hence the agreeableness arising from the cessation of an uneasiness is *a state of joy*. But this, depending upon deliverance from a danger, is a rejoicing accompanied with a resolve never again to put oneself in the way of the danger: in fact we do not like bringing back to mind how we felt on that occasion – not to speak of going in search of an opportunity for experiencing it again.

Bold, overhanging, and, as it were, threatening rocks, thunder-clouds piled up the vault of heaven, borne along with flashes and peals, volcanoes in all their violence of destruction, hurricanes leaving desolation in their track, the boundless ocean rising with rebellious force, the high waterfall of some mighty river, and the like, make our power of resistance of trifling moment in comparison with their might. But, provided our own position is secure, their aspect is all the more attractive for its fearfulness; and we readily call these objects sublime, because they raise the forces of the soul above the height of vulgar commonplace, and discover within us a power of resistance of quite another kind, which gives us courage to be able to measure ourselves against the seeming omnipotence of nature.

In the immeasurableness of nature and the incompetence of our faculty for adopting a standard proportionate to the aesthetic estimation of the magnitude of its *realm*, we found our own limitation. But with this we also found in our rational faculty another non-sensuous standard, one which has that infinity itself under it as unit, and in comparison with which everything in nature is small, and so found in our minds a pre-eminence over nature even in its immeasurability. Now in just the same way the irresistibility of the might of nature forces upon us the recognition of our physical helplessness as beings of nature, but at the same time reveals a faculty of estimating ourselves as independent of nature, and discovers a pre-eminence above nature that is the foundation of a self-preservation of quite another kind from that which may be assailed and brought into danger by external nature. This saves humanity in our own person from humiliation, even though as mortal men we have to submit to external violence. In this way external nature is not estimated in our aesthetic judgement as sublime so far as exciting fear, but rather because it challenges our power (one not of nature) to regard as small those things of which we are wont to be solicitous (worldly goods, health, and life), and hence to regard its might (to which in these matters we are no doubt subject) as exercising over us and our personality no such rude dominion that we should bow down before it, once the question becomes one of our highest principles and of our asserting or forsaking them. Therefore nature is here called sublime merely because it raises the imagination to a presentation of those cases in which the mind can make itself sensible of the appropriate sublimity of the sphere of its own being, even above nature.

This estimation of ourselves loses nothing by the fact that we must see ourselves safe in order to feel this soul-stirring delight – a fact from which it might be plausibly argued that, as there is no seriousness in the danger, so there is just as little seriousness in the sublimity of our faculty of soul. For here the delight only concerns the *province* of our faculty disclosed in such a case, so far as this faculty has its root in our nature; notwithstanding that its development and exercise is left to ourselves and remains an obligation. Here indeed there is truth – no matter how conscious a man, when he stretches his reflection so far abroad, may be of his actual present helplessness.

[. . .]

Sublimity, therefore, does not reside in any of the things of nature, but only in our own mind, in so far as we may become conscious of our superiority over nature within, and thus also over nature without us (as exerting influence upon us). Everything that provokes this feeling in us, including the *might* of nature which challenges our strength, is then, though improperly, called sublime, and it is only under presupposition of this idea within us, and in relation to it, that we are capable of attaining to the idea of the sublimity of that Being [i.e. God. Ed.] which inspires deep respect in us, not by the mere display of its might in nature, but more by the faculty which is planted in us of estimating that might without fear, and of regarding our estate as exalted above it.

Note

1 Kant is here rehearsing the main point made by Burke in his *Philosophical Enquiry into the Origin of our Ideas of the Sublime and the Beautiful*, a work which had already influenced Kant's 1763 essay, *Observations on the Feeling of the Beautiful and Sublime* (trans. J. Goldthwait, Berkeley, Calif.: University of California Press, 1960).

Friedrich Schiller, *On the Aesthetic Education of Man*, Letters 26–7

8

From Friedrich Schiller, *On the Aesthetic Education of Man*, trans. E. Wilkinson & L. Willoughby. Oxford: Oxford University Press, 1967, pp. 191–219 [footnote is Schiller's].

As I have already indicated, Kant intended his third critique to be a 'bridge' between his earlier doctrines, especially between the conception of human beings as natural, sensuous creatures rooted in the empirical world and the conviction that, in exercising moral reason, they transcend this natural condition. The message seems to be that, in the experience of beauty, the sensuous and rational are equally involved. But the discussion is an extremely abstract one and, despite the hint that beauty is a 'symbol of morality', no account is developed as to how art and beauty may be conducive to moral life.

It was left to Germany's most famous playwright and Goethe's closest friend, Friedrich Schiller (1759–1805), in a series of twenty-seven letters to his ducal patron (1795), to provide such an account and to 'bridge', in more concrete terms, the depressing divide between human nature and moral reason. In doing so, he was the first in a chain of German thinkers – Hölderlin and Schelling, for example – who saw in art the promise of unity or harmony within both the individual and society at large. Here, Schiller is at the opposite pole from Plato, an intended target surely in letter 26.5, where those who 'despise' art because it involves 'semblance' are castigated.

In the early letters, Schiller paints a dark picture of a 'barbarous', egotistic and materialist eighteenth century Europe in which men have lost their most precious possession – freedom. It is 'only through beauty that man makes his way to freedom' (2.5), and 'fine art' will be the 'instrument' for the moral and political 'education' of man (9.2). ('Cultivation' might be a better word, for Schiller's letters have little to do with the curriculum of colleges of art.) Letters 26–7 try to make good these proclamations. In the interim, Schiller has argued that most of the time people live unhappy, divided lives, set against one another and themselves. They are torn between feeling and thought, material preoccupations and reason, by two opposing drives – the 'drive to sense' and the 'drive to form': meaning, roughly, a passive surrender to natural 'reality' at the expense of freedom and integrity of the self, and a wilful imposition of categories and forms at the expense of concrete appreciation of sensuous 'reality'. Succour is at hand, however, in a third drive, the 'play drive', whereby people can at once be open to the natural world, yet lend form and meaning to their experience. This 'play drive', Schiller tells us, aims at 'living form' and this, in turn, is what 'we call "beauty"' (15.2).

This is best treated, perhaps, as characterizing the beautiful *person*, who has properly harmonized his different facets through 'play'. Artworks and natural objects are then beautiful to the degree that they help to cultivate such a personality.[1] In letter 26, it becomes clear that it is through art and aesthetic sensibility that this cultivation will be effected. This is because they pertain to 'semblance', by which Schiller means not only the semblances created by artists, but the visual and auditory appearances of things which, with sufficient practice in Kantian 'disinterestedness', we can focus on in abstraction from the material and utilitarian aspects of things. Released from such preoccupations, we attain freedom in the production and contemplation of form. In the final letter, which climaxes in exaltation of the 'Aesthetic State' where 'playful' human beings live in freedom, justice and social harmony, Schiller argues that the path to such a state is a thoroughly natural one to tread – thereby dispelling the Kantian opposition between nature and morality.

I cited Schiller's impact upon a generation of German romantics who also looked to art for a cure for spiritual and social disharmony, and this influence is apparent on other thinkers, like Benedetto Croce, for whom it is through art that human beings become what they most truly are. Given his insistence on the moral benefits of art, it would be misleading to count Schiller as an early advocate of 'art for art's sake': on the other hand, his view of what it is to be moral is itself an aestheticized one. Also influential have been his remarks on 'semblance'. By sharply distinguishing semblance from representation, he reinforced the Kantian emphasis on form which later art theorists used as an apology for abstract art. His confidence in the civilizing effects of a concern with the perceptual appearances of things anticipates Oscar Wilde's 'The decay of lying', while the equally Wildean – and Nietzschean – notion of the self as a creative work of art is implicit in the 'living form' aspired to by the beautiful person.

[1] See Anthony Savile, *Aesthetic Reconstructions: the seminal writings of Lessing, Kant and Schiller*, Oxford: Blackwell, 1987, ch. 7.

Twenty-Sixth Letter

1. Since, as I have argued in the preceding Letters, it is the aesthetic mode of the psyche which first gives rise to freedom, it is obvious that it cannot itself derive from freedom and cannot, in consequence, be of moral origin. It must be a gift of nature; the favour of fortune alone can unloose the fetters of that first physical stage and lead the savage towards beauty.

2. The germ of beauty is as little likely to develop where nature in her niggardliness deprives man of quickening refreshment, as where in her bounty she relieves him of any exertion – alike where sense is too blunted to feel any need, as where violence of appetite is denied satisfaction. Not where man hides himself, a troglodyte, in caves, eternally an isolated unit, never finding humanity outside himself; nor yet there where, a nomad, he roams in vast hordes over the face of the earth, eternally but one of a number, never finding humanity within himself – but only there, where, in his own hut, he discourses silently with himself and, from the moment he steps out of it, with all the rest of his kind, only there will the tender blossom of beauty unfold. There, where a limpid atmosphere opens his senses to every delicate contact, and an energizing warmth animates the exuberance of matter – there where, even in inanimate nature, the sway of blind mass has been overthrown, and form triumphant ennobles even the lowest orders of creation – there, amid the most joyous surroundings, and in that favoured zone where activity alone leads to enjoyment, and enjoyment alone to activity, where out of life itself the sanctity of order springs, and out of the law of order nothing but life can develop – where imagination ever flees actuality yet never strays from the simplicity of nature – here alone will sense and spirit, the receptive and the formative power, develop in that happy equilibrium which is the soul of beauty and the condition of all humanity.

3. And what are the outward and visible signs of the savage's entry upon humanity? If we enquire of history, however far back, we find that they are the same in all races which have emerged from the slavery of the animal condition: delight in semblance, and a propensity to ornamentation and play.

4. Supreme stupidity and supreme intelligence have a certain affinity with each other in that both of them seek only the real and are completely insensitive to mere semblance. Only by objects which are actually present to the senses is stupidity jerked out of its quiescence; only when its concepts can be referred back to the facts of experience is intelligence to be pacified. In a word, stupidity cannot rise above actuality, and intelligence

cannot stop short of truth. Inasmuch as need of reality and attachment to the actual are merely consequences of some deficiency, then indifference to reality and interest in semblance may be regarded as a genuine enlargement of humanity and a decisive step towards culture. In the first place, this affords evidence of outward freedom: for as long as necessity dictates, and need drives, imagination remains tied to reality with powerful bonds; only when wants are stilled does it develop its unlimited potential. But it affords evidence, too, of inner freedom, since it makes us aware of a power which is able to move of its own accord, independently of any material stimulus from without, and which is sufficiently in control of energy to hold at arm's length the importunate pressure of matter. The reality of things is the work of things themselves; the semblance of things is the work of man; and a nature which delights in semblance is no longer taking pleasure in what it receives, but in what it does.

5. It goes without saying that the only kind of semblance I am here concerned with is aesthetic semblance (which we distinguish from actuality and truth) and not logical semblance (which we confuse with these): semblance, therefore, which we love just because it is semblance, and not because we take it to be something better. Only the first is play, whereas the latter is mere deception. To attach value to semblance of the first kind can never be prejudicial to truth, because one is never in danger of substituting it for truth, which is after all the only way in which truth can ever be impaired. To despise it, is to despise the fine arts altogether, the very essence of which is semblance. All the same, it sometimes happens that intelligence will carry its zeal for reality to such a pitch of intolerance, that it pronounces a disparaging judgement upon the whole art of aesthetic semblance just because it is semblance. But this only happens to intelligence when it recalls the above mentioned affinity. Of the necessary limits of aesthetic semblance I shall treat separately on some other occasion.

6. It is nature herself which raises man from reality to semblance, by furnishing him with two senses which lead him to knowledge of the real world through semblance alone. In the case of the eye and the ear, she herself has driven importunate matter back from the organs of sense, and the object, with which in the case of our more animal senses we have direct contact, is set at a distance from us. What we actually see with the eye is something different from the sensation we receive; for the mind leaps out across light to objects. The object of touch is a force to which we are subjected; the object of eye and ear a form that we engender. As long as man is still a savage he enjoys by means of these tactile senses alone, and at this stage the senses of semblance are merely the servants of these. Either he does not rise to the level of seeing at all, or he is at all events not satisfied

with it. Once he does begin to enjoy through the eye, and seeing acquires for him a value of its own, he is already aesthetically free and the play-drive has started to develop.

7. And as soon as the play-drive begins to stir, with its pleasure in semblance, it will be followed by the shaping spirit of imitation, which treats semblance as something autonomous. Once man has got to the point of distinguishing semblance from reality, form from body, he is also in a position to abstract the one from the other, and has indeed already done so by the very fact of distinguishing between them. The capacity for imitative art is thus given with the capacity for form in general; the urge towards it rests upon a quite different endowment which I need not discuss here. Whether the artistic impulse is to develop early or late, will depend solely upon the degree of loving attachment with which man is capable of abiding with sheer semblance.

8. Since all actual existence derives from nature considered as alien force, whereas all semblance originates in man considered as perceiving subject, he is only availing himself of the undisputed rights of ownership when he reclaims Semblance from Substance, and deals with it according to laws of his own. With unrestricted freedom he is able, can he but imagine them together, actually to join together things which nature put asunder; and, conversely, to separate, can he but abstract them in his mind, things which nature has joined together. Nothing need here be sacred to him except his own law, if he but observes the demarcation separating his territory from the actual existence of things, that is to say from the realm of nature.

9. This sovereign human right he exercises in the art of semblance; and the more strictly he here distinguishes between mine and thine, the more scrupulously he separates form from substance, and the more complete the autonomy he is able to give to the former, then the more he will not only extend the realm of beauty, but actually preserve intact the frontiers of truth. For he cannot keep semblance clear of actuality without at the same time setting actuality free from semblance.

10. But it is in the world of semblance alone that he possesses this sovereign right, in the insubstantial realm of the imagination; and he possesses it there only as long as he scrupulously refrains from predicating real existence of it in theory, and as long as he renounces all idea of imparting real existence through it in practice. From this you see that the poet transgresses his proper limits, alike when he attributes existence to his ideal world, as when he aims at bringing about some determinate existence by means of it. For he can bring neither of these things to pass without either exceeding his rights as a poet (encroaching with his ideal upon the

territory of experience, and presuming to determine actual existence by means of what is merely possible) or surrendering his rights as a poet (allowing experience to encroach upon the territory of the ideal, and restricting the possible to the conditions of the actual).

11. Only inasmuch as it is honest (expressly renounces all claims to reality), and only inasmuch as it is autonomous (dispenses with all support from reality), is semblance aesthetic. From the moment it is dishonest, and simulates reality, or from the moment it is impure, and has need of reality to make its effect, it is nothing but a base instrument for material ends, and affords no evidence whatsoever of any freedom of the spirit. This does not, of course, imply that an object in which we discover aesthetic semblance must be devoid of reality; all that is required is that our judgement of it should take no account of that reality; for inasmuch as it does take account of it, it is not an aesthetic judgement. The beauty of a living woman will please us as well, or even a little better, than a mere painting of one equally beautiful; but inasmuch as the living beauty pleases better than the painted, she is no longer pleasing us as autonomous semblance, no longer pleasing the purely aesthetic sense; for the appeal to this sense, even by living things, must be through sheer appearance, even by real things, purely in virtue of their existence as idea. But it does, admittedly, require an incomparably higher degree of aesthetic culture to perceive nothing but sheer semblance in what is actually alive, than it does to dispense with the element of life in sheer semblance.

12. In whatever individual or whole people we find this honest and autonomous kind of semblance, we may assume both understanding and taste, and every kindred excellence. There we shall see actual life governed by the ideal, honour triumphant over possessions, thought over enjoyment, dreams of immortality over existence. There public opinion will be the only thing to be feared, and an olive wreath bestow greater honour than a purple robe. Only impotence and perversity will have recourse to dishonest and dependent semblance; and single individuals, as well as whole peoples, who either 'eke out reality with semblance, or (aesthetic) semblance with reality' – the two often go together – give evidence alike of their moral worthlessness and of their aesthetic incapacity.

13. To the question. 'How far can semblance legitimately exist in the moral world?' the answer is then, briefly and simply, this: To the extent that it is aesthetic semblance; that is to say, semblance which neither seeks to represent reality nor needs to be represented by it. Aesthetic semblance can never be a threat to the truth of morals; and where it might seem to be otherwise, it can be shown without difficulty that the semblance was not aesthetic. Only a stranger to polite society, for example, will take the prot-

estations of courtesy, which are common form, for tokens of personal regard, and when deceived complain of dissimulation. But only a bungler in polite society will, for the sake of courtesy, call deceit to his aid, and produce flattery in order to please. The first still lacks all sense of autonomous semblance; hence he can only lend it significance by endowing it with some content of truth. The second is himself lacking in reality and would fain, therefore, replace it by semblance.

14. Nothing is more common than to hear certain shallow critics of our age voicing the complaint that the solid virtues have disappeared from the face of the world, and that Being is neglected for the sake of Seeming. Though I feel no call to defend our age against such accusations, it is obvious enough from the sweeping way in which these severe moralizers tend to generalize their indictment, that they reproach the age not only for dishonest but for honest semblance too. And even the exceptions they might possibly be prepared to make for the sake of beauty refer rather to dependent, than to autonomous, semblance. They do not merely attack the lying colours which mask the face of truth and are bold enough to masquerade as reality; they also inveigh against that beneficent semblance with which we fill out our emptiness and cover up our wretchedness, and against that ideal semblance which ennobles the reality of common day. The hypocrisy of our morals rightly offends their strict sense of truth; it is only regrettable that, in their eyes, politeness too should count as hypocrisy. They dislike the superficial glitter which so often eclipses true merit; but it irks them no less that we should require genuine merit to have style, and refuse to absolve inward substance from having a pleasing outward form. They regret the sincerity, soundness, and solidity of former times; but they would like to see reintroduced with these the uncouthness and bluntness of primitive manners, the heavy awkwardness of ancient forms, and the lost exuberance of a Gothick Age. With judgements of this kind they show a respect for substance as such which is unworthy of man, who is meant to value matter only to the extent that it is capable of taking on form and extending the realm of ideas. To such voices, therefore, the taste of our century need pay no undue heed, so long as it can stand its ground before a higher tribunal. What a more rigoristic judge of beauty could well reproach us with, is not that we attach value to aesthetic semblance (we do not attach nearly enough), but that we have not yet attained to the level of pure semblance at all, that we have not sufficiently distinguished existence from appearance, and thereby made the frontiers of each secure for ever. We shall deserve this reproach as long as we cannot enjoy the beauty of living nature without coveting it, or admire the beauty of imitative art without enquiring after its purpose – as long as we still refuse Imagination

any absolute legislative rights of her own, and, by the kind of respect we accord to her works, go on referring her instead to the dignity of her office.

Twenty-Seventh Letter

1. You need have no fear for either reality or truth if the lofty conception of aesthetic semblance which I put forward in the last Letter were to become universal. It will not become universal as long as man is still uncultivated enough to be in a position to misuse it; and should it become universal, this could only be brought about by the kind of culture which would automatically make any misuse of it impossible. To strive after autonomous semblance demands higher powers of abstraction, greater freedom of heart, more energy of will, than man ever needs when he confines himself to reality; and he must already have left this reality behind if he would arrive at that kind of semblance. How ill-advised he would be, then, to take the path towards the ideal in order to save himself the way to the real! From semblance as here understood we should thus have little cause to fear for reality; all the more to be feared, I would suggest, is the threat from reality to semblance. Chained as he is to the material world, man subordinates semblance to ends of his own long before he allows it autonomous existence in the ideal realm of art. For this latter to happen a complete revolution in his whole way of feeling is required, without which he would not even find himself on the way to the ideal. Wherever, then, we find traces of a disinterested and unconditional appreciation of pure semblance, we may infer that a revolution of this order has taken place in his nature, and that he has started to become truly human. Traces of this kind are, however, actually to be found even in his first crude attempts at embellishing his existence, attempts made even at the risk of possibly worsening it from the material point of view. As soon as ever he starts preferring form to substance, and jeopardizing reality for the sake of semblance (which he must, however, recognize as such), a breach has been effected in the cycle of his animal behaviour, and he finds himself set upon a path to which there is no end.

2. Not just content with what satisfies nature, and meets his instinctual needs, he demands something over and above this: to begin with, admittedly, only a superfluity of material things, in order to conceal from appetite the fact that it has limits, and ensure enjoyment beyond the satisfaction of immediate needs; soon, however, a superfluity in material things, an aesthetic surplus, in order to satisfy the formal impulse too, and extend enjoyment beyond the satisfaction of every need. By merely gathering

supplies around him for future use, and enjoying them in anticipation, he does, it is true, transcend the present moment – but without transcending time altogether. He enjoys more, but he does not enjoy differently. But when he also lets form enter into his enjoyment, and begins to notice the outward appearance of the things which satisfy his desires, then he has not merely enhanced his enjoyment in scope and degree, but also ennobled it in kind.

3. It is true that Nature has given even to creatures without reason more than the bare necessities of existence, and shed a glimmer of freedom even into the darkness of animal life. When the lion is not gnawed by hunger, nor provoked to battle by any beast of prey, his idle strength creates an object for itself: he fills the echoing desert with a roaring that speaks defiance, and his exuberant energy enjoys its *self* in purposeless display. With what enjoyment of life do insects swarm in the sunbeam; and it is certainly not the cry of desire that we hear in the melodious warbling of the songbird. Without doubt there is freedom in these activities; but not freedom from compulsion altogether, merely from a certain kind of compulsion, compulsion from without. An animal may be said to be at work, when the stimulus to activity is some lack; it may be said to be at play, when the stimulus is sheer plenitude of vitality, when superabundance of life is its own incentive to action. Even inanimate nature exhibits a similar luxuriance of forces, coupled with a laxity of determination which, in that material sense, might well be called play. The tree puts forth innumerable buds which perish without ever unfolding, and sends out far more roots, branches, and leaves in search of nourishment than are ever used for the sustaining of itself or its species. Such portion of its prodigal profusion as it returns, unused and unenjoyed, to the elements, is the overplus which living things are entitled to squander in a movement of carefree joy. Thus does Nature, even in her material kingdom, offer us a prelude of the Illimitable, and even here remove in part the chains which, in the realm of form, she casts away entirely. From the compulsion of want, or physical earnestness, she makes the transition via the compulsion of superfluity, or physical play, to aesthetic play; and before she soars, in the sublime freedom of beauty, beyond the fetters of ends and purposes altogether, she makes some approach to this independence, at least from afar, in that kind of free activity which is at once its own end and its own means.

4. Like the bodily organs in man, his imagination, too, has its free movement and its material play, an activity in which, without any reference to form, it simply delights in its own absolute and unfettered power. Inasmuch as form does not yet enter this fantasy play at all, its whole charm residing in a free association of images, such play – although the

prerogative of man alone – belongs merely to his animal life, and simply affords evidence of his liberation from all external physical compulsion, without as yet warranting the inference that there is any autonomous shaping power within him.* From this play of freely associated ideas, which is still of a wholly material kind, and to be explained by purely natural laws, the imagination, in its attempt at a free form, finally makes the leap to aesthetic play. A leap it must be called, since a completely new power now goes into action; for here, for the first time, mind takes a hand as lawgiver in the operations of blind instinct, subjects the arbitrary activity of the imagination to its own immutable and eternal unity, introduces its own autonomy into the transient, and its own infinity into the life of sense. But as long as brute nature still has too much power, knowing no other law but restless hastening from change to change, it will oppose to that necessity of the spirit its own unstable caprice, to that stability its own unrest, to that autonomy its own subservience, to that sublime self-sufficiency its own insatiable discontent. The aesthetic play-drive, therefore, will in its first attempts be scarcely recognizable, since the physical play-drive, with its wilful moods and its unruly appetites, constantly gets in the way. Hence we see uncultivated taste first seizing upon what is new and startling – on the colourful, fantastic, and bizarre, the violent and the savage – and shunning nothing so much as tranquil simplicity. It fashions grotesque shapes, loves swift transitions, exuberant forms, glaring contrasts, garish lights, and a song full of feeling. At this stage what man calls beautiful is only what excites him, what offers him material – but excites him to a resistance involving autonomous activity, but offers him material for possible shaping. Otherwise it would not be beauty – even for him. The form of his judgements has thus undergone an astonishing change: he seeks these objects, not because they give him something to enjoy passively, but because they provide an incentive to respond actively. They please him, not because they

* Most of the imaginative play which goes on in everyday life is either entirely based on this feeling for free association of ideas, or at any rate derives therefrom its greatest charm. This may not in itself be proof of a higher nature, and it may well be that it is just the most flaccid natures who tend to surrender to such unimpeded flow of images; it is nevertheless this very independence of the fantasy from external stimuli, which constitutes at least the negative condition of its creative power. Only by tearing itself free from reality does the formative power raise itself up to the ideal; and before the imagination, in its productive capacity, can act according to its own laws, it must first, in its reproductive procedures, have freed itself from alien laws. From mere lawlessness to autonomous law-giving from within, there is, admittedly, still a big step to be taken; and a completely new power, the faculty for ideas, must first be brought into play. But this power, too, can now develop with greater ease, since the senses are not working against it, and the indefinite does, at least negatively, border upon the infinite.

meet a need, but because they satisfy a law which speaks, though softly as yet, within his breast.

5. Soon he is no longer content that things should please him; he himself wants to please. At first, indeed, only through that which is his; finally through that which he is. The things he possesses, the things he produces, may no longer bear upon them the marks of their use, their form no longer be merely a timid expression of their function; in addition to the service they exist to render, they must at the same time reflect the genial mind which conceived them, the loving hand which wrought them, the serene and liberal spirit which chose and displayed them. Now the ancient German goes in search of glossier skins, statelier antlers, more elaborate drinking horns; and the Caledonian selects for his feasts the prettiest shells. Even weapons may no longer be mere objects of terror; they must be objects of delight as well, and the cunningly ornamented sword-belt claims no less attention than the deadly blade of the sword. Not content with introducing aesthetic superfluity into objects of necessity, the play-drive as it becomes ever freer finally tears itself away from the fetters of utility altogether, and beauty in and for itself alone begins to be an object of his striving. Man adorns himself. Disinterested and undirected pleasure is now numbered among the necessities of existence, and what is in fact unnecessary soon becomes the best part of his delight.

6. And as form gradually comes upon him from without – in his dwelling, his household goods, and his apparel – so finally it begins to take possession of him himself, transforming at first only the outer, but ultimately the inner, man too. Uncoordinated leaps of joy turn into dance, the unformed movements of the body into the graceful and harmonious language of gesture; the confused and indistinct cries of feeling become articulate, begin to obey the laws of rhythm, and to take on the contours of song. If the Trojan host storms on to the battlefield with piercing shrieks like a flock of cranes, the Greek army approaches it in silence, with noble and measured tread. In the former case we see only the exuberance of blind forces; in the latter, the triumph of form and the simple majesty of law.

7. Now compulsion of a lovelier kind binds the sexes together, and a communion of hearts helps sustain a connection but intermittently established by the fickle caprice of desire. Released from its dark bondage, the eye, less troubled now by passion, can apprehend the form of the beloved; soul looks deep into soul, and out of a selfish exchange of lust there grows a generous interchange of affection. Desire widens, and is exalted into love, once humanity has dawned in its object; and a base advantage over sense is now disdained for the sake of a nobler victory over will. The need to please subjects the all-conquering male to the gentle tribunal of taste; lust he can

steal, but love must come as a gift. For this loftier prize he can only contend by virtue of form, never by virtue of matter. From being a force impinging upon feeling, he must become a form confronting the mind; he must be willing to concede freedom, because it is freedom he wishes to please. And even as beauty resolves the conflict between opposing natures in this simplest and clearest paradigm, the eternal antagonism of the sexes, so too does it resolve it – or at least aims at resolving it – in the complex whole of society, endeavouring to reconcile the gentle with the violent in the moral world after the pattern of the free union it there contrives between the strength of man and the gentleness of woman. Now weakness becomes sacred, and unbridled strength dishonorable; the injustice of nature is rectified by the magnanimity of the chivalric code. He whom no violence may alarm is disarmed by the tender blush of modesty, and tears stifle a revenge which no blood was able to assuage. Even hatred pays heed to the gentle voice of honour; the sword of the victor spares the disarmed foe, and a friendly hearth sends forth welcoming smoke to greet the stranger on that dread shore where of old only murder lay in wait for him.

8. In the midst of the fearful kingdom of forces, and in the midst of the sacred kingdom of laws, the aesthetic impulse to form is at work, unnoticed, on the building of a third joyous kingdom of play and of semblance, in which man is relieved of the shackles of circumstance, and released from all that might be called constraint, alike in the physical and in the moral sphere.

9. If in the dynamic State of rights it is as force that one man encounters another, and imposes limits upon his activities; if in the ethical State of duties Man sets himself over against man with all the majesty of the law, and puts a curb upon his desires: in those circles where conduct is governed by beauty, in the aesthetic State, none may appear to the other except as form, or confront him except as an object of free play. To bestow freedom by means of freedom is the fundamental law of this kingdom.

10. The dynamic State can merely make society possible, by letting one nature be curbed by another; the ethical State can merely make it (morally) necessary, by subjecting the individual will to the general; the aesthetic State alone can make it real, because it consummates the will of the whole through the nature of the individual. Though it may be his needs which drive man into society, and reason which implants within him the principles of social behaviour, beauty alone can confer upon him a social character. Taste alone brings harmony into society, because it fosters harmony in the individual. All other forms of perception divide man, because they are founded exclusively either upon the sensuous or upon the spiritual part of his being; only the aesthetic mode of perception makes of

him a whole, because both his natures must be in harmony if he is to achieve it. All other forms of communication divide society, because they relate exclusively either to the private receptivity or to the private proficiency of its individual members, hence to that which distinguishes man from man; only the aesthetic mode of communication unites society, because it relates to that which is common to all. The pleasures of the senses we enjoy merely as individuals, without the genus which is immanent within us having any share in them at all; hence we cannot make the pleasures of sense universal, because we are unable to universalize our own individuality. The pleasures of knowledge we enjoy merely as genus, and by carefully removing from our judgement all trace of individuality; hence we cannot make the pleasures of reason universal, because we cannot eliminate traces of individuality from the judgements of others as we can from our own. Beauty alone do we enjoy at once as individual and as genus, i.e., as representatives of the human genus. The good of the Senses can only make one man happy, since it is founded on appropriation, and this always involves exclusion; and it can only make this one man one-sidedly happy, since his Personality has no part in it. Absolute good can only bring happiness under conditions which we cannot presume to be universal; for truth is the prize of abnegation alone, and only the pure in heart believe in the pure will. Beauty alone makes the whole world happy, and each and every being forgets its limitations while under its spell.

11. No privilege, no autocracy of any kind, is tolerated where taste rules, and the realm of aesthetic semblance extends its sway. This realm stretches upwards to the point where reason governs with unconditioned necessity, and all that is mere matter ceases to be. It stretches downwards to the point where natural impulse reigns with blind compulsion, and form has not yet begun to appear. And even at these furthermost confines, where taste is deprived of all legislative power, it still does not allow the executive power to be wrested from it. A social appetite must renounce its self-seeking, and the Agreeable, whose normal function is to seduce the senses, must cast toils of Grace over the mind as well. Duty, stern voice of Necessity, must moderate the censorious tone of its precepts – a tone only justified by the resistance they encounter – and show greater respect for Nature through a nobler confidence in her willingness to obey them. From within the Mysteries of Science, taste leads knowledge out into the broad daylight of Common Sense, and transforms a monopoly of the Schools into the common possession of Human Society as a whole. In the kingdom of taste even the mightiest genius must divest itself of its majesty, and stoop in all humility to the mind of a little child. Strength must allow itself to be bound by the Graces, and the lion have its defiance curbed by the bridle of a

Cupid. In return, taste throws a veil of decorum over those physical desires which, in their naked form, affront the dignity of free beings; and, by a delightful illusion of freedom, conceals from us our degrading kinship with matter. On the wings of taste even that art which must cringe for payment can lift itself out of the dust; and, at the touch of her wand, the fetters of serfdom fall away from the lifeless and the living alike. In the Aesthetic State everything – even the tool which serves – is a free citizen, having equal rights with the noblest; and the mind, which would force the patient mass beneath the yoke of its purposes, must here first obtain its assent. Here, therefore, in the realm of Aesthetic Semblance, we find that ideal of equality fulfilled which the Enthusiast would fain see realized in substance. And if it is true that it is in the proximity of thrones that fine breeding comes most quickly and most perfectly to maturity, would one not have to recognize in this, as in much else, a kindly dispensation which often seems to be imposing limits upon man in the real world, only in order to spur him on to realization in an ideal world?

12. But does such a State of Aesthetic Semblance really exist? And if so, where is it to be found? As a need, it exists in every finely attuned soul; as a realized fact, we are likely to find it, like the pure Church and the pure Republic, only in some few chosen circles, where conduct is governed, not by some soulless imitation of the manners and morals of others, but by the aesthetic nature we have made our own; where men make their way, with undismayed simplicity and tranquil innocence, through even the most involved and complex situations, free alike of the compulsion to infringe the freedom of others in order to assert their own, as of the necessity to shed their Dignity in order to manifest Grace.

G. W. F. Hegel, *Introduction to Aesthetics*, Chapters 1–3

9

From Hegel's Introduction to Aesthetics, being the Introduction to the Berlin Aesthetics Lectures of the 1820s, trans. T. M. Knox. Oxford: Clarendon Press, 1975, pp. 1–14 [words and phrases in square brackets, unless followed by 'Ed.', are the translator's].

In chapter 7 of these lectures, Hegel congratulates Schiller on recognizing art's role in effecting 'unity and reconciliation' between seemingly conflicting sides of human existence, such as reason and feeling, duty and desire. However, by focusing on formal features of art, at the expense of 'message', and on its contribution to human betterment, Schiller fails to appreciate the essential nature of serious art. For the beauty it presents is nothing less than the 'sensible manifestation of the Idea', one of Hegel's names (alongside 'the Absolute', 'God' and 'Spirit' (*Geist*)) for the ultimate, rational reality which underlies or structures everything we experience.

Such comments suggest firstly, and rightly, that his remarks on art are integrated in the vast metaphysical system developed by Georg Wilhelm Friedrich Hegel (1770–1831), greatest of the post-Kantian German idealists. (The *Introduction to Aesthetics*, based on Hegel's and his students' notes, is, mercifully, fairly free from the heavyweight terminology of his metaphysics.) But they might also suggest, wrongly, that Hegel follows Schiller and Schelling in regarding art as the highest human activity. The 'paradox' in Hegel is that while art is held to be 'the self-revelation of God', it is also held to be 'coming to an end' – indeed, to be 'a thing of the past' (chapter 3).[1] In the opening sections of the *Introduction* included below, we find Hegel defending art against its detractors, yet refusing to lament its demise. To understand this 'paradoxical' manoeuvre we need to look further afield than these pages.

In Hegelspeak, art belongs, with religion and philosophy, to the realm of 'Absolute Spirit', since it is through these three activities, in that order, that

Reprinted by permission of Oxford University Press.

[1] Michael Inwood, 'Introduction' to *Hegel: introductory lectures on aesthetics*, trans. B. Bosanquet, Harmondsworth: Penguin, 1993, p. ix.

Geist or God – and we humans, its 'vehicles' – eventually arrives at rational, 'self-conscious freedom at peace with itself' (*Phenomenology of Spirit*, § 12). It does so through recognizing that there is no 'out-and-out other' to itself: that everything in nature is shot through with *Geist*. Such recognition is only complete when given explicit philosophical articulation, but in a metaphorical manner it is exhibited in the great religions, especially Christianity. However, as Charles Taylor explains, 'there is a still lower level' of implicit recognition, embodied not 'in a discourse of myth or theology', but 'in sensuous form, as objects of intuition'.[2] This level is art. In other words, art inarticulately expresses philosophic truth in the form of sensible products. In classical Greek statues of the gods in human shape, for example, is implicitly expressed the recognition that the divine, like ourselves, is rational. (See chapter 8 of the lectures.)

Art, then, like religion, is a crucial stage on the arduous journey to man's – and *Geist's* – self-understanding. But precisely because this understanding *can* be given reasoned articulation – because there is nothing finally 'mystical' or 'inaccessible to thinking' (*The Encyclopedia Logic*, § 82) – art cannot, *pace* Schelling, be 'higher' than philosophy. And because this understanding *has* now been articulated – by Hegel himself – 'art has ceased to be the supreme need of the spirit' which it was in a less rational and self-conscious age.[3] Imagery becomes redundant when the truths it intimates can be stated. Art is no longer the mode of expression appropriate to the prevailing level of understanding, as it was for the Greeks.

Although few later writers on art subscribed to Hegel's metaphysics, his influence has been enormous. As Ernst Gombrich reminds us, Hegel was 'the father of art history',[4] for not only does he give to art a role within history, but art itself develops, each epoch deploying the images which express the prevailing mode of comprehension. Equally, as we have seen, he is responsible for the 'death of art' thesis, much discussed by commentators on twentieth century art.[5] Hegel would surely applaud the point that 'Conceptual Art' is the *reductio ad absurdum* of art – the substitution for the 'sensuous' creations of art of philosophical ideas better located in an aesthetics journal than on a canvas. More generally, Hegel is the inspiration for those who, left cold by the Kantian emphasis on form, seek the importance of artworks in the ideas they embody and their involvement with the age to which they belong.

[2] *Hegel*, Cambridge: Cambridge University Press, 1975, p. 468.

[3] Hegel, *Aesthetics: lectures on fine art*, vol. I, trans. T.M. Knox Oxford: Clarendon Press, 1975, p. 103.

[4] *Tributes: interpreters of our cultural tradition*, Ithaca, NY: Cornell University Press, 1984.

[5] See Arthur C. Danto's transparently titled *The Philosophical Disenfranchisement of Art*, New York: Columbia University Press, 1986.

[1] Prefatory Remarks

These lectures are devoted to Aesthetics. Their topic is the spacious ***realm of the beautiful***; more precisely, their province is ***art***, or, rather, ***fine art***.

For this topic, it is true, the word Aesthetics, taken literally, is not wholly satisfactory, since 'Aesthetics' means, more precisely, the science of sensation, of feeling. In this sense it had its origin as a new science, or rather as something which for the first time was to become a philosophical discipline, in the school of [Christian] Wolff [1679–1750. A follower of Leibniz. Ed.] at the period in Germany when works of art were treated with regard to the feelings they were supposed to produce, as, for instance, the feeling of pleasure, admiration, fear, pity, and so on. Because of the unsatisfactoriness, or more accurately, the superficiality of this word, attempts were made after all to frame others, e.g. 'Callistics'. But this too appears inadequate because the science which is meant deals not with the beautiful as such but simply with the beauty of art. We will therefore let the word 'Aesthetics' stand; as a mere name it is a matter of indifference to us, and besides it has meanwhile passed over into common speech. As a name then it may be retained, but the proper expression for our science is *Philosophy of Art* and, more definitely, *Philosophy of Fine Art*.

[2] Limitation and Defence of Aesthetics

By adopting this expression we at once exclude the beauty of nature. Such a limitation of our topic may appear to be laid down arbitrarily, on the principle that every science has authority to demarcate its scope at will. But this is not the sense in which we should take this limitation of aesthetics to the beauty of art. In ordinary life we are of course accustomed to speak of a beautiful colour, a beautiful sky, a beautiful river; likewise of beautiful flowers, beautiful animals, and even more of beautiful people. We will not here enter upon the controversy about how far the attribute of beauty is justifiably ascribed to these and the like, and how far, in general, natural beauty may be put alongside the beauty of art. But we may assert against this view, even at this stage, that the beauty of art is ***higher*** than nature. The beauty of art is beauty ***born of the spirit and born again***,[1] and the higher the spirit and its productions stand above nature and its phenomena, the higher too is the beauty of art above that of nature. Indeed, considered ***formally*** [i.e. no matter what it says], even a useless notion that enters a man's head is higher than any product of nature, because in such a notion spirituality and freedom are always present. Of course, considered in its *content*, the sun, for example, appears as an absolutely necessary factor [in the universe] while a false notion vanishes as *accidental* and transitory. But, taken by itself, a natural existent like the sun is indifferent, not free and self-conscious in itself; and if we treat it in its necessary connection with other things, then we are not treating it by itself, and therefore not as beautiful.

Now if we said in general that spirit and its artistic beauty stands *higher* than natural beauty, then of course virtually nothing is settled, because 'higher' is a quite vague expression which describes natural and artistic beauty as still standing side by side in the space of imagination and differing only quantitatively and therefore externally. But what is *higher* about the spirit and its artistic beauty is not something merely relative in comparison with nature. On the contrary, spirit is alone the *true*, comprehending everything in itself, so that everything beautiful is truly beautiful only as sharing in this higher sphere and generated by it. In this sense the beauty of nature appears only as a reflection of the beauty that belongs to spirit, as an imperfect incomplete mode [of beauty], a mode which in its *substance* is contained in the spirit itself. – Besides we shall find that a limitation to fine art arises very naturally, since, however much is said about the beauties of nature (less by the ancients than by us), it has not yet entered anyone's head to concentrate on the *beauty* of natural objects and make a science, a systematic exposition, of these beauties. A treatment from the point of view of *utility* has indeed been made and, for example, a scientific account of natural objects useful against diseases has been composed, a *materia medica*, a description of the minerals, chemical products, plants, or animals, which are useful for cures. But the realms of nature have not been classified and examined from the point of view of beauty. In [discussing] natural beauty we feel ourselves too much in a vague sphere, without a *criterion*, and therefore such a classification would provide too little interest for us to undertake it.

These preliminary remarks on beauty in nature and art, on the relation of the two, and the exclusion of the former from the scope of our proper subject, should dispose of the idea that the limitation is due merely to caprice and arbitrariness. The proof of this relation should not come here yet, since its consideration falls within our science itself and is therefore not to be further explained and proved until later [see Part I, ch. II].

But if we now limit ourselves provisionally to the beauty of art, this first step brings us at once up against new difficulties.

[3] Refutation of Objections

The *first* that we may encounter is the doubt whether fine art shows itself *deserving* of a scientific treatment.[2] Beauty and art does indeed pervade all the business of life like a friendly genius and brightly adorns all our surroundings whether inner or outer, mitigating the seriousness of our circumstances and the complexities of the actual world, extinguishing idleness in an entertaining way, and, where there is nothing good to be done, filling the place of evil always better than evil itself. Yet even though art intersperses with its pleasing forms everything from the war-paint of the savages to the splendour of temples with all their riches of adornment, these forms themselves nevertheless seem to fall outside the true ends and aims of life. Even if artistic creations are not detrimental to these serious purposes, if indeed they sometimes even seem to further them, at least by keeping evil away, still, art belongs rather to the indulgence and relaxation of the spirit, whereas substantial interests require its exertion. Thus it may look as if it would be inappropriate and pedantic to propose to treat with scientific seriousness what is not itself of a serious nature. In any case, on this view, art appears as a superfluity, even if the softening of the heart which preoccupation with beauty can produce does not altogether become exactly deleterious as downright effeminacy. From this point of view, granted that the fine arts are a luxury, it has frequently been necessary to defend them in their relation to practical necessities in general, and in particular to morality and piety, and, since it is impossible to prove their harmlessness, at least to give grounds for believing that this luxury of the spirit may afford a greater sum of advantages than disadvantages. With this in view, serious aims have been ascribed to art itself, and it has frequently been recommended as a mediator between reason and sense, between inclination and duty, as a reconciler of these colliding elements in their grim strife and opposition. But it may be maintained that in the case of these aims of art, admittedly more serious, nothing is gained for reason and duty by this attempt at mediation, because by their very nature reason and duty permit of no mixture with anything else; they could not enter into such a transaction, and they demand the same purity which they have in themselves. Besides, it may be argued, art is not by this means made any worthier of scientific discussion, since it always remains a servant on both sides [between which it is supposed to mediate], and along with higher aims it all the same also promotes idleness and frivolity. Indeed, to put it simply, in this service, instead of being an end in itself, it can appear only as a means. – If, finally, art is regarded as a means, then there always remains in the form of the means a disadvantageous aspect, namely that even if art subordinates itself to more serious aims in fact, and produces more serious effects, the means that it uses for this purpose is *deception*. The beautiful [*Schöne*] has its being in pure appearance [*Schein*].[3] But an inherently true end and aim, as is easily recognized, must not be achieved by deception, and even if here and there it may be furthered by this means, this should be only in a limited way; and even in that case deception will be unable to count as the right means. For the means should correspond to the dignity of the end, and not pure appearance and deception but only the truth can create the truth, just as science too has to treat the true interests of the spirit in accordance with the true mode of actuality and the true mode of envisaging it.

In these respects it may look as if fine art is unworthy of scientific treatment because [it is alleged] it remains only a pleasing play, and, even if it pursues more serious ends, it still contradicts their nature; but [the allegation proceeds] in general it is only a servant both of that play and of these ends, and alike for the element of its being and the means of its effectiveness it can avail itself of nothing but deception and pure appearance.

But, *secondly*, it is still more likely to seem that even if fine art in general is a proper object of philosophical reflection, it is yet no appropriate topic for *strictly* scientific treatment. For the beauty of art presents itself to *sense*, feeling, intuition, imagination; it has a different sphere from thought, and the apprehension of its activity and its products demands an organ other than scientific thinking. Further, it is precisely the *freedom* of production and configurations that we enjoy in the beauty of art. In the production as well as in the perception of works of art, it seems as if we escape from every fetter of rule and regularity. In place of the strictness of conformity to law, and the dark inwardness of thought, we seek peace and enlivenment in the forms of art; we exchange the shadow realm of the Idea for bright and vigorous reality. Finally, the source of works of art is the free activity of fancy which in its imaginations is itself more free than nature is. Art has at its command not only the whole wealth of natural formations in their manifold and variegated appearance; but in addition the creative imagination has power to launch out beyond them *inexhaustibly* in productions of its own. In face of this immeasurable fullness of fancy and its free products, it looks as if thought must lose courage to bring them *completely* before itself, to criticize them, and arrange them under its universal formulae.

Science on the contrary, the objectors admit, has, in its form, to do with the thinking which abstracts from a mass of details. The result is that, on the one hand, imagination with its whim and caprice, the organ, i.e., of artistic activity and enjoyment, remains excluded from science. On the other hand, they say that while art does brighten and vivify the unillumined and withered dryness of the Concept, does reconcile its abstractions and its conflict with reality, does enrich the Concept with reality, a *purely* intellectual treatment [of art] removes this means of enrichment, destroys it, and carries the Concept back to its simplicity without reality and to its shadowy abstractness. Further, in its content, science is occupied with what is inherently *necessary*. If aesthetics leaves natural beauty aside, we have in this respect apparently not only not gained anything, but rather have removed ourselves still further from the necessary. For the very word 'nature' already gives us the idea of necessity and conformity to law, and so of a state of affairs which, it can be hoped, is nearer to scientific treatment and susceptible of it. But in the sphere of the spirit in general, especially in the imagination, what seems, in comparison with nature, to be peculiarly at home is caprice and the absence of law, and this is automatically incapable of any scientific explanation.

In all these respects, therefore [the argument runs], fine art, alike in its origin, its effect, and its scope, instead of showing itself fitted for scientific endeavour, seems rather in its own right to resist thought's regulating activity and *not* to be suitable for scientific discussion.

These scruples, and others like them, against a truly scientific preoccupation with fine art are derived from common ideas, points of view, and considerations; their more prolix elaboration you can read *ad nauseam* in older books, especially French ones,[4] about beauty and the fine arts. And in part they contain facts that are right enough, and, in part too, argumentation is derived from them which at first sight seems plausible as well. Thus, for example, it is a fact that the shapes that beauty takes on are as multifarious as its occurrence is universal. If you like, you can infer from this a universal bent in human nature for the beautiful, and then go on to the further inference that because the ideas of the beautiful are so infinitely various, and, therefore, at first sight, something *particular*, there cannot be any *universal* laws of beauty and taste.

Now before we can turn away from such considerations to our proper subject, our next task must consist in a short introductory discussion of the scruples and doubts that have been raised.

[i] As regards the *worthiness* of art to be treated scientifically, it is of course the case that art can be used as a fleeting play, affording recreation and entertainment, decorating our surroundings, giving pleasantness to the externals of our life, and making other objects stand out by artistic adornment. Thus regarded, art is indeed not independent, not free, but ancillary. But what *we* want to consider is art which is *free* alike in its end and its means. The fact that art in general can serve other ends and be in

that case a mere passing amusement is something which it shares equally with thought. For, on the one hand, science may indeed be used as an intellectual servant for finite ends and accidental means, and it then acquires its character not from itself but from other objects and circumstances. Yet, on the other hand, it also cuts itself free from this servitude in order to raise itself, in free independence, to the truth in which it fulfils itself independently and conformably with its own ends alone.

Now, in this its freedom alone is fine art truly art, and it only fulfils its supreme task when it has placed itself in the same sphere as religion and philosophy, and when it is simply one way of bringing to our minds and expressing the *Divine*, the deepest interests of mankind, and the most comprehensive truths of the spirit. In works of art the nations have deposited their richest inner intuitions and ideas, and art is often the key, and in many nations the sole key, to understanding their philosophy and religion. Art shares this vocation with religion and philosophy, but in a special way, namely by displaying even the highest [reality] sensuously, bringing it thereby nearer to the senses, to feeling, and to nature's mode of appearance. What is thus displayed is the depth of a supra-sensuous world which thought pierces and sets up at first as a *beyond* in contrast with immediate consciousness and present feeling; it is the freedom of intellectual reflection which rescues itself from the *here* and now, called sensuous reality and finitude. But this breach, to which the spirit proceeds, it is also able to heal. It generates out of itself works of fine art as the first reconciling middle term between pure thought and what is merely external, sensuous, and transient, between nature and finite reality and the infinite freedom of conceptual thinking.

[ii] So far as concerns the unworthiness of the *element* of art in general, namely its pure appearance and *deceptions*, this objection would of course have its justification if pure appearance could be claimed as something wrong. But appearance itself is essential to essence. Truth would not be truth if it did not show itself and appear, if it were not truth *for* someone and *for* itself, as well as for the spirit in general too. Consequently, not pure appearance in general, but only the special kind of appearance in which art gives reality to what is inherently true can be the subject of reproof. If in this connection the pure appearance in which art brings its conceptions into existence is to be described as 'deception', this reproof first acquires its meaning in comparison with the phenomena of the *external world* and its immediate materiality, as well as in relation to our own world of feeling, i.e. the *inner world of sense*. To both these worlds, in our life of experience, our own phenomenal life, we are accustomed to ascribe the value and name of actuality, reality, and truth, in contrast to art which lacks such reality and

truth. But it is precisely this whole sphere of the empirical inner and outer world which is not the world of genuine actuality; on the contrary, we must call it, in a stricter sense than we call art, a pure appearance and a harsher deception. Only beyond the immediacy of feeling and external objects is genuine actuality to be found. For the truly actual is only that which has being in and for itself, the substance of nature and spirit, which indeed gives itself presence and existence, but in this existence remains in and for itself and only so is truly actual. It is precisely the dominion of these universal powers which art emphasizes and reveals. In the ordinary external and internal world essentiality does indeed appear too, but in the form of a chaos of accidents, afflicted by the immediacy of the sensuous and by the capriciousness of situations, events, characters, etc. Art liberates the true content of phenomena from the pure appearance and deception of this bad, transitory world, and gives them a higher actuality, born of the spirit. Thus, far from being mere pure appearance, a higher reality and truer existence is to be ascribed to the phenomena of art in comparison with [those of] ordinary reality.

Neither can the representations of art be called a deceptive appearance in comparison with the truer representations of historiography. For the latter has not even immediate existence but only the spiritual pure appearance thereof as the element of its portrayals, and its content remains burdened with the entire contingency of ordinary life and its events, complications, and individualities, whereas the work of art brings before us the eternal powers that govern history without this appendage of the immediate sensuous present and its unstable appearance.

But if the mode in which artistic forms appear is called a deception in comparison with philosophical thinking and with religious and moral principles, of course the form of appearance acquired by a topic in the sphere of *thinking* is the truest reality; but in comparison with the appearance of immediate existence and of historiography, the pure appearance of art has the advantage that it points through and beyond itself, and itself hints at something spiritual of which it is to give us an idea, whereas immediate appearance does not present itself as deceptive but rather as the real and the true, although the truth is in fact contaminated and concealed by the immediacy of sense. The hard shell of nature and the ordinary world make it more difficult for the spirit to penetrate through them to the Idea than works of art do.

But while on the one hand we give this high position to art, it is on the other hand just as necessary to remember that neither in content nor in form is art the highest and absolute mode of bringing to our minds the true interests of the spirit. For precisely on account of its form, art is limited to a specific content. Only one sphere and stage of truth is capable of being represented in the element of art. In order to be a genuine content for art, such truth must in virtue of its own specific character be able to go forth into [the sphere of] sense and remain adequate to itself there. This is the case, for example, with the gods of Greece. On the other hand, there is a deeper comprehension of truth which is no longer so akin and friendly to sense as to be capable of appropriate adoption and expression in this medium. The Christian view of truth is of this kind, and, above all, the spirit of our world today, or, more particularly, of our religion and the development of our reason, appears as beyond the stage at which art is the supreme mode of our knowledge of the Absolute. The peculiar nature of artistic production and of works of art no longer fills our highest need. We have got beyond venerating works of art as divine and worshipping them. The impression they make is of a more reflective kind, and what they arouse in us needs a higher touchstone and a different test. Thought and reflection have spread their wings above fine art. Those who delight in lamenting and blaming may regard this phenomenon as a corruption and ascribe it to the predominance of passions and selfish interests which scare away the seriousness of art as well as its cheerfulness; or they may accuse the distress of the present time, the complicated state of civil and political life which does not permit a heart entangled in petty interests to free itself to the higher ends of art. This is because intelligence itself subserves this distress, and its interests, in sciences which are useful for such ends alone, and it allows itself to be seduced into confining itself to this desert.

However all this may be, it is certainly the case that art no longer affords that satisfaction of spiritual needs which earlier ages and nations sought in it, and found in it alone, a satisfaction that, at least on the part of religion, was most intimately linked with art. The beautiful days of Greek art, like the golden age of the later Middle Ages, are gone. The development of reflection in our life today has made it a need of ours, in relation both to our will and judgement, to cling to general considerations and to regulate the particular by them, with the result that universal forms, laws, duties, rights, maxims, prevail as determining reasons and are the chief regulator. But for artistic interest and production we demand in general rather a quality of life in which the universal is not present in the form of law and maxim, but which gives the impression of being one with the senses and the feelings, just as the universal and the rational is contained in the imagination by being brought into unity with a concrete sensuous appearance. Consequently the conditions of our present time are not favourable to art. It is not, as might be supposed, merely that the practising artist himself is infected by the loud voice of reflection all around him and by the opinions and judgements on art that have become customary everywhere, so that he is misled into introducing more thoughts into his work; the point is that our whole spiritual culture is of such a kind that he himself stands within the world of reflection and its relations, and could not by any act of will and decision abstract himself from it; nor could he by special education or removal from the relations of life contrive and organize a special solitude to replace what he has lost.

In all these respects art, considered in its highest vocation,is and remains for us a thing of the past. Thereby it has lost for us genuine truth and life, and has rather been transferred into our *ideas* instead of maintaining its earlier necessity in reality and occupying its higher place. What is now aroused in us by works of art is not just immediate enjoyment but our judgement also, since we subject to our intellectual consideration (i) the content of art, and (ii) the work of art's means of presentation, and the appropriateness or inappropriateness of both to one another. The *philosophy* of art is therefore a greater need in our day than it was in days when art by itself as art yielded full satisfaction. Art invites us to intellectual consideration, and that not for the purpose of creating art again, but for knowing philosophically what art is.

But as soon as we propose to accept this invitation, we are met by the suspicion, already touched upon, that while art may well be a suitable subject for philosophical reflection in a general way, it may not be suitable for strictly systematic and scientific treatment. But this implies at once the false idea that a philosophical discussion can also be unscientific. On this point I can only say in brief that, whatever ideas others may have about philosophy and philosophizing, my view is that philosophizing is throughout inseparable from scientific procedure. Philosophy has to consider an object in its necessity, not merely according to subjective necessity or external ordering, classification, etc.; it has to unfold and prove the object, according to the necessity of its own inner nature. It is only this unfolding which constitutes the scientific element in the treatment of a subject. But in so far as the objective necessity of an object lies essentially in its logical and metaphysical nature, the treatment of art in isolation may, and indeed must, be exempt from absolute scientific rigour; art has so many preconditions both in respect of its content and in respect of its material and its medium, whereby it always simultaneously touches on the accidental; and so it is only in relation to the essential inner progress of its content and means of expression that we may refer to its *necessary* formation.

[iii] But what of the objection that works of fine art are not susceptible of a scientific and intellectual treatment because they have their origin in the heart and unregulated imagination, and, incalculable in number and

variety, exercise their effect only on feeling and imagination? This is a perplexity which even now still seems to carry some weight. For the beauty of art does in fact appear in a form which is expressly opposed to thought and which thought is compelled to destroy in order to pursue its own characteristic activity. This idea hangs together with the view that the real in general, the life of nature and spirit, is marred and killed by comprehension; that instead of being brought nearer to us by conceptual thinking, it is all the more removed from us, with the result that, by using thinking as a means of grasping what the live phenomenon is, man defeats his own purpose. At this point we cannot deal with this matter exhaustively; we can only indicate the point of view from which this difficulty or impossibility or unadaptability can be removed.

This much at least will be granted at once, that the spirit is capable of considering itself, and of possessing a consciousness, a *thinking* consciousness, of itself and of everything originating in itself. Thinking is precisely what constitutes the inmost essential nature of spirit. In this thinking consciousness of itself and its products, however much freedom and caprice these may always have, the spirit is acting in accordance with its essential nature, provided that it be genuinely in them. Now art and works of art, by springing from and being created by the spirit, are themselves of a spiritual kind, even if their presentation assumes an appearance of sensuousness and pervades the sensuous with the spirit. In this respect art already lies nearer to the spirit and its thinking than purely external spiritless nature does. In the products of art, the spirit has to do solely with its own. And even if works of art are not thought or the Concept, but a development of the Concept out of itself, a shift of the Concept from its own ground to that of sense, still the power of the thinking spirit lies in being able not only to grasp itself in its proper form as thinking, but to know itself again just as much when it has surrendered its proper form to feeling and sense, to comprehend itself in its opposite, because it changes into thoughts what has been estranged and so reverts to itself. And in this preoccupation with its opposite the thinking spirit is not false to itself at all as if it were forgetting and abandoning itself thereby, nor is it so powerless as to be unable to grasp what is different from itself; on the contrary, it comprehends both itself and its opposite. For the Concept is the universal which maintains itself in its particularizations, overreaches itself and its opposite, and so it is also the power and activity of cancelling again the estrangement in which it gets involved. Thus the work of art too, in which thought expresses itself, belongs to the sphere of conceptual thinking, and the spirit, by subjecting it to philosophic treatment, is thereby merely satisfying the need of the spirit's inmost nature. For since thinking is the essence and Concept of spirit, the spirit in the last resort is only satisfied when it has permeated all products of its activity with thought too and so only then has made them genuinely its own. But art, far removed . . . from being the highest form of spirit, acquires its real ratification only in philosophy.

Nor does art elude philosophical treatment by lawless caprice, since, as has been already hinted, its true task is to bring the highest interests of spirit to our minds. From this it follows at once that, so far as *content* is concerned, fine art cannot range in wild unfettered fancy since these spiritual interests set firm stopping-places to it for its content, no matter how multifarious and inexhaustible its forms and configurations. The same holds good for the forms themselves. They too are not left to pure chance. Not every artistic configuration is capable of expressing and displaying those interests, of absorbing and reproducing them; on the contrary, by a definite content the form appropriate to it is also made definite.

And so, after all, seen from this angle, we are able to orientate ourselves by process of thought in what seemed the impossibly vast mass of works and forms of art. Thus we have now stated, in relation to our science, the content to which we propose to restrict ourselves and we have seen that neither is fine art unworthy of philosophical treatment, nor is philosophical treatment incapable of descrying the essence of fine art.

Notes

1 i.e. 'born' first in the artist's mind and then in the work he creates.

2 'Science', 'scientific' etc. translate *Wissenschaft* and its cognates, but the German word is wider in scope than our 'science', referring as much to history and sociology as to physics. Hegel soon explains what he means by a 'scientific' treatment of art.

3 See Schiller's twenty-sixth letter above for a discussion of *Schein*, there translated as 'semblance'.

4 Particularly Charles Batteux's *Les Beaux Arts réduits à un même principe* (1746).

10 Arthur Schopenhauer, *The World as Will and Representation*, Vol. I, Section 52

From Arthur Schopenhauer, *The World as Will and Representation*, 2 vols, trans. E. F. J. Payne. New York: Dover, 1969, pp. 255–67 [some Greek, Latin and other sentences replaced by English translations; some footnotes omitted].

If Kant is the philosopher's philosopher, our fourth German in a row, Arthur Schopenhauer (1788–1850), is the artist's: for no philosopher has attributed a more exalted role to art, especially music – not, at any rate, in such eloquent and powerful prose. For Schopenhauer, as for his predecessors, art affords opportunities for 'disinterested' contemplation, but unlike them he holds that such contemplation at once enhances our condition and provides direct knowledge of reality. (Recall that Hegel, whom Schopenhauer regarded as a bloated charlatan, saw artworks only as 'images' or symbols of truths awaiting philosophical articulation, not as direct, indispensable vehicles of truth.)

As with his predecessors, Schopenhauer's aesthetics is rooted in a wider metaphysics, a highly original one even if eclectically constructed from Platonic, Kantian and Indian materials. Like Kant, he sharply distinguishes between reality 'in itself' and the world as we are bound to represent or experience it. The former is non-spatial, non-temporal and non-plural, the 'illusion' of space, time and plurality being the result of the subjective imposition on reality of a *principium individuationis* (principle of individuality). He differs from Kant in holding that the 'thing in itself' can be known, albeit not through ordinary perception: it is *will*, something we observe at work in our own activities and may reasonably infer to be at work, though not in a conscious form, in the universe at large. ('Energy' or 'power' might have been wiser terms to use.) Precisely because everything, ourselves included, is governed by a blind, relentless 'will-to-live', Schopenhauer – here displaying his debt to the Buddha – regards the universe as a theatre of suffering and life as a 'mistake', a febrile, frustrating search for satisfaction, punctuated by occasional moments of respite which soon sour into boredom.

Although escape from this predicament is only finally achievable through an ascetic 'denial of the will-to-live', partial relief is afforded by the contemplation of artworks, enabling us to 'celebrate the Sabbath of the penal servitude of the will' (Vol. I, § 38). In the case of all the arts except music, this is because we rise above the hurly-burly of ordinary life through contemplation of the abiding Platonic Forms of things which the artist of genius is able to make present to us. Since these Forms are more 'objective' than the subjectively conditioned objects of perception, the genius thereby communicates knowledge. His notorious mysogyny aside, Schopenhauer would surely have applauded Degas' ambition to paint, not women, but *woman*.

It is the two chapters on music (Vol. I, § 52; Vol. II, Ch. 39), however, which mark Schopenhauer's most famous contribution to aesthetics. 'No other philosopher', it is rightly said, 'has given music such a weighty role',[1] nor prior to him really tackled the difficult question of how this generally non-mimetic artform communicates so powerfully to human beings. Schopenhauer's answer, elaborated in the pages which follow, is that, in a sense, music *is* mimetic: what it 'copies', however, is not the familiar world, rather it is 'a copy of the will itself' – first and foremost by 'copying' and capturing the essence of those emotions (joy, pain, horror and so on) through which the will does its worst in human life. Quite why music, in directly acquainting us with something so allegedly ghastly as the will, should give us pleasure is not made entirely clear.[2] Nor does Schopenhauer explain why it is in the jolly tunes of Rossini, not the fateful chords of Beethoven, that music achieves its 'full effect'.

Schopenhauer's chapters on music had a profound impact on both musical practice and theory. Wagner's *Tristan and Isolde*, with its tortuously delayed climaxes, is patently inspired by Schopenhauerian maxims on how music may convey certain emotions, just as the composer's later views on the relation between words and music are prompted by Schopenhauer's stress on the pre-eminence of music. When Thomas Mann speaks of music as a language, of 'the advantage that music, which says nothing and everything' has over the 'bareness and baldness' of verbal language, and of its 'saving responsibility', it is Schopenhauer's voice one hears[3] – as one hears also in the resilient claim, despite the efforts of the music critic of Eduard Hanslick and of Igor Stravinsky to discredit it, that music is an expression, not of this or that composer's particular feelings, but of the 'essential nature' of the emotions, as it were 'in the abstract'.

[1] Christopher Janaway, *Schopenhauer* (Oxford: Oxford University Press, 1994), p. 72.

[2] See Michael Tanner, 'Schopenhauer', in D.E. Cooper (ed.), *A Companion to Aesthetics* (Oxford: Blackwell, 1992), pp. 389.

[3] *Doctor Faustus* (Harmondsworth: Penguin, 1968), p. 159, p. 477.

We have now considered all the fine arts in the general way suitable to our point of view. We began with architecture, whose aim as such is to elucidate the objectification of the will at the lowest grade of its visibility, where it shows itself as the dumb striving of the mass, devoid of knowledge and conforming to law; yet it already reveals discord with itself and conflict, namely that between gravity and rigidity. Our observations ended with tragedy, which presents to us in terrible magnitude and distinctness at the highest grade of the will's objectification that very conflict of the will with itself. After this, we find that there is yet another fine art that remains excluded, and was bound to be excluded, from our consideration, for in the systematic connection of our discussion there was no fitting place for it; this art is *music*. It stands quite apart from all the others. In it we do not recognize the copy, the repetition, of any Idea of the inner nature of the world. Yet it is such a great and exceedingly fine art, its effect on man's innermost nature is so powerful, and it is so completely and profoundly understood by him in his innermost being as an entirely universal language, whose distinctness surpasses even that of the world of perception itself, that in it we certainly have to look for more than that 'unconscious exercise in arithmetic in which the mind does not know it is counting', which Leibniz took it to be. Yet he was quite right, in so far as he considered only its immediate and outward significance, its exterior. But if it were nothing more, the satisfaction afforded by it would inevitably be similar to that which we feel when a sum in arithmetic comes out right, and could not be that profound pleasure with which we see the deepest recesses of our nature find expression. Therefore, from our standpoint, where the aesthetic effect is the thing we have in mind, we must attribute to music a far more serious and profound significance that refers to the innermost being of the world and of our own self. In this regard the numerical ratios into which it can be resolved are related not as the thing signified, but only as the sign. That in some sense music must be related to the world as the depiction to the thing depicted, as the copy to the original, we can infer from the analogy with the remaining arts, to all of which this character is peculiar; from their effect on us, it can be inferred that that of music is on the whole of the same nature, only stronger, more rapid, more necessary and infallible. Further, its imitative reference to the world must be very profound, infinitely true, and really striking, since it is instantly understood by everyone, and presents a certain infallibility by the fact that its form can be reduced to quite definite rules expressible in numbers, from which it cannot possibly depart without entirely ceasing to be music. Yet the point of comparison between music and the world, the regard in which it stands to the world in the relation of a copy or a repetition, is very obscure. Men have practised music at all times without being able to give an account of this; content to understand it immediately, they renounce any abstract conception of this direct understanding itself.

I have devoted my mind entirely to the impression of music in its many different forms; and then I have returned again to reflection and to the train of my thought expounded in the present work, and have arrived at an explanation of the inner essence of music, and the nature of its imitative relation to the world, necessarily to be presupposed from analogy. This explanation is quite sufficient for me, and satisfactory for my investigation, and will be just as illuminating also to the man who has followed me thus far, and has agreed with my view of the world. I recognize, however, that it is essentially impossible to demonstrate this explanation, for it assumes and establishes a relation of music as a representation to that which of its essence can never be representation, and claims to regard music as the copy of an original that can itself never be directly represented. Therefore, I can do no more than state here at the end of this third book, devoted mainly to a consideration of the arts, this explanation of the wonderful art of tones which is sufficient for me. I must leave the acceptance or denial of my view to the effect that both music and the whole thought communicated in this work have on each reader. Moreover, I regard it as necessary, in order that a man may assent with genuine conviction to the explanation of the significance of music here to be given, that he should often listen to music with constant reflection on this; and this again requires that he should be already very familiar with the whole thought which I expound.

The (Platonic) Ideas are the adequate objectification of the will. To stimulate the knowledge of these by depicting individual things (for works of art are themselves always such) is the aim of all the other arts (and is possible with a corresponding change in the knowing subject). Hence all of them objectify the will only indirectly, in other words, by means of the Ideas. As our world is nothing but the phenomenon or appearance of the Ideas in plurality through entrance into the *principium individuationis* (the form of knowledge possible to the individual as such), music, since it passes over the Ideas, is also quite independent of the phenomenal world, positively ignores it, and, to a certain extent, could still exist even if there were no world at all, which cannot be said of the other arts. Thus music is as *immediate* an objectification and copy of the whole *will* as the world itself is, indeed as the Ideas are, the multiplied phenomenon of which constitutes the world of individual things. Therefore music is by no means like the other arts, namely a copy of the Ideas, but a *copy of the will itself*, the objectivity of which are the Ideas. For this reason the effect of music is so very much more powerful and penetrating than is that of the other arts, for these others speak only of the shadow, but music of the essence. However, as it is the same will that objectifies itself both in the Ideas and in music, though in quite a different way in each, there must be, not indeed an absolutely direct likeness, but yet a parallel, an analogy, between music and the Ideas, the phenomenon of which in plurality and in incompleteness is the visible world. The demonstration of this analogy will make easier, as an illustration, an understanding of this explanation, which is difficult because of the obscurity of the subject.

I recognize in the deepest tones of harmony, in the ground-bass, the lowest grades of the will's objectification, inorganic nature, the mass of the planet. It is well known that all the high notes, light, tremulous, and dying away more rapidly, may be regarded as resulting from the simultaneous vibrations of the deep bass-note. With the sounding of the low note, the high notes always sound faintly at the same time, and it is a law of harmony that a bass-note may be accompanied only by those high notes that actually sound automatically and simultaneously with it (its 'harmonics'), through the accompanying vibrations. Now this is analogous to the fact that all the bodies and organizations of nature must be regarded as having come into existence through gradual development out of the mass of the planet. This is both their supporter and their source, and the high notes have the same relation to the ground-bass. There is a limit to the depth, beyond which no sound is any longer audible. This corresponds to the fact that no matter is perceivable without form and quality, in other words, without the manifestation of a force incapable of further explanation, in which an Idea expresses itself, and, more generally, that no matter can be entirely without will. Therefore, just as a certain degree of pitch is inseparable from the tone as such, so a certain grade of the will's manifestation is inseparable from matter. Therefore, for us the ground-bass is in harmony what inorganic nature, the crudest mass on which everything rests and from which everything originates and develops, is in the world. Further, in the whole of the ripienos [*i.e. tutti* accompaniments. Ed.] that produce the harmony, between the bass and the leading voice singing the melody, I recognize the whole gradation of the Ideas in which the will objectifies itself. Those nearer to the bass are the lower of those grades, namely the still inorganic bodies manifesting themselves, however, in many ways. Those that are higher represent to me the plant and animal worlds. The definite intervals of the scale are parallel to the definite grades of the will's objectification, the definite species in nature. The departure from the arithmetical correctness of the intervals through some temperament, or produced by the selected key, is analogous to the departure of the individual from the type of the species. In fact, the impure discords, giving no definite interval, can be compared to the monstrous abortions between two species of animals, or between man and animal. But all these bass-notes and ripienos that constitute the *harmony*, lack that sequence and continuity of progress which belong only to the upper voice that sings the *melody*. This voice alone moves rapidly and lightly in modulations and runs, while all the others have only a slower movement without a connection existing in each by itself. The deep bass moves most ponderously, the representative of the crudest mass; its rising and falling occur only in large intervals, in thirds, fourths, fifths, never by *one* tone, unless it be a bass transposed by double counterpoint. This slow movement is also physically essential to it; a quick run or trill in the low notes cannot even be imagined. The higher ripienos, running parallel to the animal world, move more rapidly, yet without melodious connection and significant progress. The disconnected course of the ripienos and their determination by laws are analogous to the fact that in the whole irrational world, from the crystal to the most perfect animal, no being has a really connected consciousness that would make its life into a significant whole. No being experiences a succession of mental developments, none perfects itself by training or instruction, but at any time everything exists uniformly according to its nature, determined by a fixed law. Finally, in the *melody*, in the high, singing, principal voice, leading the whole and progressing with unrestrained freedom, in the uninterrupted significant connection of *one* thought from beginning to end, and expressing a whole, I recognize the highest grade of the will's objectification, the intellectual life and endeavour of man. He alone, because endowed with the faculty of reason, is always looking before and after on the path of his actual life and of its innumerable possibilities, and so achieves a course of life that is intellectual, and is thus connected as a whole. In keeping with this, *melody* alone has significant and intentional connection from beginning to end. Consequently, it relates the story of the intellectually enlightened will, the copy or impression whereof in actual life is the series of its deeds. Melody, however, says more; it relates the most secret history of the intellectually enlightened will, portrays every agitation, every effort, every movement of the will, everything which the faculty of reason summarizes under the wide and negative concept of feeling, and which cannot be further taken up into the abstractions of reason. Hence it has always been said that music is the language of feeling and of passion, just as words are the language of reason. Plato explains it as 'The movement of the melody which it imitates, when the soul is stirred by passions', *Laws*, VIII [812c]; and Aristotle also says 'How is it that rhythms and melodies, although only sound, resemble states of the soul?', *Problemata*, c. 19.

Now the nature of man consists in the fact that his will strives, is satisfied, strives anew, and so on and on; in fact his happiness and well-being consist only in the transition from desire to satisfaction, and from this to a fresh desire, such transition going forward rapidly. For the non-appearance of satisfaction is suffering; the empty longing for a new desire is languor, boredom. Thus, corresponding to this, the nature of melody is a constant digression and deviation from the keynote in a thousand ways, not only to the harmonious intervals, the third and dominant, but to every tone, to the dissonant seventh, and to the extreme intervals; yet there always follows a final return to the keynote. In all these ways, melody expresses the many different forms of the will's efforts, but also its satisfaction by ultimately finding again a harmonious interval, and still more the keynote. The invention of melody, the disclosure in it of all the deepest secrets of human willing and feeling, is the work of genius, whose effect is more apparent here than anywhere else, is far removed from all reflection and conscious intention, and might be called an inspiration. Here, as everywhere in art, the concept is unproductive. The composer reveals the innermost nature of the world, and expresses the profoundest wisdom in a language that his reasoning faculty does not understand, just as a magnetic somnambulist gives information about things of which she has no conception when she is awake. Therefore in the composer, more than in any other artist, the man is entirely separate and distinct from the artist. Even in the explanation of this wonderful art, the concept shows its inadequacy and its limits; however, I will try to carry out our analogy. Now, as rapid transition from wish to satisfaction and from this to a new wish are happiness and well-being, so rapid melodies without great deviations are cheerful. Slow melodies that strike painful discords and wind back to the keynote only through many bars, are sad, on the analogy of delayed and hard-won satisfaction. Delay in the new excitement of the will, namely languor, could have no other expression than the sustained keynote, the effect of which would soon be intolerable; very monotonous and meaningless melodies approximate to this. The short, intelligible phrases of rapid dance music seem to speak only of ordinary happiness which is easy of attainment. On the other hand, the *allegro maestoso* in great phrases, long passages, and wide deviations expresses a greater, nobler effort towards a distant goal, and its final attainment. The *adagio* speaks of the suffering of a great and noble endeavour that disdains all trifling happiness. But how marvellous is the effect of *minor and major*! How astonishing that the change of half a tone, the entrance of a minor third instead of a major, at once and inevitably forces on us an anxious and painful feeling, from which we are again delivered just as instantaneously by the major! The *adagio* in the minor key reaches the expression of the keenest pain, and becomes the most convulsive lament. Dance music in the minor key seems to express the failure of the trifling happiness that we ought rather to disdain; it appears to speak of the attainment of a low end with toil and trouble. The inexhaustibleness of possible melodies corresponds to the inexhaustibleness of nature in the difference of individuals, physiognomies, and courses of life. The transition from one key into quite a different one, since it entirely abolishes the connection with what went before, is like death inasmuch as the individual ends in it. Yet the will that appeared in this individual lives on just the same as before, appearing in other individuals, whose consciousness, however, has no connection with that of the first.

But we must never forget when referring to all these analogies I have brought forward, that music has no direct relation to them, but only an indirect one; for it never expresses the phenomenon, but only the inner nature, the in-itself, of every phenomenon, the will itself. Therefore music does not express this or that particular and definite pleasure, this or that affliction, pain, sorrow, horror, gaiety, merriment, or peace of mind, but joy, pain sorrow, horror, gaiety, merriment, peace of mind *themselves*, to a certain extent in the abstract, their essential nature, without any accessories, and so also without the motives for them. Nevertheless, we understand them perfectly in this extracted quintessence. Hence it arises that our imagination is so easily stirred by music, and tries to shape that invisible, yet vividly aroused, spirit-world that speaks to us directly, to clothe it with flesh and bone, and thus to embody it in an analogous example. This is the origin of the song with words, and finally of the opera. For this reason they should never forsake that subordinate position in order to make themselves the chief thing, and the music a mere means of expressing the song, since this is a great misconception and an utter absurdity. Everywhere music expresses only the quintessence of life and of its events, never these themselves, and therefore their differences do not always influence it. It is just this universality that belongs uniquely to music, together with the most precise distinctness, that gives it that high value as the panacea of all our sorrows. Therefore, if music tries to stick too closely to the words, and to mould itself according to the events, it is endeavouring to speak a language not its own. No one has kept so free from this mistake as Rossini; hence his music speaks its *own* language so distinctly and purely that it requires no words at all, and therefore produces its full effect even when rendered by instruments alone.

As a result of all this, we can regard the phenomenal world, or nature, and music as two different expressions of the same thing; and this thing itself is therefore the only medium of their analogy, a knowledge of which is required if we are to understand that analogy. Accordingly, music, if regarded as an expression of the world, is in the highest degree a universal language that is related to the universality of concepts much as these are related to the particular things. Yet its universality is by no means that empty universality of abstraction, but is of quite a different kind; it is united with thorough and unmistakable distinctness. In this respect it is like geometrical figures and numbers, which are the universal forms of all possible objects of experience and are *a priori* applicable to them all, and yet are not abstract, but perceptible and thoroughly definite. All possible efforts, stirrings, and manifestations of the will, all the events that occur within man himself and are included by the reasoning faculty in the wide, negative concept of feeling, can be expressed by the infinite number of possible melodies, but always in the universality of mere form without the material, always only according to the in-itself, not to the phenomenon, as it were the innermost soul of the phenomenon without the body. This close relation that music has to the true nature of all things can also explain the fact that, when music suitable to any scene, action, event, or environment is played, it seems to disclose to us its most secret meaning, and appears to be the most accurate and distinct commentary on it. Moreover, to the man who gives himself up entirely to the impression of a symphony, it is as if he saw all the possible events of life and of the world passing by within himself. Yet if he reflects, he cannot assert any likeness between that piece of music and the things that passed through his mind. For, as we have said, music differs from all the other arts by the fact that it is not a copy of the phenomenon, or, more exactly, of the will's adequate objectivity, but is directly a copy of the will itself, and therefore expresses the metaphysical to everything physical in the world, the thing-in-itself to every phenomenon. Accordingly, we could just as well call the world embodied music as embodied will; this is the reason why music makes every picture, indeed every scene from real life and from the world, at once appear in enhanced significance, and this is, of course, all the greater, the more analogous its melody is to the inner spirit of the given phenomenon. It is due to this that we are able to set a poem to music as a song, or a perceptive presentation as a pantomime, or both as an opera. Such individual pictures of human life, set to the universal language of music, are never bound to it or correspond to it with absolute necessity, but stand to it only in the relation of an example, chosen at random, to a universal concept. They express in the distinctness of reality what music asserts in the universality of mere form. For, to a certain extent, melodies are, like universal concepts, an abstraction from reality. This reality, and hence the world of particular things, furnishes what is perceptive, special, and individual, the particular case, both to the universality of the concepts and to that of the melodies. These two universalities, however, are in a certain respect opposed to each other, since the concepts contain only the forms, first of all abstracted from perception, so to speak the stripped-off outer shell of things; hence they are quite properly *abstracta*. Music, on the other hand, gives the innermost kernel preceding all form, or the heart of things. This relation could very well be expressed in the language of the scholastics by saying that the concepts are the *universalia post rem*, but music gives the *universalia ante rem*, and reality the *universalia in re*.[1] Even other examples, just as arbitrarily chosen, of the universal expressed in a poem could correspond in the same degree to the general significance of the melody assigned to this poem; and so the same composition is suitable to many verses; hence also the *vaudeville*. But that generally a relation between a composition and a perceptive expression is possible is due, as we have said, to the fact that the two are simply quite different expressions of the same inner nature of the world. Now when in the particular case such a relation actually exists, thus when the composer has known how to express in the universal language of music the stirrings of will that constitute the kernel of an event, then the melody of the song, the music of the opera, is expressive. But the analogy discovered by the composer between these two must have come from the immediate knowledge of the inner nature of the world unknown to his faculty of reason; it cannot be an imitation brought about with conscious intention by means of concepts, otherwise the music does not express the inner nature of the will itself, but merely imitates its phenomenon inadequately. All really imitative music does this; for example, *The Seasons* by Haydn, also many passages of his *Creation*, where phenomena of the world of perception are directly imitated; also in all battle pieces. All this is to be entirely rejected.

The inexpressible depth of all music, by virtue of which it floats past us as a paradise quite familiar and yet eternally remote, and is so easy to understand and yet so inexplicable, is due to the fact that it reproduces all the emotions of our innermost being, but entirely without reality and remote from its pain. In the same way, the seriousness essential to it and wholly excluding the ludicrous from its direct and peculiar province is to be explained from the fact that its object is not the representation, in regard to which deception and ridiculousness alone are possible, but that this object is directly the will; and this is essentially the most serious of all things, as being that on which all depends. How full of meaning and significance the language of music is we see from the repetition signs, as well as from the *Da capo* ['repeat from the beginning'. Ed.] which would be intolerable in the case of works composed in the language of words. In music, however, they are very appropriate and beneficial; for to comprehend it fully, we must hear it twice.

In the whole of this discussion on music I have been trying to make it clear that music expresses in an exceedingly universal language, in a homogeneous material, that is, in mere tones, and with the greatest distinctness and truth, the inner being, the in-itself, of the world, which we think of under the concept of will, according to its most distinct manifestation. Further, according to my view and contention, philosophy is nothing but a complete and accurate repetition and expression of the inner nature of the world in very general concepts, for only in these is it possible to obtain a view of that entire inner nature which is everywhere adequate and applicable. Thus whoever has followed me and has entered into my way of thinking will not find it so very paradoxical when I say that, supposing we succeeded in giving a perfectly accurate and complete explanation of music which goes into detail, and thus a detailed repetition in concepts of what it expresses, this would also be at once a sufficient repetition and explanation of the world in concepts, or one wholly corresponding thereto, and hence the true philosophy. Consequently, we can parody in the following way the above-mentioned saying of Leibniz, in the sense of our higher view of music, for it is quite correct from a lower point of view: 'Music is an unconscious exercise in metaphysics in which the mind does not know it is philosophizing.' For *scire*, to know, always means to have couched in abstract concepts. But further, in virtue of the truth of the saying of Leibniz, corroborated in many ways, music, apart from its aesthetic or inner significance, and considered merely externally and purely empirically, is nothing but the means of grasping, immediately and in the concrete, larger numbers and more complex numerical ratios that we can otherwise know only indirectly by comprehension in concepts. Therefore, by the union of these two very different yet correct views of music, we can now arrive at a conception of the possibility of a philosophy of numbers, like that of Pythagoras and of the Chinese in the *I Ching* [*Book of changes.* Ed.], and then interpret in this sense that saying of the Pythagoreans quoted by Sextus Empiricus (*Adversus Mathematicos*, Bk. vii [§ 94]: 'All things are similar to number.' And if, finally, we apply this view to our above-mentioned interpretation of harmony and melody, we shall find a mere moral philosophy without an explanation of nature, such as Socrates tried to introduce, to be wholly analogous to a melody without harmony, desired exclusively by Rousseau; and in contrast to this, mere physics and metaphysics without ethics will correspond to mere harmony without melody. Allow me to add to these occasional observations a few more remarks concerning the analogy of music with the phenomenal world. We found in the previous book that the highest grade of the will's objectification, namely man, could not appear alone and isolated, but that this presupposed the grades under him, and these again presupposed lower and lower grades. Now music, which, like the world, immediately objectifies the will, is also perfect only in complete harmony. In order to produce its full impression, the high leading voice of melody requires the accompaniment of all the other voices down to the lowest bass which is to be regarded as the origin of all. The melody itself intervenes as an integral part in the harmony, as the harmony does in the melody, and only thus, in the full-toned whole, does music express what it intends to express. Thus the one will outside time finds its complete objectification only in the complete union of all the grades that reveal its inner nature in the innumerable degrees of enhanced distinctness. The following analogy is also remarkable. In the previous book we saw that, notwithstanding the self-adaptation of all the phenomena of the will to one another as regards the species, which gives rise to the teleological view, there yet remains an unending conflict between those phenomena as individuals. It is visible at all grades of individuals, and makes the world a permanent battlefield of all those phenomena of one and the same will; and in this way the will's inner contradiction with itself becomes visible. In music there is also something corresponding to this; thus a perfectly pure harmonious system of tones is impossible not only physically, but even arithmetically. The numbers themselves, by which the tones can be expressed, have insoluble irrationalities. No scale can ever be computed within which every fifth would be related to the keynote as 2 to 3, every major third as 4 to 5, every minor third as 5 to 6, and so on. For if the tones are correctly related to the keynote, they no longer are so to one another, because, for example, the fifth would have to be the minor third to the third, and so on. For the notes of the scale can be compared to actors, who have to play now one part, now another. Therefore a perfectly correct music cannot even be conceived, much less worked out; and for this reason all possible music deviates from perfect purity. It can merely conceal the discords essential to it by dividing these among all the notes, i.e., by temperament. [See vol. II, ch. 39. Ed.]

I might still have much to add on the way in which music is perceived, namely in and through time alone, with absolute exclusion of space, even without the influence of the knowledge of causality, and thus of the understanding. For the tones make the aesthetic impression as effect, and this without our going back to their causes, as in the case of perception. But I do not wish to make these remarks still more lengthy, as I have perhaps already gone too much into detail with regard to many things in this third book, or have dwelt too much on particulars. However, my aim made it necessary, and will be the less disapproved of, if the importance and high value of art, seldom sufficiently recognized, are realized. According to our view, the whole of the visible world is only the objectification, the mirror, of the will, accompanying it to knowledge of itself, and indeed, as we shall soon see, to the possibility of its salvation. At the same time, the world as representation, if we consider it in isolation, by tearing ourselves from willing, and letting it alone take possession of our consciousness, is the most delightful, and the only innocent, side of life. We have to regard art as the greater enhancement, the more perfect development, of all this; for essentially it achieves just the same thing as is achieved by the visible world itself, only with greater concentration, perfection, intention, and intelligence; and therefore, in the full sense of the world, it may be called the flower of life. If the whole world as representation is only the visibility of the will, then art is the elucidation of this visibility, the *camera obscura* which shows the objects more purely, and enables us to survey and comprehend them better. It is the play within the play, the stage on the stage in *Hamlet*.

The pleasure of everything beautiful, the consolation afforded by art, the enthusiasm of the artist which enables him to forget the cares of life, this one advantage of the genius over other men alone compensating him for the suffering that is heightened in proportion to the clearness of consciousness, and for the desert loneliness among a different race of men, all this is due to the fact that, as we shall see later on, the in-itself of life, the will, existence itself, is a constant suffering, and is partly woeful, partly fearful. The same thing, on the other hand, as representation alone, purely contemplated, or repeated through art, free from pain, presents us with a significant spectacle. This purely knowable side of the world and its repetition in any art is the element of the artist. He is captivated by a consideration of the spectacle of the will's objectification. He sticks to this, and does not get tired of contemplating it, and of repeating it in his descriptions. Meanwhile, he himself bears the cost of producing that play; in other words, he himself is the will objectifying itself and remaining in constant suffering. That pure, true, and profound knowledge of the inner nature of the world now becomes for him an end in itself; at it he stops. Therefore it does not become for him a quieter of the will, as we shall see in the following book in the case of the saint who has attained resignation; it does not deliver him from life for ever, but only for a few moments. For him it is not the way out of life, but only an occasional consolation in it, until his power, enhanced by this contemplation, finally becomes tired of the spectacle, and seizes the serious side of things. The St. Cecilia of Raphael can be regarded as a symbol of this transition. Therefore we will now in the following book turn to the serious side. [The following Fourth Book discusses ethics and 'the denial of the will-to-live'. Ed.]

Note

1 This somewhat fanciful comparison between reality, music and concepts on the one side and *in re*, *ante rem* and *post rem* universals on the other refers to the distinction, first drawn by Avicenna (980–1037), between the essences embodied in things and these essences first as conceived in the mind of God and then as abstractions of human thought.

11 Leo Tolstoy, 'On art'

From Leo Tolstoy, *What is Art? and Essays on Art*, trans. A. Maude. London: Oxford University Press, 1930, pp. 46–61 [footnotes are Tolstoy's].

One might expect an essay on art by the author of *War and Peace* and *Anna Karenin* to expound on literary genius or the craft of the novel. But like the larger, slightly later *What is Art?*, 'On art' (*c.* 1896) belongs to the last, 'messianic' period in the long life of Leo Tolstoy (1828–1910). Already, in *A Confession* some fifteen years earlier, Tolstoy had come to regard his great novels as trifling achievements. Now he was to deny them – along with the works of Beethoven, Wagner, Baudelaire and many others in the Western canon – the very title of 'art'. It is a great irony that arguably the greatest of novelists should also have been the author of essays regarded by many as manifestos of extreme philistinism, as 'the petulant, almost fanatical outburst of an old man with pretensions to sainthood'.[1]

Tolstoy figures in textbooks on aesthetics nearly always as the author's whipping-boy – indeed, as two whipping-boys, for he is accused of especially extreme and implausible versions of both 'expressionism' and 'moralism'. The idea that artworks serve to express feelings is not, of course, novel. We have already encountered it in Schopenhauer's discussion of music. But whereas, for the German, these feelings are expressed 'as it were, in the abstract', for Tolstoy artworks serve to transmit, and arouse in others, the particular emotions of the artist. Moreover, this function is definitive of art. As Tolstoy famously puts it in *What is Art?*:

> Art is a human activity consisting in this, that one man consciously by means of certain external signs, hands on to others feelings he has lived through, and that others are infected by these feelings and also experience them. (p. 123)

[1] Robert Wilkinson, 'Art, emotion and expression', in Oswald Hanfling (ed.), *Philosophical Aesthetics: an introduction*, Oxford: Blackwell, 1992, p. 186.

Art, then, does not, as for other 'expression' theorists, tell us about feelings: it induces them, rather as – to use Tolstoy's own example – one man's yawn infects others with his tiredness. His is an 'arousal' version of 'expressionism', not a 'cognitivist' one.[2]

Since art is essentially 'infectious', it follows that artists have a moral responsibility for the emotional and spiritual health of their fellows, so that, as Tolstoy wrote in his diary of 1896, 'the aesthetic is merely one expression of the ethical'. Whereas for Plato, aesthetic criteria were subordinate to moral ones, for Tolstoy works which 'infect' people adversely are not genuine art at all. Moreover, since we *all* need to be 'infected' with the good and the moral, effete and obscure works which communicate only to the few are, for that reason alone, bad art or non-art. In *What is Art?* this claim becomes the demand that authentic art must promote the Christian ideal of 'the brotherhood of man'.

One reason for selecting the essay 'On art' in preference to snippets from its wilder, more exuberant successor is that the theses usually ascribed to Tolstoy are here stated in a more measured and qualified manner that does much to scotch the familiar criticisms. Two objections which the short essay pre-empts, for example, are that Tolstoy is concerned with the content and expressive power of artworks to the exclusion of their form, and that artworks serve merely to transmit feelings that are fully-fledged prior to the works' creation. For Tolstoy, attention to form is necessary in order for feelings accurately to be conveyed and, indeed, for the very elucidation of feelings that are, to begin with, only dimly and inchoately experienced. Moreover, while art must indeed serve to increase 'spiritual wealth', there is as yet no specific commitment to a Christian construal of what that 'wealth' consists in.

While Tolstoy may have become the critical butt of contemporary philosophers of art, he has also been an inspiration to many practitioners and theorists of art. Both inside and outside Russia – in India, for example, where Gandhi and Tagore were among his admirers – Tolstoy helped to inspire 'arts and crafts' movements, enthusiasts for folk art, and others groups disaffected with the effete decadence of 'high' culture. The important idea that a work of art may not only arouse feeling, but serve to crystallize the artist's own emotion, is taken up by later writers, such as Collingwood. More generally, it is Tolstoy's spectre which still looms when people press the question, so annoying and embarrassing to others, of just what it is that justifies the immense expenditure and effort devoted to the production and consumption of works that most men and women find disgusting or risible, and in which only a handful of *aficionados* even pretend to discern something worthwhile.

[2] See Alan H. Goldman, *Aesthetic Value*, Boulder, Co.: Westview, 1995, pp. 46ff.

What is and what is not Art; And when is Art Important, and when is it Trivial?

I

In our life there are many insignificant or even harmful activities which enjoy a respect they do not deserve, or are tolerated merely because they are considered to be of importance. The copying of flowers, horses, and landscapes, such clumsy learning of musical pieces as is carried on in most of our so-called educated families, and the writing of feeble stories and bad verses, hundreds of which appear in the newspapers and magazines, are obviously not artistic activities; and the painting of indecent, pornographic pictures stimulating sensuality, or the composition of songs and stories of that nature, even if they have artistic qualities, is not a worthy activity deserving of respect.

And therefore, taking all the productions which are considered among us to be artistic, I think it would be useful, first, to separate what really is art from what has no right to that name; and secondly, taking what really is art, to distinguish what is important and good from what is insignificant and bad.

The question of how and where to draw the line separating Art from Non-Art, and the good and important in art from the insignificant and evil, is one of enormous importance in life.

A great many of the wrong-doings and mistakes in our life result from our calling things Art which are not Art. We accord an unmerited respect to things which not only do not deserve it, but deserve condemnation and contempt. Apart from the enormous amount of human labour spent on the preparation of articles needed for the production of art – studios, paints, canvas, marble, musical instruments, and the theatres with their scenery and appliances – even the lives of human beings are actually perverted by the one-sided labours demanded in the preparation of those who train for the arts. Hundreds of thousands if not millions of children are forced to one-sided toil, practising the so-called arts of dancing and music. Not to speak of the children of the educated classes who pay their tribute to art in the form of tormenting lessons – children devoted to the ballet and musical professions are simply distorted in the name of Art to which they are dedicated. If it is possible to compel children of seven or eight to play an instrument, and for ten or fifteen years to continue to do so for seven or eight hours a day; if it is possible to place girls in the schools for the ballet, and then to make them cut capers during the first months of their pregnancy, and if all this is done in the name of art, then it is certainly necessary to define, first of all, what really is art – lest under the guise of art a counterfeit should be produced – and then also to prove that art is a matter of importance to mankind.

Where then is the line dividing art, an important and necessary matter valuable to humanity, from useless occupations, commercial productions, and even from immorality? In what does the essence and importance of true art lie?

II

One theory – which its opponents call 'tendencious' – says that the essence of true art lies in the importance of the subject treated of: that for art to be art, it is necessary that its content should be something important, necessary to man, good, moral, and instructive.

According to that theory the artist – that is to say the man who possesses a certain skill – by taking the most important theme which interests society at the time, can, by clothing it in what looks like artistic form, produce a work of true art. According to that theory religious, moral, social, and political truths clothed in what seems like artistic form are artistic productions.

Another theory, which calls itself 'aesthetic', or 'art for art's sake', holds that the essence of true art lies in the beauty of its form; that for art to be true, it is necessary that what it presents should be beautiful.

According to that theory it is necessary for the production of art that an artist should possess technique, and should depict an object which produces in the highest degree a pleasant impression; and therefore a beautiful landscape, flowers, fruit, a nude figure, and ballets, will be works of art.

A third theory – which calls itself 'realistic' – says that the essence of art consists in the truthful, exact, presentation of reality: that for art to be true it is necessary that it should depict life as it really is.

According to that theory, it follows that works of art may be anything an artist sees or hears, all that he is able to make use of in his function of reproduction, independently of the importance of the subject or beauty of the form.

Such are the theories; and on the basis of each of them so-called works of art appear which fit the first, the second, or the third. But, apart from the fact that each of these theories contradicts the others, not one of them satisfies the chief demand, namely, to ascertain the boundary which divides art from commercial, insignificant, or even harmful productions.

In accordance with each of these theories, works can be produced unceasingly, as in any handicraft, and they may be insignificant or harmful.

As to the first theory ('tendency'), important subjects – religious, moral, social, or political – can always be found ready to hand, and therefore one can continually produce works of so-called art. Moreover, such subjects may be presented so obscurely and insincerely that works treating of the most important of them will prove insignificant and even harmful, the lofty content being degraded by insincere expression.

Similarly according to the second theory ('aesthetic') any man having learned the technique of any branch of art can incessantly produce something beautiful and pleasant, but again this beautiful and pleasant thing may be insignificant and harmful.

Just in the same way according to the third theory ('realistic'), every one who wishes to be an artist can incessantly produce objects of so-called art, because everybody is always interested in something. If the author is interested in what is insignificant and evil, then his work will be insignificant and evil.

The chief point is that, according to each of these three theories, 'works of art' can be produced incessantly, as in every handicraft, and that they actually are being so produced. So that these three dominant and discordant theories not merely fail to fix the line that separates art from non-art, but on the contrary they, more than anything else, serve to stretch the domain of art and bring within it all that is insignificant and harmful.

III

Where then is the boundary dividing art that is needful, important, and deserving of respect, from that which is unnecessary, unimportant, and deserving not of respect but of contempt – such as productions which have a plainly depraving effect? In what does true artistic activity consist?

To answer this question clearly we must first discriminate between artistic activity and another activity (usually confused with it), namely, that of handing on impressions and perceptions received from preceding generations – separating such activity as that, from the reception of new impressions: those, namely, which will thereafter be handed on from generation to generation.

The handing on of what was known to former generations, in the sphere of art as in the sphere of science, is an activity of teaching and learning. But the production of something *new* is creation – the real artistic activity.

The business of handing on knowledge – teaching – has not an independent significance, but depends entirely on the importance people attach to that which has been created – what it is they consider necessary to hand on from generation to generation. And therefore the definition of what a creation is, will also define what it is that should be handed on. Moreover, the teacher's business is not usually considered to be artistic; the importance of artistic activity is properly attributed to creation – that is, to artistic production.*

What then is artistic (and scientific) creation?

Artistic (and also scientific) creation is such mental activity as brings dimly-perceived feelings (or thoughts) to such a degree of clearness that these feelings (or thoughts) are transmitted to other people.

The process of 'creation' – one common to all men and therefore known to each of us by inner experience – occurs as follows: a man surmises or dimly feels something that is perfectly new to him, which he has never heard of from anybody. This something new impresses him, and in ordinary conversation he points out to others what he perceives, and to his surprise finds that what is apparent to him is quite unseen by them. They do not see or do not feel what he tells them of. This isolation, discord, disunion from others, at first disturbs him, and verifying his own perception the man tries in different ways to communicate to others what he has seen, felt, or understood; but these others still do not understand what he communicates to them, or do not understand it as he understands or feels it. And the man begins to be troubled by a doubt as to whether he imagines and dimly feels something that does not really exist, or whether others

* The most usual and widely diffused definition of art is that art is a particular activity not aiming at material utility, but affording pleasure to people; a pleasure, it is usually added, 'ennobling and elevating to the soul'.

This definition corresponds to the conception of art held by the majority of people; but it is inexact and not quite clear, and admits of very arbitrary interpretation.

It is not clear, for it fuses in one conception art as a human activity producing objects of art, and also the feelings of the recipient; and it admits of arbitrary interpretation, because it does not define wherein lies the pleasure that 'ennobles and elevates the soul'. So that one person may declare that he receives such pleasure from a certain production from which another does not receive it at all.

And therefore to define art it is necessary to define the peculiarity of that activity, both in its origin in the soul of the producer and in the peculiarity of its action on the souls of the recipients. This activity is distinguished from any other activity of craftsmanship, or trade, or even science (though it has great affinity with this last), in that it is not evoked by any material need, but supplies to both producer and recipient a special kind of so-called 'artistic satisfaction'. To explain to oneself this characteristic one must understand what impels people to this activity – that is, how artistic production originates.

do not see and do not feel something that does exist. And to solve this doubt he directs his whole strength to the task of making his discovery so clear that there cannot be the smallest doubt, either for himself or for other people, as to the existence of that which he perceives; and as soon as this elucidation is completed and the man himself no longer doubts the existence of what he has seen, understood, or felt, others at once see, understand, and feel as he does, and it is this effort to make clear and indubitable to himself and to others what both to others and to him had been dim and obscure, that is the source from which flows the production of man's spiritual activity in general, or what we call works of art – which widen man's horizon and oblige him to see what had not been perceived before.*

It is in this that the activity of an artist consists; and to this activity is related the feeling of the recipient. This feeling has its source in imitativeness, or rather in a capacity to be infected, and in a certain hypnotism – that is to say in the fact that the artist's stress of spirit elucidating to himself the subject that had been doubtful to him, communicates itself, through the artistic production, to the recipients. A work of art is then finished when it has been brought to such clearness that it communicates itself to others and evokes in them the same feeling that the artist experienced while creating it.

What was formerly unperceived, unfelt, and uncomprehended by them, is by intensity of feeling brought to such a degree of clearness that it becomes acceptable to all, and the production is a work of art.

The satisfaction of the intense feeling of the artist who has achieved his aim gives pleasure to him. Participation in this same stress of feeling and in its satisfaction, a yielding to this feeling, the imitation of it and infection by it (as by a yawn), the experiencing in brief moments what the artist has lived through while creating his work, is the enjoyment those who assimilate a work of art obtain.

Such in my opinion is the peculiarity that distinguishes art from any other activity.

* The division of the results of man's mental activity into scientific, philosophic, theological, hortatory, artistic, and other groups, is made for convenience of observation. But such divisions do not exist in reality; just as the divisions of the River Vólga into the Tver, Nizhnigórod, Simb'rsk and Sarátov sections, are not divisions of the river itself, but divisions we make for our own convenience.

IV

According to this division, all that imparts to mankind something new, achieved by an artist's stress of feeling and thought, is a work of art. But that this mental activity should really have the importance people attach to it, it is necessary that it should contribute what is good to humanity, for it is evident that to a new evil, to a new temptation leading people into evil, we cannot attribute the value given to art as to something that benefits mankind. The importance, the value, of art consists in widening man's outlook, in increasing the spiritual wealth that is humanity's capital.

Therefore, though a work of art must always include something new, yet the revelation of something new will not always be a work of art. That it should be a work of art, it is necessary:

(1) That the new idea, the content of the work, should be of importance to mankind.
(2) That this content should be expressed so clearly that people may understand it.
(3) That what incites the author to work at his production should be an inner need and not an external inducement.

And therefore that in which no new thing is disclosed will not be a work of art; and that which has for its content what is insignificant and therefore unimportant to man will not be a work of art however intelligibly it may be expressed, and even if the author has worked at it sincerely from an inner impulse. Nor will that be a work of art which is so expressed as to be unintelligible, however sincere may be the author's relation to it; nor that which has been produced by its author not from an inner impulse but for an external aim, however important may be its content and however intelligible its expression.

That is a work of art which discloses something new and at the same time in some degree satisfies the three conditions: content, form, and sincerity.

And here we come to the problem of how to define that lowest degree of content, beauty, and sincerity, which a production must possess to be a work of art.

To be a work of art it must, in the first place, be a thing which has for its content something hitherto unknown but of which man has need; secondly, it must show this so intelligibly that it becomes generally accessible; and thirdly, it must result from the author's need to solve an inner doubt.

A work in which all three conditions are present even to a slight degree, will be a work of art; but a production from which even one of them is absent will not be a work of art.

But it will be said that every work contains something needed by man, and every work will be to some extent intelligible, and that an author's relation to every work has some degree of sincerity. Where is the limit of needful content, intelligible expression, and sincerity of treatment? A reply to this question will be given us by a clear perception of the highest limit to which art may attain: the opposite of the highest limit will show the lowest limit, dividing all that cannot be accounted art from what is art. The highest limit of content is such as is always necessary to all men. That which is always necessary to all men is what is good or moral.* The lowest limit of content, consequently, will be such as is not needed by men, and is a bad and immoral content. The highest limit of expression will be such as is always intelligible to all men. What is thus intelligible is that which has nothing in it obscure, superfluous, or indefinite, but only what is clear, concise, and definite – what is called beautiful. Conversely, the lowest limit of expression will be such as is obscure, diffuse, and indefinite – that is to say formless. The highest limit of the artist's relation to his subject will be such as evokes in the soul of all men an impression of reality – the reality not so much of what exists, as of what goes on in the soul of the artist. This impression of reality is produced by truth only, and therefore the highest relation of an author to his subject is *sincerity*. The lowest limit, conversely, will be that in which the author's relation to his subject is not genuine but false. All works of art lie between these two limits.

A perfect work of art will be one in which the content is important and significant to all men, and therefore it will be *moral*. The expression will be quite clear, intelligible to all, and therefore *beautiful*; the author's relation to his work will be altogether sincere and heartfelt, and therefore true. Imperfect works, but still works of art, will be such productions as satisfy all three conditions though it be but in unequal degree. That alone will be

* Half-a-century ago no explanation would have been needed of the words 'important', 'good', and 'moral', but in our time nine out of ten educated people, at these words, will ask with a triumphant air: 'What *is* important, good or moral?' assuming that these words express something conditional and not admitting of definition, and therefore I must answer this anticipated objection.

That which unites people not by violence but by love: that which serves to disclose the joy of the union of men with one another, is 'important', 'good', or 'moral'. 'Evil' and 'immoral' is that which divides them, that leads men to the suffering produced by disunion. 'Important' is that which causes people to understand and to love what they previously did not understand or love.

no work of art, in which either the content is quite insignificant and unnecessary to man, or the expression quite unintelligible, or the relation of the author to the work quite insincere. In the degree of perfection attained in each of these respects lies the difference in quality between all true works of art. Sometimes the first predominates, sometimes the second, and sometimes the third.

All the remaining imperfect productions fall naturally, according to the three fundamental conditions of art, into three chief kinds: (1) those which stand out by the importance of their content, (2) those which stand out by their beauty of form, and (3) those which stand out by their heartfelt sincerity. These three kinds all yield approximations to perfect art, and are inevitably produced wherever there is art.

Thus among young artists heartfelt sincerity chiefly prevails, coupled with insignificance of content and more or less beauty of form. Among older artists, on the contrary, the importance of the content often predominates over beauty of form and sincerity. Among laborious artists beauty of form predominates over content and sincerity.

All works of art may be appraised by the prevalence in them of the first, the second, or the third quality, and they may all be subdivided into (1) those that have content and are beautiful, but have little sincerity; (2) those that have content, but little beauty and little sincerity; (3) those that have little content, but are beautiful and sincere, and so on, in all possible combinations and permutations.

All works of art, and in general all the mental activities of man, can be appraised on the basis of these three fundamental qualities; and they have been and are so appraised.

The differences in valuation have resulted, and do result, from the extent of the demand presented to art by certain people at a certain time in regard to these three conditions.

So for instance in classical times the demand for significance of content was much higher, and the demand for clearness and sincerity much lower than they subsequently became, especially in our time. The demand for beauty became greater in the Middle Ages, but on the other hand the demand for significance and sincerity became lower; and in our time the demand for sincerity and truthfulness has become much greater, but on the other hand the demand for beauty, and especially for significance, has been lowered.

V

The evaluation of works of art is necessarily correct when all three conditions are taken into account, and inevitably incorrect when works are valued not on the basis of all three conditions but only of one or two of them.

And yet such evaluation of works of art on the basis of only one of the three conditions is an error particularly prevalent in our time, lowering the general level of what is demanded from art to what can be reached by a mere imitation of it, and confusing the minds of critics, and of the public, and of artists themselves, as to what is really art and as to where its boundary lies – the line that divides it from craftsmanship and from mere amusement.

This confusion arises from the fact that people who lack the capacity to understand true art, judge of works of art from one side only, and according to their own characters and training observe in them the first, the second, or the third side only, imagining and assuming that this one side perceptible to them – and the significance of art based on this one condition – defines the whole of art. Some see only the importance of the content, others only the beauty of form, and others again only the artist's sincerity and therefore truthfulness. And according to what they see they define the nature of art itself, construct their theories, and praise and encourage those who, like themselves, not understanding wherein a work of art consists, turn them out like pancakes and inundate our world with foul floods of all kinds of follies and abominations which they call 'works of art'.

Such are the majority of people and, as representatives of that majority, such were the originators of the three aesthetic theories already alluded to, which meet the perceptions and demands of that majority.

All these theories are based on a misunderstanding of the whole importance of art and on severing its three fundamental conditions; and therefore these three false theories of art clash, as a result of the fact that real art has three fundamental conditions of which each of those theories accepts but one.

The first theory, of so-called 'tendencious' art, accepts as a work of art one that has for its subject something which, though it be not new, is important to all men by its moral content, independently of its beauty and spiritual depth.

The second ('art for art's sake') recognizes as a work of art only that which has beauty of form, independently of its novelty, the importance of its content, or its sincerity.

The third theory, the 'realistic', recognizes as a work of art only that in which the author's relation to his subject is sincere, and which is therefore truthful. The last theory says that however insignificant or even foul may be the content, with a more or less beautiful form the work will be good, if the author's relation to what he depicts is sincere and therefore truthful.

VI

All these theories forget one chief thing – that neither importance, nor beauty, nor sincerity, provides the requisite for works of art, but that the basic condition of the production of such works is that the artist should be conscious of something new and important; and that therefore, just as it always has been, so it always will be, necessary for a true artist to be able to perceive something quite new and important. For the artist to see what is new, it is necessary that he should observe and think, and not occupy his life with trifles which hinder his attentive penetration into, and meditation on, life's phenomena. In order that the new things he sees may be important ones, the artist must be a morally enlightened man, and he must not live a selfish life but must share the common life of humanity.

If only he sees what is new and important he will be sure to find a form which will express it, and the sincerity which is an essential content of artistic production will be present. He must be able to express the new subject so that all may understand it. For this he must have such mastery of his craft that when working he will think as little about the rules of that craft as a man when walking thinks of the laws of motion. And in order to attain this, the artist must not look round on his work and admire it, must not make technique his aim – as one who is walking should not contemplate and admire his gait – but should be concerned only to express his subject clearly, and in such a way as to be intelligible to all.

Finally, to work at his subject not for external ends but to satisfy his inner need, the artist must rise superior to motives of avarice and vanity. He must love with his own heart and not with another's, and not pretend that he loves what others love or consider worthy of love.

And to attain all this the artist must do as Balaam did when the messengers came to him and he went apart awaiting God so as to say only what God commanded; and he must not do as that same Balaam afterwards did when, tempted by gifts, he went to the king against God's command, as was evident even to the ass on which he rode, though not perceived by him while blinded by avarice and vanity.

VII

In our time nothing of that kind is demanded. A man who wishes to follow art need not wait for some important and new perception to arise in his soul, which he can sincerely love and having loved can clothe in suitable form. In our time a man who wishes to follow art either takes a subject current at the time and praised by people who in his opinion are clever, and clothes it as best he can in what is called 'artistic form'; or he chooses a subject which gives him most opportunity to display his technical skill, and with toil and patience produces what he considers to be a work of art; or having received some chance impression he takes what caused that impression for his subject, imagining that it will yield a work of art since it happened to produce an impression on him.

And so there appear an innumerable quantity of so-called works of art which, as in every mechanical craft, can be produced without the least intermission. There are always current fashionable notions in society, and with patience a technique can always be learnt, and something or other will always seem interesting to some one. Having separated the conditions that should be united in a true work of art, people have produced so many works of pseudo-art that the public, the critics, and the pseudo-artists themselves, are left quite without any definition of what they themselves hold to be art.

The people of to-day have, as it were, said to themselves: 'Works of art are good and useful; so it is necessary to produce more of them.' It would indeed be a very good thing if there were more; but the trouble is that you can only produce to order works which are no better than works of mere craftsmanship because of their lack of the essential conditions of art.

A really artistic production cannot be made to order, for a true work of art is the revelation (by laws beyond our grasp) of a new conception of life arising in the artist's soul, which, when expressed, lights up the path along which humanity progresses.

Clive Bell, 'The aesthetic hypothesis' 12

From Clive Bell, *Art*. New York: Chatto & Windus, 1981, pp. 15–34 [some footnotes omitted].

Had Tolstoy lived a little longer, he would doubtless have counted the author of this 1913 essay, the English art critic Clive Bell (1881–1964), among the élitist connoisseurs he so despised – and this despite Bell's seemingly Tolstoyan view that artworks move us because 'they express an emotion that the artist has felt' (*Art*, p. 49). Bell would not have minded Tolstoy's charge. He and his friend Roger Fry were leading critics of the contemporary popular taste for the allegedly moralizing, sentimental or trivial paintings of such nineteenth century 'photographic' artists as Frith and Alma-Tadema, and champions of both the generally ignored works of primitive artists and the 'shocking' works of Cézanne, Gauguin and Matisse. (It was Fry who coined the term 'post-impressionist' for these Frenchmen.)

It was as a result of being 'carried off [his] feet' by Cézanne that Bell arrived at his 'aesthetic hypothesis': 'significant form', a certain combination of lines and colours, is 'the one quality common to all works of visual art'. It is this form alone which 'provokes' that distinctive 'aesthetic emotion' experienced before genuine works of art. The implication, which Bell draws out at length, is that the representational aspects of a painting, its content and its message – if it has any of these – are irrelevant to its status or value as art. Bell is often accused of offering no argument for his hypothesis, but there is surely an implicit one. Represented content is *clearly* irrelevant in some cases – in Persian bowls, the Chartres windows and later Cézanne, for example – just as, in some cases, beauty, moral elevation, and so on, are. Eventually, there remains only one candidate, significant form, to be that single quality which all artworks – even the ones which *are* representational, beautiful or whatever – must have in common in order to be recognized as such. It is, of course, debatable whether the abstraction Bell demands from a painting's content is either feasible or desirable, whether indeed the form of a painting can always be discerned in isolation from content. After all, the formal achievement might consist in the artist's organization of the elements of the scene – a battle, say – which he is depicting.[1]

Bell's exclusive emphasis on form has a Kantian pedigree, as indeed does his 'metaphysical hypothesis', later on in *Art*, that it is the artist's and viewer's 'complete detachment from the concerns of life' which is responsible for a work's capacity to provoke a distinctively aesthetic response (p. 54). But there are also differences from Kant. First, according to the admittedly tentative metaphysical hypothesis, artworks have a cognitive import denied by Kant, for they make us aware of 'essential reality, of the God in everything, of the universal in the particular' (*ibid.*). Second, aesthetic pleasure for Kant is satisfaction in our own mental activity (the 'free play' of understanding and imagination); for Bell, however, the object of the aesthetic emotion is something objective, a quality of works of art themselves – their significant form. This second point also serves to distinguish Bell's view from Tolstoy's brand of 'expressionism'. For Bell, a painting is not a means employed by an artist to 'infect' us with ordinary human emotions, like joy and anger, which he has felt. Rather, he paints in response to a *sui generis* emotional response to the formal features of things around him, and the significant form he produces on the canvas then provokes, and indeed is the object of, the viewer's aesthetic emotion.

Bell and Fry, as the history of twentieth century art confirms, were remarkably successful in their championship of the new art, including abstract art, of their day. Bell's own 'aesthetic hypothesis', however, is often accused of circularity: significant form is what provokes the aesthetic emotion, and the aesthetic emotion is what is provoked by significant form.[2] That may be unfair: asked to define 'significant form', Bell's response would surely be to take us by the hand, put us before Cézanne's *Mont Sainte-Victoire* paintings or a Persian bowl and say 'Look! That's what it is!' Be that as it may, Bell's combination of formalism and expressionism has inspired many later writers, such as Suzanne Langer,[3] to amplify the provocative hypotheses of *Art*, that 'classic book' which, according to its excusably hyperbolic cover-blurb, 'pulled critical theory of the arts out of the nineteenth century into the twentieth'.

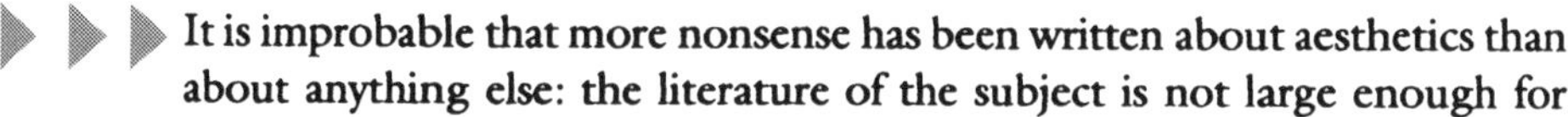

It is improbable that more nonsense has been written about aesthetics than about anything else: the literature of the subject is not large enough for

[1] See Anne Sheppard, *Aesthetics: an introduction to the philosophy of art*, Oxford: Oxford University Press, 1987, pp. 45ff.
[2] See the articles in the special Bell issue of *The British Journal of Aesthetics*, 2 (1965).
[3] See her *Feeling and Form*, New York: Scribner, 1953.

that. It is certain, however, that about no subject with which I am acquainted has so little been said that is at all to the purpose. The explanation is discoverable. He who would elaborate a plausible theory of aesthetics must possess two qualities – artistic sensibility and a turn for clear thinking. Without sensibility a man can have no aesthetic experience, and, obviously, theories not based on broad and deep aesthetic experience are worthless. Only those for whom art is a constant source of passionate emotion can possess the data from which profitable theories may be deduced; but to deduce profitable theories even from accurate data involves a certain amount of brain-work, and, unfortunately, robust intellects and delicate sensibilities are not inseparable. As often as not, the hardest thinkers have had no aesthetic experience whatever. I have a friend blessed with an intellect as keen as a drill, who, though he takes an interest in aesthetics, has never during a life of almost forty years been guilty of an aesthetic emotion. So, having no faculty for distinguishing a work of art from a handsaw, he is apt to rear up a pyramid of irrefragable argument on the hypothesis that a handsaw is a work of art. This defect robs his perspicuous and subtle reasoning of much of its value; for it has ever been a maxim that faultless logic can win but little credit for conclusions that are based on premises notoriously false. Every cloud, however, has its silver lining, and this insensibility, though unlucky in that it makes my friend incapable of choosing a sound basis for his argument, mercifully blinds him to the absurdity of his conclusions while leaving him in full enjoyment of his masterly dialectic. People who set out from the hypothesis that Sir Edwin Landseer was the finest painter that ever lived will feel no uneasiness about an aesthetic which proves that Giotto was the worst. So, my friend, when he arrives very logically at the conclusion that a work of art should be small or round or smooth, or that to appreciate fully a picture you should pace smartly before it or set it spinning like a top, cannot guess why I ask him whether he has lately been to Cambridge, a place he sometimes visits.

On the other hand, people who respond immediately and surely to works of art, though, in my judgement, more enviable than men of massive intellect but slight sensibility, are often quite as incapable of talking sense about aesthetics. Their heads are not always very clear. They possess the data on which any system must be based; but, generally, they want the power that draws correct inferences from true data. Having received aesthetic emotions from works of art, they are in a position to seek out the quality common to all that have moved them, but, in fact, they do nothing of the sort. I do not blame them. Why should they bother to examine their feelings when for them to feel is enough? Why should they stop to think when they are not very good at thinking? Why should they hunt for a common quality in all objects that move them in a particular way when they can linger over the many delicious and peculiar charms of each as it comes? So, if they write criticism and call it aesthetics, if they imagine that they are talking about Art when they are talking about particular works of art or even about the technique of painting, if loving particular works they find tedious the consideration of art in general, perhaps they have chosen the better part. If they are not curious about the nature of their emotion, nor about the quality common to all objects that provoke it, they have my sympathy, and, as what they say is often charming and suggestive, my admiration too. Only let no one suppose that what they write and talk is aesthetics; it is criticism, or just 'shop'.

The starting-point for all systems of aesthetics must be the personal experience of a peculiar emotion. The objects that provoke this emotion we call works of art. All sensitive people agree that there is a peculiar emotion provoked by works of art. I do not mean, of course, that all works provoke the same emotion. On the contrary, every work produces a different emotion. But all these emotions are recognizably the same in kind; so far, at any rate, the best opinion is on my side. That there is a particular kind of emotion provoked by works of visual art, and that this emotion is provoked by every kind of visual art, by pictures, sculptures, buildings, pots, carvings, textiles, &c., &c., is not disputed, I think, by anyone capable of feeling it. This emotion is called the aesthetic emotion; and if we can discover some quality common and peculiar to all the objects that provoke it, we shall have solved what I take to be the central problem of aesthetics. We shall have discovered the essential quality in a work of art, the quality that distinguishes works of art from all other classes of objects.

For either all works of visual art have some common quality, or when we speak of 'works of art' we gibber. Everyone speaks of 'art', making a mental classification by which he distinguishes the class 'works of art' from all other classes. What is the justification of this classification? What is the quality common and peculiar to all members of this class? Whatever it be, no doubt it is often found in company with other qualities; but they are adventitious – it it is essential. There must be some one quality without which a work of art cannot exist; possessing which, in the least degree, no work is altogether worthless. What is this quality? What quality is shared by all objects that provoke our aesthetic emotions? What quality is common to Sta. Sophia and the windows at Chartres, Mexican sculpture, a Persian bowl, Chinese carpets, Giotto's frescoes at Padua, and the masterpieces of Poussin, Piero della Francesca, and Cézanne? Only one answer seems possible – significant form. In each, lines and colours combined in a particular way, certain forms and relations of forms, stir our aesthetic emotions. These relations and combinations of lines and colours, these aesthetically moving forms, I call 'Significant Form'; and 'Significant Form' is the one quality common to all works of visual art.

At this point it may be objected that I am making aesthetics a purely subjective business, since my only data are personal experiences of a particular emotion. It will be said that the objects that provoke this emotion vary with each individual, and that therefore a system of aesthetics can have no objective validity. It must be replied that any system of aesthetics which pretends to be based on some objective truth is so palpably ridiculous as not to be worth discussing. We have no other means of recognizing a work of art than our feeling for it. The objects that provoke aesthetic emotion vary with each individual. Aesthetic judgements are, as the saying goes, matters of taste; and about tastes, as everyone is proud to admit, there is no disputing. A good critic may be able to make me see in a picture that had left me cold things that I had overlooked, till at last, receiving the aesthetic emotion, I recognize it as a work of art. To be continually pointing out those parts, the sum, or rather the combination, of which unite to produce significant form, is the function of criticism. But it is useless for a critic to tell me that something is a work of art; he must make me feel it for myself. This he can do only by making me see; he must get at my emotions through my eyes. Unless he can make me see something that moves me, he cannot force my emotions. I have no right to consider anything a work of art to which I cannot react emotionally; and I have no right to look for the essential quality in anything that I have not *felt* to be a work of art. The critic can affect my aesthetic theories only by affecting my aesthetic experience. All systems of aesthetics must be based on personal experience – that is to say, they must be subjective.

Yet, though all aesthetic theories must be based on aesthetic judgements, and ultimately all aesthetic judgements must be matters of personal taste, it would be rash to assert that no theory of aesthetics can have general validity. For, though A, B, C, D are the works that move me, and A, D, E, F the works that move you, it may well be that *x* is the only quality believed by either of us to be common to all the works in his list. We may all agree about aesthetics, and yet differ about particular works of art. We may differ as to the presence or absence of the quality *x*. My immediate object will be to show that significant form is the only quality common and peculiar to all the works of visual art that move me; and I will ask those whose aesthetic experience does not tally with mine to see whether this quality is not also, in their judgement, common to all works that move them, and whether they can discover any other quality of which the same can be said.

Also at this point a query arises, irrelevant indeed, but hardly to be suppressed: 'Why are we so profoundly moved by forms related in a particular way?' The question is extremely interesting, but irrelevant to aesthetics. In pure aesthetics we have only to consider our emotion and its object: for the purposes of aesthetics we have no right, neither is there any necessity, to pry behind the object into the state of mind of him who made it. Later [*Art*, I. III. 'The Metaphysical hypothesis'. Ed.] I shall attempt to answer the question; for by so doing I may be able to develop my theory of the relation of art to life. I shall not, however, be under the delusion that I am rounding off my theory of aesthetics. For a discussion of aesthetics, it need be agreed only that forms arranged and combined according to certain unknown and mysterious laws do move us in a particular way, and that it is the business of an artist so to combine and arrange them that they shall move us. These moving combinations and arrangements I have called, for the sake of convenience and for a reason that will appear later, 'Significant Form'.

A third interruption has to be met.

'Are you forgetting about colour?' someone enquires. Certainly not; my term 'significant form' included combinations of lines and of colours. The distinction between form and colour is an unreal one; you cannot conceive a colourless line or a colourless space; neither can you conceive a formless relation of colours. In a black and white drawing the spaces are all white and all are bounded by black lines; in most oil paintings the spaces are multi-coloured and so are the boundaries; you cannot imagine a boundary line without any content, or a content without a boundary line. Therefore, when I speak of significant form, I mean a combination of lines and colours (counting white and black as colours) that moves me aesthetically.

Some people may be surprised at my not having called this 'beauty'. Of course, to those who define beauty as 'combinations of lines and colours that provoke aesthetic emotion', I willingly concede the right of substituting their word for mine. But most of us, however strict we may be, are apt to apply the epithet 'beautiful' to objects that do not provoke that peculiar emotion produced by works of art. Everyone, I suspect, has called a butterfly or a flower beautiful. Does anyone feel the same kind of emotion for a butterfly or a flower that he feels for a cathedral or a picture? Surely, it is not what I call an aesthetic emotion that most of us feel, generally, for natural beauty. I shall suggest, later, that some people may, occasionally, see in nature what we see in art, and feel for her an aesthetic emotion; but I am satisfied that, as a rule, most people feel a very different kind of emotion for birds and flowers and the wings of butterflies from that which they feel for pictures, pots, temples and statues. Why these beautiful things do not move us as works of art move is another, and not an aesthetic, question. For our immediate purpose we have to discover only what quality is common to objects that do move us as works of art. In the last part of this chapter, when I try to answer the question – 'Why are we so profoundly moved by some combinations of lines and colours?' I shall hope to offer an acceptable explanation of why we are less profoundly moved by others.

Since we call a quality that does not raise the characteristic aesthetic emotion 'Beauty', it would be misleading to call by the same name the quality that does. To make 'beauty' the object of the aesthetic emotion, we must give to the word an over-strict and unfamiliar definition. Everyone sometimes uses 'beauty' in an unaesthetic sense; most people habitually do so. To everyone, except perhaps here and there an occasional aesthete, the commonest sense of the word is unaesthetic. Of its grosser abuse, patent in our chatter about 'beautiful huntin'' and 'beautiful shootin'', I need not take account; it would be open to the precious to reply that they never do so abuse it. Besides, here there is no danger of confusion between the aesthetic and the non-aesthetic use; but when we speak of a beautiful woman there is. When an ordinary man speaks of a beautiful woman he certainly does not mean only that she moves him aesthetically; but when an artist calls a withered old hag beautiful he may sometimes mean what he means when he calls a battered torso beautiful. The ordinary man, if he be also a man of taste, will call the battered torso beautiful, but he will not call a withered hag beautiful because, in the matter of women, it is not to the aesthetic quality that the hag may possess, but to some other quality that he assigns the epithet. Indeed, most of us never dream of going for aesthetic emotions to human beings, from whom we ask something very different. This 'something', when we find it in a young woman, we are apt to call 'beauty'. We live in a nice age. With the man-in-the-street 'beautiful' is more often than not synonymous with 'desirable'; the word does not necessarily connote any aesthetic reaction whatever, and I am tempted to believe that in the minds of many the sexual flavour of the word is stronger than the aesthetic. I have noticed a consistency in those to whom the most beautiful thing in the world is a beautiful woman, and the next most beautiful thing a picture of one. The confusion between aesthetic and sensual beauty is not in their case so great as might be supposed. Perhaps there is none; for perhaps they have never had an aesthetic emotion to confuse with their other emotions. The art that they call 'beautiful' is generally closely related to the women. A beautiful picture is a photograph of a pretty girl; beautiful music, the music that provokes emotions similar to those provoked by young ladies in musical farces; and beautiful poetry, the poetry that recalls the same emotions felt, twenty years earlier, for the rector's daughter. Clearly the word 'beauty' is used to connote the objects of quite distinguishable emotions, and that is a reason for not employing a term which would land me inevitably in confusions and misunderstandings with my readers.

On the other hand, with those who judge it more exact to call these combinations and arrangements of form that provoke our aesthetic emotions, not 'significant form', but 'significant relations of form', and then try to make the best of two worlds, the aesthetic and the metaphysical, by calling these relations 'rhythm', I have no quarrel whatever. Having made it clear that by 'significant form' I mean arrangements and combinations that move us in a particular way, I willingly join hands with those who prefer to give a different name to the same thing.

The hypothesis that significant form is the essential quality in a work of art has at least one merit denied to many more famous and more striking – it does help to explain things. We are all familiar with pictures that interest us and excite our admiration, but do not move us as works of art. To this class belongs what I call 'Descriptive Painting' – that is, painting in which forms are used not as objects of emotion, but as means of suggesting emotion or conveying information. Portraits of psychological and historical value, topographical works, pictures that tell stories and suggest situations, illustrations of all sorts, belong to this class. That we all recognize the distinction is clear, for who has not said that such and such a drawing was excellent as illustration, but as a work of art worthless? Of course many descriptive pictures possess, amongst other qualities, formal significance, and are therefore works of art: but many more do not. They interest us; they may move us too in a hundred different ways, but they do not move us aesthetically. According to my hypothesis they are not works of art. They leave untouched our aesthetic emotions because it is not their forms but the ideas or information suggested or conveyed by their forms that affect us.

Few pictures are better known or liked than Frith's 'Paddington Station'; certainly I should be the last to grudge it its popularity. Many a weary forty minutes have I whiled away disentangling its fascinating incidents and forging for each an imaginary past and an improbable future. But certain though it is that Frith's masterpiece, or engravings of it, have provided thousands with half-hours of curious and fanciful pleasure, it is not less certain that no one has experienced before it one half-second of aesthetic rapture – and this although the picture contains several pretty passages of colour, and is by no means badly painted. 'Paddington Station' is not a work of art; it is an interesting and amusing document. In it line and colour are used to recount anecdotes, suggest ideas, and indicate the manners and customs of an age: they are not used to provoke aesthetic emotion. Forms and the relations of forms were for Frith not objects of emotion, but means of suggesting emotion and conveying ideas.

The ideas and information conveyed by 'Paddington Station' are so amusing and so well presented that the picture has considerable value and is well worth preserving. But, with the perfection of photographic processes and of the cinematograph, pictures of this sort are becoming otiose. Who doubts that one of those *Daily Mirror* photographers in collaboration with a *Daily Mail* reporter can tell us far more about 'London day by day' than any Royal Academician? For an account of manners and fashions we shall go, in future, to photographs, supported by a little bright journalism, rather than to descriptive painting. Had the imperial academicians of Nero, instead of manufacturing incredibly loathsome imitations of the antique, recorded in fresco and mosaic the manners and fashions of their day, their stuff, though artistic rubbish, would now be an historical gold-mine. If only they had been Friths instead of being Alma-Tademas! But photography has made impossible any such transmutation of modern rubbish. Therefore it must be confessed that pictures in the Frith tradition are grown superfluous; they merely waste the hours of able men who might be more profitably employed in works of a wider beneficence. Still, they are not unpleasant, which is more than can be said for that kind of descriptive painting of which 'The Doctor' is the most flagrant example. Of course 'The Doctor' is not a work of art. In it form is not used as an object of emotion, but as a means of suggesting emotions. This alone suffices to make it nugatory; it is worse than nugatory because the emotion it suggests is false. What it suggests is not pity and admiration but a sense of complacency in our own pitifulness and generosity. It is sentimental. Art is above morals, or, rather, all art is moral because, as I hope to show presently, works of art are immediate means to good. Once we have judged a thing a work of art, we have judged it ethically of the first importance and put it beyond the reach of the moralist. But descriptive pictures which are not works of art, and, therefore, are not necessarily means to good states of mind, are proper objects of the ethical philosopher's attention. Not being a work of art, 'The Doctor' has none of the immense ethical value possessed by all objects that provoke aesthetic ecstasy; and the state of mind to which it is a means, as illustration, appears to me undesirable.

The works of those enterprising young men, the Italian Futurists, are notable examples of descriptive painting. Like the Royal Academicians, they use form, not to provoke aesthetic emotions, but to convey information and ideas. Indeed, the published theories of the Futurists prove that their pictures ought to have nothing whatever to do with art.[1] Their social and political theories are respectable, but I would suggest to young

Italian painters that it is possible to become a Futurist in thought and action and yet remain an artist, if one has the luck to be born one. To associate art with politics is always a mistake. Futurist pictures are descriptive because they aim at presenting in line and colour the chaos of the mind at a particular moment; their forms are not intended to promote aesthetic emotion but to convey information. These forms, by the way, whatever may be the nature of the ideas they suggest, are themselves anything but revolutionary. In such Futurist pictures as I have seen – perhaps I should except some by Severini – the drawing, whenever it becomes representative as it frequently does, is found to be in that soft and common convention brought into fashion by Besnard some thirty years ago, and much affected by Beaux-Art students ever since. As works of art, the Futurist pictures are negligible; but they are not to be judged as works of art. A good Futurist picture would succeed as a good piece of psychology succeeds; it would reveal, through line and colour, the complexities of an interesting state of mind. If Futurist pictures seem to fail, we must seek an explanation, not in a lack of artistic qualities that they never were intended to possess, but rather in the minds the states of which they are intended to reveal.

Most people who care much about art find that of the work that moves them most the greater part is what scholars call 'Primitive'. Of course there are bad primitives. For instance, I remember going, full of enthusiasm, to see one of the earliest Romanesque churches in Poitiers (Notre-Dame-la-Grande), and finding it as ill-proportioned, over-decorated, coarse, fat and heavy as any better class building by one of those highly civilized architects who flourished a thousand years earlier or eight hundred later. But such exceptions are rare. As a rule primitive art is good – and here again my hypothesis is helpful – for, as a rule, it is also free from descriptive qualities. In primitive art you will find no accurate representation; you will find only significant form. Yet no other art moves us so profoundly. Whether we consider Sumerian sculpture or pre-dynastic Egyptian art, or archaic Greek, or the Wei and T'ang masterpieces, or those early Japanese works of which I had the luck to see a few superb examples (especially two wooden Bodhisattvas) at the Shepherd's Bush Exhibition in 1910, or whether, coming nearer home, we consider the primitive Byzantine art of the sixth century and its primitive developments amongst the Western barbarians, or, turning far afield, we consider that mysterious and majestic art that flourished in Central and South America before the coming of the white men, in every case we observe three common characteristics – absence of representation, absence of technical swagger, sublimely impressive form. Nor is it hard to discover the connection between these three. Formal significance loses itself in preoccupation with exact representation and ostentatious cunning.*

Naturally, it is said that if there is little representation and less saltimbancery [quackery. Ed.] in primitive art, that is because the primitives were unable to catch a likeness or cut intellectual capers. The contention is beside the point. There is truth in it, no doubt, though, were I a critic whose reputation depended on a power of impressing the public with a semblance of knowledge, I should be more cautious about urging it than such people generally are. For to suppose that the Byzantine masters wanted skill, or could not have created an illusion had they wished to do so, seems to imply ignorance of the amazingly dexterous realism of the notoriously bad works of that age. Very often, I fear, the misrepresentation of the primitives must be attributed to what the critics call, 'wilful distortion'. Be that as it may, the point is that, either from want of skill or want of will, primitives neither create illusions, nor make display of extravagant accomplishment, but concentrate their energies on the one thing needful – the creation of form. Thus have they created the finest works of art that we possess.

Let no one imagine that representation is bad in itself; a realistic form may be as significant, in its place as part of the design, as an abstract. But if a representative form has value, it is as form, not as representation. The representative element in a work of art may or may not be harmful; always it is irrelevant. For, to appreciate a work of art we need bring with us nothing from life, no knowledge of its ideas and affairs, no familiarity with its emotions. Art transports us from the world of man's activity to a world of aesthetic exaltation. For a moment we are shut off from human interests; our anticipations and memories are arrested; we are lifted above the stream of life. The pure mathematician rapt in his studies knows a state of mind which I take to be similar, if not identical. He feels an emotion for his speculations which arises from no perceived relation between them and the lives of men, but springs, inhuman or super-human, from the heart of an abstract science. I wonder, sometimes, whether the appreciators of art and of mathematical solutions are not even more closely allied. Before we feel an aesthetic emotion for a combination of forms, do we not perceive intellectually the rightness and necessity of the combination? If we do, it would explain the fact that passing rapidly through a room we recognize a picture to be good, although we cannot say that it has provoked much emotion. We seem to have recognized intellectually the rightness of its forms without staying to fix our attention, and collect, as it were, their emotional

* This is not to say that exact representation is bad in itself. It is indifferent. A perfectly represented form may be significant, only it is fatal to sacrifice significance to representation.

significance. If this were so, it would be permissible to enquire whether it was the forms themselves or our perception of their rightness and necessity that caused aesthetic emotion. But I do not think I need linger to discuss the matter here. I have been enquiring why certain combinations of forms move us; I should not have travelled by other roads had I enquired, instead, why certain combinations are perceived to be right and necessary, and why our perception of their rightness and necessity is moving. What I have to say is this: the rapt philosopher, and he who contemplates a work of art, inhabit a world with an intense and peculiar significance of its own; that significance is unrelated to the significance of life. In this world the emotions of life find no place. It is a world with emotions of its own.

To appreciate a work of art we need bring with us nothing but a sense of form and colour and a knowledge of three-dimensional space. That bit of knowledge, I admit, is essential to the appreciation of many great works, since many of the most moving forms ever created are in three dimensions. To see a cube or a rhomboid as a flat pattern is to lower its significance, and a sense of three-dimensional space is essential to the full appreciation of most architectural forms. Pictures which would be insignificant if we saw them as flat patterns are profoundly moving because, in fact, we see them as related planes. If the representation of three-dimensional space is to be called 'representation', then I agree that there is one kind of representation which is not irrelevant. Also, I agree that along with our feeling for line and colour we must bring with us our knowledge of space if we are to make the most of every kind of form. Nevertheless, there are magnificent designs to an appreciation of which this knowledge is not necessary: so, though it is not irrelevant to the appreciation of some works of art it is not essential to the appreciation of all. What we must say is that the representation of three-dimensional space is neither irrelevant nor essential to all art, and that every other sort of representation is irrelevant.

That there is an irrelevant representative or descriptive element in many great works of art is not in the least surprising. . . . Representation is not of necessity baneful, and highly realistic forms may be extremely significant. Very often, however, representation is a sign of weakness in an artist. A painter too feeble to create forms that provoke more than a little aesthetic emotion will try to eke that little out by suggesting the emotions of life. To evoke the emotions of life he must use representation. Thus a man will paint an execution, and, fearing to miss with his first barrel of significant form, will try to hit with his second by raising an emotion of fear or pity. But if in the artist an inclination to play upon the emotions of life is often the sign of a flickering inspiration, in the spectator a tendency to seek, behind form, the emotions of life is a sign of defective sensibility always. It means that his aesthetic emotions are weak or, at any rate, imperfect. Before a work of art people who feel little or no emotion for pure form find themselves at a loss. They are deaf men at a concert. They know that they are in the presence of something great, but they lack the power of apprehending it. They know that they ought to feel for it a tremendous emotion, but it happens that the particular kind of emotion it can raise is one that they can feel hardly or not at all. And so they read into the forms of the work those facts and ideas for which they are capable of feeling emotion, and feel for them the emotions that they can feel – the ordinary emotions of life. When confronted by a picture, instinctively they refer back its forms to the world from which they came. They treat created form as though it were imitated form, a picture as though it were a photograph. Instead of going out on the stream of art into a new world of aesthetic experience, they turn a sharp corner and come straight home to the world of human interests. For them the significance of a work of art depends on what they bring to it; no new thing is added to their lives, only the old material is stirred. A good work of visual art carries a person who is capable of appreciating it out of life into ecstasy: to use art as a means to the emotions of life is to use a telescope for reading the news. You will notice that people who cannot feel pure aesthetic emotions remember pictures by their subjects; whereas people who can, as often as not, have no idea what the subject of a picture is. They have never noticed the representative element, and so when they discuss pictures they talk about the shapes of forms and the relations and quantities of colours. Often they can tell by the quality of a single line whether or no a man is a good artist. They are concerned only with lines and colours, their relations and quantities and qualities; but from these they win an emotion more profound and far more sublime than any that can be given by the description of facts and ideas.

This last sentence has a very confident ring – over-confident, some may think. Perhaps I shall be able to justify it, and make my meaning clearer too, if I give an account of my own feelings about music. I am not really musical. I do not understand music well. I find musical form exceedingly difficult to apprehend, and I am sure that the profounder subtleties of harmony and rhythm more often than not escape me. The form of a musical composition must be simple indeed if I am to grasp it honestly. My opinion about music is not worth having. Yet, sometimes, at a concert, though my appreciation of the music is limited and humble, it is pure. Sometimes, though I have a poor understanding, I have a clean palate. Consequently, when I am feeling bright and clear and intent, at the beginning of a concert for instance, when something that I can grasp is being played, I get from music that pure aesthetic emotion that I get from visual art. It is less intense, and the rapture is evanescent; I understand music too ill for music to transport me far into the world of pure aesthetic ecstasy. But at moments I do appreciate music as pure musical form, as sounds combined according to the laws of a mysterious necessity, as pure art with a tremendous significance of its own and no relation whatever to the significance of life; and in those moments I lose myself in that infinitely sublime state of mind to which pure visual form transports me. How inferior is my normal state of mind at a concert. Tired or perplexed, I let slip my sense of form, my aesthetic emotion collapses, and I begin weaving into the harmonies, that I cannot grasp, the ideas of life. Incapable of feeling the austere emotions of art, I begin to read into the musical forms human emotions of terror and mystery, love and hate, and spend the minutes, pleasantly enough, in a world of turbid and inferior feeling. At such times, were the grossest pieces of onomatopoeic representation – the song of a bird, the galloping of horses, the cries of children, or the laughing of demons – to be introduced into the symphony, I should not be offended. Very likely I should be pleased; they would afford new points of departure for new trains of romantic feeling or heroic thought. I know very well what has happened. I have been using art as a means to the emotions of life and reading into it the ideas of life. I have been cutting blocks with a razor. I have tumbled from the superb peaks of aesthetic exaltation to the snug foothills of warm humanity. It is a jolly country. No one need be ashamed of enjoying himself there. Only no one who has ever been on the heights can help feeling a little crestfallen in the cosy valleys. And let no one imagine, because he has made merry in the warm tilth and quaint nooks of romance, that he can even guess at the austere and thrilling raptures of those who have climbed the cold, white peaks of art.

About music most people are as willing to be humble as I am. If they cannot grasp musical form and win from it a pure aesthetic emotion, they confess that they understand music imperfectly or not at all. They recognize quite clearly that there is a difference between the feeling of the musician for pure music and that of the cheerful concert-goer for what music suggests. The latter enjoys his own emotions, as he has every right to do, and recognizes their inferiority. Unfortunately, people are apt to be less modest about their powers of appreciating visual art. Everyone is inclined to believe that out of pictures, at any rate, he can get all that there is to be got; everyone is ready to cry 'humbug' and 'impostor' at those who say that more can be had. The good faith of people who feel pure aesthetic emotions is called in question by those who have never felt anything of the sort. It is the prevalence of the representative element, I suppose, that makes the man in the street so sure that he knows a good picture when he sees one. For I have noticed that in matters of architecture, pottery, textiles, &c., ignorance and ineptitude are more willing to defer to the opinions of those who have been blest with peculiar sensibility. It is a pity that cultivated and intelligent men and women cannot be induced to believe that a great gift of aesthetic appreciation is at least as rare in visual as in musical art. A comparison of my own experience in both has enabled me to discriminate very clearly between pure and impure appreciation. Is it too much to ask that others should be as honest about their feelings for pictures as I have been about mine for music? For I am certain that most of those who visit galleries do feel very much what I feel at concerts. They have their moments of pure ecstasy; but the moments are short and unsure. Soon they fall back into the world of human interests and feel emotions, good no doubt, but inferior. I do not dream of saying that what they get from art is bad or nugatory; I say that they do not get the best that art can give. I do not say that they cannot understand art; rather I say that they cannot understand the state of mind of those who understand it best. I do not say that art means nothing or little to them; I say they miss its full significance. I do not suggest for one moment that their appreciation of art is a thing to be ashamed of; the majority of the charming and intelligent people with whom I am acquainted appreciate visual art impurely; and, by the way, the appreciation of almost all great writers has been impure. But provided that there be some fraction of pure aesthetic emotion, even a mixed and minor appreciation of art is, I am sure, one of the most valuable things in the world – so valuable, indeed, that in my giddier moments I have been tempted to believe that art might prove the world's salvation.

Yet, though the echoes and shadows of art enrich the life of the plains, her spirit dwells on the mountains. To him who woos, but woos impurely, she returns enriched what is brought. Like the sun, she warms the good seed in good soil and causes it to bring forth good fruit. But only to the perfect lover does she give a new strange gift – a gift beyond all price. Imperfect lovers bring to art and take away the ideas and emotions of their own age and civilization. In twelfth-century Europe a man might have been greatly moved by a Romanesque church and found nothing in a T'ang picture. To a man of a later age, Greek sculpture meant much and Mexican nothing, for only to the former could he bring a crowd of associated ideas to be the objects of familiar emotions. But the perfect lover, he who can feel the profound significance of form, is raised above the accidents of time and place. To him the problems of archaeology, history, and hagiography are impertinent. If the forms of a work are significant its provenance is irrelevant. Before the grandeur of those Sumerian figures in the Louvre he is carried on the same flood of emotion to the same aesthetic ecstasy as, more than four thousand years ago, the Chaldean lover was carried. It is the mark of great art that its appeal is universal and eternal.* Significant form stands charged with the power to provoke aesthetic emotion in anyone capable of feeling it. The ideas of men go buzz and die like gnats; men change their institutions and their customs as they change their coats; the intellectual triumphs of one age are the follies of another; only great art remains stable and unobscure. Great art remains stable and unobscure because the feelings that it awakens are independent of time and place, because its kingdom is not of this world. To those who have and hold a sense of the significance of form what does it matter whether the forms that move them were created in Paris the day before yesterday or in Babylon fifty centuries ago? The forms of art are inexhaustible; but all lead by the same road of aesthetic emotion to the same world of aesthetic ecstasy.

Note

1 See especially 'The Futurist manifesto' and related pieces in the futurists' leader F. T. Marinetti's *Selected Writings*, London: Secker & Warburg, 1972.

* Mr. Roger Fry permits me to make use of an interesting story that will illustrate my view. When Mr. Okakura, the Government editor of *The Temple Treasures of Japan*, first came to Europe, he found no difficulty in appreciating the pictures of those who from want of will or want of skill did not create illusions but concentrated their energies on the creation of form. He understood immediately the Byzantine masters and the French and Italian Primitives. In the Renaissance painters, on the other hand, with their descriptive preoccupations, their literary and anecdotic interests, he could see nothing but vulgarity and muddle. The universal and essential quality of art, significant form, was missing, or rather had dwindled to a shallow stream, overlaid and hidden beneath weeds, so the universal response, aesthetic emotion, was not evoked. It was not till he came on to Henri Matisse that he again found himself in the familiar world of pure art. Similarly, sensitive Europeans who respond immediately to the significant forms of great Oriental art, are left cold by the trivial pieces of anecdote and social criticism so lovingly cherished by Chinese dilettanti. It would be easy to multiply instances did not decency forbid the labouring of so obvious a truth.

A. K. Coomaraswamy, *The Dance of Śiva*, Essays 3–4. 13

From Ananda K. Coomaraswamy, *The Dance of Śiva: essays on Indian art and culture*. New York: Dover, 1985, pp. 30–45 [some footnotes omitted].

It's a long way from Clive Bell's Bloomsbury to the India of the author of this 1924 collection of essays, the philosopher, art historian and museum curator, A. K. Coomaraswamy (1877–1947). Yet we find him citing with approval the Englishman's notion of 'significant form' and his 'metaphysical thesis' on art's power to communicate 'essential reality'. This is less surprising if we recall Romain Rolland's description of Coomaraswamy as 'one of those great Hindus ... working for the union of Eastern and Western thought'.[1] But the importance of the essays is less in the attempt to relate the Indian aesthetic tradition to modern Western writers like Bell and Benedetto Croce than in the succinct restatement and development of the main theme of that tradition. With the publication of *The Dance of Śiva*, the largely forgotten classical texts on which Coomaraswamy drew were to enjoy a renaissance of interest.

As Coomaraswamy explains in the essay preceding those selected here, the earliest Indian discussions of art relegated it to an instrumental role, a device for achieving 'the Four Ends' – 'function, prosperity, pleasure, and spiritual freedom'. Things change, however, with the appearance of the *Nāṭyaśāstra (The Treatise on Drama)*, attributed to one Bharata, probably around the beginning of the first millennium CE and perhaps inspired by the great playwright, Kālidāsa. Coomaraswamy copiously cites this treatise, as well as later ones such as the *Sāhita Darpaṇa* of Viśvanātha (*circa* fifteenth century).

According to *The Treatise on Drama*, 'the chief goal of drama is to produce *rasa*, the aesthetic emotion ... emotion re-presented, distilled by art'.[2] And it is upon *rasa* (literally, 'flavour' or 'taste'), the 'principal term of Indian aesthetics',

[1] Foreword to *The Dance of Śiva*, p. xii.

[2] Chandra Rajan, Introduction to Kālidāsa, *The Loom of Time: a selection of his plays and poems*, Harmondsworth: Penguin, 1989, p. 29.

that the essays focus. Just as our word 'taste' can refer to something's taste or to our taste of it, so *rasa*, to quote a contemporary of Coomaraswamy, 'means either aesthetic enjoyment or that which is aesthetically enjoyed' – though the warning is at once given that *rasa*, unlike ordinary gustatory experience, stands 'on a new level altogether as compared with other feelings'.[3]

The main issue for Indian aestheticians has been to explore the nature of this aesthetic experience and its object(s). Because *rasa* is *sui generis* or 'altogether new', the issue is a difficult one. In a manner Kant would admire, Indian thinkers dissociate this experience from mere agreeableness, satisfaction or moral glow, and stress the 'self-forgetfulness' which belongs to it. This means, Coomaraswamy argues, that *rasa* is independent of appreciation of technical skill, ornamentation, and nobility or baseness of subject-matter. The failure to make these distinctions, he adds, is largely responsible for the view that *rasa* or beauty is only 'subjective' or 'relative'. Kant would also applaud the refusal to infer from this that beauty is therefore an objective property of things which the *rasika* ('true critic') perceives. *Rasa*, Coomaraswamy stresses, 'does not exist apart from the artist . . . and the *rasika* who enters into his experience' (p. 41). The very Kantian problem therefore emerges of how aesthetic enjoyment, if it is not 'objective' in this sense, can fail to be personal and idiosyncratic.

The solution is roughly as follows. Although the *rasa* or beauty we experience is not a property of objects, it is nevertheless a dimension of reality – or, better, 'absolute' beauty *is* true reality experienced through feeling rather than cognition or religious devotion. Because the 'object' of aesthetic experience is the same as that of religious experience, 'we are justified in . . . identifying . . . beauty with God' or Brahman (p. 45). Far from being 'personal', such experience is possible only for someone who 'forgets' himself and therefore identifies with the monistic whole which true reality, Brahman, is. A work of art, it seems, by depicting certain 'permanent moods', like wonder and terror, induces in the *rasika* a sense of this reality. *Rasa*, it emerges, does not strictly refer *both* to a person's experience and to what he experiences: for in that experience the distinction between subject and object, between individual and Brahman, is transcended.

One might ask why art cannot be bypassed in favour of direct, perhaps mystical, experience of Brahman. Coomaraswamy's reply is that most of us, at least, cannot 'find our way by a mere denial of things, but only by learning to see those things as they really are, infinite or beautiful' (p. 37) – in other words, by finding God *in* works of art and the beauties of nature, not through retreat from the everyday world. Only then, in the words of the great Bengali poet Rabindranath Tagore, can we experience 'the bliss of the touch of the play of the one in the many'.[4]

[3] K. C. Bhattacharyya, 'The concept of *rasa*' in his *Studies in Philosophy*, Delhi: Motilal Banarsidass, 1983, p. 349.

[4] *Gitanjali*, London: Unwin, 1986, p. 59.

Coomaraswamy played an important role in communicating the central aesthetic tradition of his culture to a wider world, but an important role, too, within his country in helping to revive Indian arts after centuries of atrophy under foreign domination. We have encountered before in this reader the thought that 'religion and art are . . . names for one and the same . . . intuition of reality and identity' (p. 36). Since that thought is surely easier to accommodate within the Hindu religious framework than our own, Coomaraswamy's defence of it has an understandable and special appeal for his countrymen.

Hindu View of Art

II. Theory of Beauty

We have so far discussed the Hindu view of art mainly from the internal evidence of the art itself. There remains, what is more exactly pertinent to the title of these chapters, to discuss the Hindu Aesthetic as it is expressly formulated and elaborated in the abundant Sanskrit and Hindī literature on Poetics and the Drama. We shall find that general conclusions are reached which are applicable, not only to literature, but to all arts alike.

The discussion begins with the Defence of Poesy. This is summed up in the statement that it may contribute to the achievement of all or any of the Four Ends of Life. A single word rightly employed and understood is compared to the 'cow of plenty', yielding every treasure; and the same poem that is of material advantage to one, may be of spiritual advantage to another or upon another occasion.

The question follows: What is the essential element in poetry? According to some authors this consists in style or figures, or in suggestion (***vyañjanā***, to which we shall recur in discussing the varieties of poetry). But the greater writers refute these views and are agreed that the one essential element in poetry is what they term ***Rasa***, or Flavour. With this term, which is the equivalent of Beauty or Aesthetic Emotion in the strict sense of the philosopher, must be considered the derivative adjective ***rasavant***, 'having rasa', applied to a work of art, and the derivative substantive ***rasika***, one who enjoys rasa, a connoisseur or lover, and finally ***rasāsvādana***, the tasting of rasa, i.e., aesthetic contemplation.

A whole literature is devoted to the discussion of rasa and the conditions of its experience. The theory, as we have remarked, is worked out in relation to poetry and drama, especially the classic drama of Kālidāsa and others. When we consider that these plays are essentially secular in subject and sensuous in expression, the position arrived at regarding its significance will seem all the more remarkable.

Aesthetic emotion – rasa – is said to result in the spectator – rasika – though it is not effectively *caused*, through the operation of determinants (*vibhāva*), consequents (*anubhāva*), moods (*bhāvā*) and involuntary emotions (*sattvabhāva*). Thus:

Determinants: the aesthetic problem, plot, theme, etc., viz: the hero and other characters and the circumstances of time and place. In the terminology of Croce these are the 'physical stimulants to aesthetic reproduction'.

Consequents: deliberate manifestations of feeling, as gestures, etc.

Moods: transient moods (thirty-three in number) induced in the characters by pleasure and pain, e.g., joy, agitation, impatience, etc. Also the permanent (nine), viz: the Erotic, Heroic, Odious, Furious, Terrible, Pathetic, Wondrous and Peaceful.

Involuntary Emotions: emotional states originating in the inner nature; involuntary expressions of emotion such as horripilation, trembling, etc. (eight in all).

In order that a work may be able to evoke rasa one [or two] of the permanent moods must form a master-motif to which all other expressions of emotion are subordinate. That is to say, the first essential of a rasavant work is unity –

> As a king to his subjects, as a guru to his disciples,
> Even so the master-motif is lord of all other motifs. [*Nāṭyaśāstra*]

If, on the contrary, a transient emotion is made the motif of the whole work, this 'extended development of a transient emotion tends to the absence of rasa', or as we should now say, the work becomes sentimental. Pretty art which emphasizes passing feelings and personal emotion is neither beautiful nor true: it tells us of meeting again in heaven, it confuses time and eternity, loveliness and beauty, partiality and love.

Let us remark in passing that while the nine permanent moods correspond to an identical classification of rasas or flavours as nine in number, the rasa of which we speak here is an absolute, and distinct from any one of these. The 'nine rasas' are no more than the various colourings of one experience, and are arbitrary terms of rhetoric used only for convenience in classification: just as we speak of poetry categorically as lyric, epic, dramatic, etc., without implying that poetry is anything but poetry. Rasa is tasted – beauty is felt – only by empathy, '*Einfühlung*' (*sādhārana*); that is to say by entering into, feeling, the permanent motif; but it is not the same as the permanent motif itself, for, from this point of view, it matters not with which of the permanent motifs we have to do.

It is just here that we see how far Hindu Aesthetic had now departed from its once practical and hedonistic character: the ***Daśarūpa*** [of Dhanamjaya. Ed.] declares plainly that Beauty is absolutely independent of the sympathetic – 'Delightful or disgusting, exalted or lowly, cruel or kindly, obscure or refined, (actual) or imaginary, there is no subject that cannot evoke rasa in man.'

Of course, a work of art may and often does afford us at the same time pleasure in a sensuous or moral way, but this sort of pleasure is derived directly from its material qualities, such as tone or texture, assonance, etc., or the ethical peculiarity of its theme, and not from its aesthetic qualities: the aesthetic experience is independent of this, and may even, as Dhanamjaya says, be derived in spite of sensuous or moral displeasure.

Incidentally we may observe that the ***fear*** of art which prevails amongst Puritans arises partly from the failure to recognize that aesthetic experience does not depend on pleasure or pain at all: and when this is not the immediate difficulty, then from the distrust of any experience which is 'beyond good and evil' and so devoid of a definitely ***moral*** purpose.

The tasting of rasa – the vision of beauty – is enjoyed, says Viśvanātha, 'only by those who are competent thereto': and he quotes Dharmadatta to the effect that 'those devoid of imagination, in the theatre, are but as the wood-work, the walls, and the stones'. It is a matter of common experience that it is possible for a man to devote a whole life time to the study of art, without having once experienced aesthetic emotion: 'historical research' as Croce expresses it, 'directed to illumine a work of art by placing us in a position to judge it, does not alone suffice to bring it to birth in our spirit', for 'pictures, poetry, and every work of art produce no effect save on souls prepared to receive them'.[1] Viśvanātha comments very pertinently on this fact when he says that 'even some of the most eager students of poetry are seen not to have a right perception of rasa'. The capacity and genius necessary for appreciation are partly native ('ancient') and partly cultivated ('contemporary'): but cultivation alone is useless, and if the poet is born, so too is the rasika, and criticism is akin to genius.

Indian theory is very clear that instruction is not the purpose of art. On this point Dhanamjaya is sufficiently sarcastic:

'As for any simple man of little intelligence', he writes, 'who says that from dramas, which distil joy, the gain is knowledge only, as in the case of history and the like (mere statement, narrative, or illustration) – homage to him, for he has averted his face from what is delightful.'

The spectator's appreciation of beauty depends on the effort of his own imagination, 'just as in the case of children playing with clay elephants'. Thus, technical elaboration (realism) in art is not by itself the cause of rasa: as remarked by Rabindranath Tagore 'in our country, those of the audience who are appreciative, are content to perfect the song in their own mind by the force of their own feeling'. This is not very different from what is said by Śukrāchārya with reference to images: 'the defects of images are constantly destroyed by the power of the virtue of the worshipper who has his heart always set on God'. If this attitude seems to us dangerously uncritical, that is to say dangerous to art, or rather to accomplishment, let us remember that it prevailed everywhere in all periods of great creative activity: and that the decline of art has always followed the decline of love and faith.

Tolerance of an imperfect work of art may arise in two ways: the one *uncritical*, powerfully swayed by the sympathetic, and too easily satisfied with a very inadequate correspondence between content and form, the other *creative*, very little swayed by considerations of charm, and able by force of true imagination to complete the correspondence of content and form which is not achieved or not preserved in the original. Uncritical tolerance is content with prettiness or edification, and recoils from beauty that is 'difficult': creative tolerance is indifferent to prettiness or edification, and is able from a mere suggestion, such as an awkward 'primitive' or a broken fragment, to create or recreate a perfect experience.

Also, 'the permanent motif becomes rasa through the rasika's own capacity for being delighted – not from the character of the hero to be imitated, nor because the work aims at the production of aesthetic emotion.' [*Daśarūpa*]. How many works which have 'aimed at the production of aesthetic emotion', that is to say, which were intended to be beautiful, have failed of their purpose!

The degrees of excellence in poetry are discussed in the *Kāvya Prakāśa* and the *Sāhitya Darpana*. The best is where there is a deeper significance than that of the literal sense. In minor poetry the sense overpowers the suggestion. In inferior poetry, significantly described as 'variegated' or 'romantic' (*chitra*), the only artistic quality consists in the ornamentation of the literal sense, which conveys no suggestion beyond its face meaning. Thus narrative and descriptive verse take a low place, just as portraiture does in plastic art: and, indeed, the *Sāhitya Darpana* [of Viśvanātha. Ed.] excludes the last kind of poetry altogether. It is to be observed that the kind of suggestion meant is something more than implication or *double entendre*: in the first case we have to do with mere abbreviation, comparable with the use of the words *et cetera*, in the second we have a mere play on words. What is understood to be suggested is one of the nine rasas.

It is worth noting that we have here a departure from, and I think, an improvement on Croce's definition '*expression is art*'. A mere statement, however completely expressive, such as: 'The man walks', or $(a+b)^2 = a^2+2ab+b^2$, is not art. Poetry is indeed a kind of sentence: but what kind of sentence? A sentence ensouled by rasa, i.e., in which one of the nine rasas is implied or suggested: and the savouring of this flavour, ***rasāsvādana***, through empathy, by those possessing the necessary sensibility is the condition of beauty.

What then are ***rasa*** and ***rasāsvādana***, beauty and aesthetic emotion? The nature of this experience is discussed by Viśvanātha in the *Sāhitya Darpana*: 'It is pure, indivisible, self-manifested, compounded equally of joy and consciousness, free of admixture with any other perception, the very twin brother of mystic experience (***Brahmāsvādana sahodarah***), and the very life of it is supersensuous (***lokottara***) wonder.' Further, 'It is enjoyed by those who are competent thereto, in identity, just as the form of God is itself the joy with which it is recognized.'[2]

For that very reason it cannot be an object of knowledge, its perception being indivisible from its very existence. Apart from perception it does not exist. It is not on that account to be regarded as eternal in time or as interrupted: it is timeless. It is again, supersensuous, hyperphysical (***alaukika***), and the only proof of its reality is to be found in experience.*

Religion and art are thus names for one and the same experience – an intuition of reality and of identity. This is not, of course, exclusively a Hindu view: it has been expounded by many others, such as the Neo-platonists, Hsieh Ho, Goethe, Blake, Schopenhauer and Schiller. Nor is it refuted by Croce. It has been recently restated as follows:

'In those moments of exaltation that art can give, it is easy to believe that we have been possessed by an emotion that comes from the world of reality. Those who take this view will have to say that there is in all things the stuff out of which art is made – reality. The peculiarity of the artist would seem to be that he possesses the power of surely and frequently seizing reality (generally behind pure form), and the power of expressing his sense of it, in pure form always!' [Clive Bell, *Art*, p. 47. Ed.]

Here pure form means form not clogged with unaesthetic matter such as associations.

It will be seen that this view is monistic: the doctrine of the universal presence of reality is that of the immanence of the Absolute. It is inconsistent with a view of the world as absolute ***māyā***, or utterly unreal, but it implies

* The rasika is therefore unable to convince the Philistine by argument: he can but say, Taste and see that it is good – for *I know* in what I have believed.

that through the false world of everyday experience may be seen by those of penetrating vision (artists, lovers and philosophers) glimpses of the real substrate.[3] This world is the formless as we perceive it, the unknowable as we know it.

Precisely as love is reality experienced by the lover, and truth is reality as experienced by the philosopher, so beauty is reality as experienced by the artist: and these are three phases of the Absolute. But it is only through the objective work of art that the artist is able to communicate his experience, and for this purpose any theme proper to himself will serve, since the Absolute is manifested equally in the little and the great, animate and inanimate, good and evil.

We have seen that the world of Beauty, like the Absolute, cannot be known objectively. Can we then reach this world by rejecting objects, by a deliberate purification of art from all associations? We have already seen, however, that the mere intention to create beauty is not sufficient: there must exist an object of devotion. Without a point of departure there can be no flight and no attainment: here also 'one does not attain to perfection by mere renunciation' [*Bhagavad Gītā*, III. 14. Ed.]. We can no more achieve Beauty than we can find Release by turning our backs on the world: we cannot find our way by a mere denial of things, but only in learning to see those things as they really are, infinite or beautiful. The artist reveals this beauty wherever the mind attaches itself: and the mind attaches itself, not directly to the Absolute, but to objects of choice.

Thus we return to the earth. If we supposed we should find the object of search elsewhere, we were mistaken. The two worlds, of spirit and matter, Purusha and Prakṛiti, are one; and this is as clear to the artist as it is to the lover or the philosopher.[4] Those Philistines to whom it is not so apparent, we should speak of as materialists or as nihilists – exclusive monists, to whom the report of the senses is either all in all, or nothing at all. The theory of rasa set forth according to Viśvanātha and other aestheticians, belongs to totalistic monism; it marches with the Vedānta. In a country like India, where thought is typically consistent with itself, this is no more than we had a right to expect.

That Beauty is a State

It is very generally held that natural objects such as human beings, animals or landscapes, and artificial objects such as factories, textiles or works of intentional art, can be classified as beautiful or ugly. And yet no general principle of classification has ever been found: and that which seems to be beautiful to one is described as ugly by another. In the words of Plato 'Everyone chooses his love out of the objects of beauty according to his own taste.'

To take, for example, the human type: every race, and to some extent every individual, has an unique ideal. Nor can we hope for a final agreement: we cannot expect the European to prefer the Mongolian features, nor the Mongolian the European. Of course, it is very easy for each to maintain the absolute value of his own taste and to speak of other types as ugly; just as the hero of chivalry maintains by force of arms that his own beloved is far more beautiful than any other. In like manner the various sects maintain the absolute value of their own ethics. But it is clear that such claims are nothing more than statements of prejudice, for who is to decide which racial ideal or which morality is 'best'? It is a little too easy to decide that our own is best; we are at the most entitled to believe it the best for us. This relativity is nowhere better suggested than in the classic saying attributed to Majñūn, when it was pointed out to him that the world at large regarded his Lailā as far from beautiful. 'To see the beauty of Lailā', he said, 'requires the eyes of Majñūn.'

It is the same with works of art. Different artists are inspired by different objects; what is attractive and stimulating to one is depressing and unattractive to another, and the choice also varies from race to race and epoch to epoch. As to the appreciation of such works, it is the same; for men in general admire only such works as by education or temperament they are predisposed to admire. To enter into the spirit of an unfamiliar art demands a greater effort than most are willing to make. The classic scholar starts convinced that the art of Greece has never been equalled or surpassed, and never will be; there are many who think, like Michelangelo, that because Italian painting is good, therefore good painting is Italian. There are many who never yet felt the beauty of Egyptian sculpture or Chinese or Indian painting or music: that they have also the hardihood to deny their beauty, however, proves nothing.

It is also possible to forget that certain works are beautiful: the eighteenth century had thus forgotten the beauty of Gothic sculpture and primitive Italian painting, and the memory of their beauty was only restored by a great effort in the course of the nineteenth. There may also exist natural objects or works of art which humanity only very slowly learns to regard as in any way beautiful; the western aesthetic appreciation of desert and mountain scenery, for example, is no older than the nineteenth century; and it is notorious that artists of the highest rank are often not understood till long after their death. So that the more we consider the variety of human election, the more we must admit the relativity of taste.

And yet there remain philosophers firmly convinced that an absolute Beauty (***rasa***) exists, just as others maintain the conceptions of absolute Goodness and absolute Truth. The lovers of God identify these absolutes with Him (or It) and maintain that He can only be known as perfect Beauty, Love and Truth. It is also widely held that the true critic (***rasika***) is able to decide which works of art are beautiful (***rasavant***) and which are not; or in simpler words, to distinguish works of genuine art from those that have no claim to be so described. At the same time we must admit the relativity of taste, and the fact that all gods (***devas*** and ***Īśvaras***) are modelled after the likeness of men.

It remains, then, to resolve the seeming contradictions. This is only to be accomplished by the use of more exact terminology. So far have I spoken of 'beauty' without defining my meaning, and have used one word to express a multiplicity of ideas. But we do not mean the same thing when we speak of a beautiful girl and a beautiful poem; it will be still more obvious that we mean two different things, if we speak of beautiful weather and a beautiful picture. In point of fact, the conception of beauty and the adjective 'beautiful' belong exclusively to aesthetic and should only be used in aesthetic judgement. We seldom make any such judgements when we speak of natural objects as beautiful; we generally mean that such objects as we call beautiful are congenial to us, practically or ethically. Too often we pretend to judge a work of art in the same way, calling it beautiful if it represents some form or activity of which we heartily approve, or if it attracts us by the tenderness or gaiety of its colour, the sweetness of its sounds or the charm of its movement. But when we thus pass judgement on the dance in accordance with our sympathetic attitude towards the dancer's charm or skill, or the meaning of the dance, we ought not to use the language of pure aesthetic. Only when we judge a work of art aesthetically may we speak of the presence or absence of beauty, we may call the work ***rasavant*** or otherwise; but when we judge it from the standpoint of activity, practical or ethical, we ought to use a corresponding terminology, calling the picture, song or actor 'lovely', that is to say lovable, or otherwise, the action 'noble', the colour 'brilliant', the gesture 'graceful', or otherwise, and so forth. And it will be seen that in doing this we are not really judging the work of art as such, but only the material and the separate parts of which it is made, the activities they represent, or the feelings they express.

Of course, when we come to choose such works of art to live with, there is no reason why we should not allow the sympathetic and ethical considerations to influence our judgement. Why should the ascetic invite annoyance by hanging in his cell some representation of the nude, or the general select a lullaby to be performed upon the eve of battle? When every ascetic and every soldier has become an artist there will be no more need for works of art: in the meanwhile ethical selection of some kind is allowable and necessary. But in this selection we must clearly understand what we are doing, if we would avoid an infinity of error, culminating in that type of sentimentality which regards the useful, the stimulating and the moral elements in works of art as the essential. We ought not to forget that he who plays the villain of the piece may be a greater artist than he who plays the hero. For beauty – in the profound words of Millet – does not arise from the subject of a work of art, but from the necessity that has been felt of representing that subject.

We should only speak of a work of art as good or bad with reference to its aesthetic quality; only the subject and the material of the work are entangled in relativity. In other words, to say that a work of art is more or less beautiful, or *rasavant*, is to define the extent to which it is a work of art, rather than a mere illustration. However important the element of sympathetic magic in such a work may be, however important its practical applications, it is not in these that its beauty consists.

What, then, is Beauty, what is *rasa*, what is it that entitles us to speak of divers works as beautiful or *rasavant?* What is this sole quality which the most dissimilar works of art possess in common? Let us recall the history of a work of art. There is (1) an aesthetic intuition on the part of the original artist, – the poet or creator; then (2) the internal expression of this intuition, – the true creation or vision of beauty (3) the indication of this by external signs (language) for the purpose of communication, – the technical activity; and finally, (4) the resulting stimulation of the critic or *rasika* to reproduction of the original intuition, or of some approximation to it.[5]

The source of the original intuition may, as we have seen, be any aspect of life whatsoever. To one creator the scales of a fish suggest a rhythmical design, another is moved by certain landscapes, a third elects to speak of hovels, a fourth to sing of palaces, a fifth may express the idea that all things are enlinked, enlaced and enamoured in terms of the General Dance, or he may express the same idea equally vividly by saying that 'not a sparrow falls to the ground without our Father's knowledge'. Every artist discovers beauty, and every critic finds it again when he tastes of the same experience through the medium of the external signs. But where is this beauty? We have seen that it cannot be said to exist in certain things and not in others. It may then be claimed that beauty exists everywhere; and this I do not deny, though I prefer the clearer statement that it may be discovered anywhere. If it could be said to exist everywhere in a material and intrinsic sense, we could pursue it with our cameras and scales, after the fashion of the experimental psychologists: but if we did so, we should only achieve a certain acquaintance with average taste – we should not discover a means of distinguishing forms that are beautiful from forms that are ugly. Beauty can never thus be measured, for it does not exist apart from the artist himself, and the *rasika* who enters into his experience. . . .

When every sympathetic consideration has been excluded, however, there still remains a pragmatic value in the classification of works of art as beautiful or ugly. But what precisely do we mean by these designations as applied to objects? In the works called beautiful we recognize a correspondence of theme and expression, content and form: while in those called ugly we find the content and form at variance. In time and space, however, the correspondence never amounts to an identity: it is our own activity, in the presence of the work of art, which completes the ideal relation, and it is in this sense that beauty is what we 'do to' a work of art rather than a quality present in the object. With reference to the object, then 'more' or 'less' beautiful will imply a greater or less correspondence between content and form, and this is all that we can say of the object as such: or in other words, art is good that is good of its kind. In the stricter sense of completed internal aesthetic activity, however, beauty is absolute and cannot have degrees.

The vision of beauty is spontaneous, in just the same sense as the inward light of the lover (*bhākta*). It is a state of grace that cannot be achieved by deliberate effort; though perhaps we can remove hindrances to its manifestation, for there are many witnesses that the secret of all art is to be found in self-forgetfulness. And we know that this state of grace is not achieved in the pursuit of pleasure; the hedonists have their reward, but they are in bondage to loveliness, while the artist is free in beauty.

It is further to be observed that when we speak seriously of works of art as beautiful, meaning that they are truly works of art, valued as such apart from subject, association, or technical charm, we still speak elliptically. We mean that the external signs – poems, pictures, dances, and so forth – are effective reminders. We may say that they possess significant form. But this can only mean that they possess that kind of form which reminds us of beauty, and awakens in us aesthetic emotion. The nearest explanation of significant form should be *such form as exhibits the inner relations of things*; or, after Hsieh Ho, 'which reveals the rhythm of the spirit in the gestures of living things'.[6] All such works as possess significant form are linguistic; and, if we remember this, we shall not fall into the error of those who advocate the use of language for language's sake, nor shall we confuse the significant forms, or their logical meaning or moral value, with the beauty of which they remind us.

Let us insist, however, that the concept of beauty has originated with the philosopher, not with the artist: *he* has been ever concerned with saying clearly what had to be said. In all ages of creation the artist has been in love with his particular subject – when it is not so, we see that his work is not 'felt' – he has never set out to achieve the Beautiful, in the strict aesthetic sense, and to have this aim is to invite disaster, as one who should seek to fly without wings.

It is not to the artist that one should say the subject is immaterial: that is for the philosopher to say to the philistine who dislikes a work of art for no other reason than that he dislikes it.

The true critic (*rasika*) perceives the beauty of which the artist has exhibited the signs. It is not necessary that the critic should appreciate the artist's meaning – every work of art is a *kāmadhenu*, yielding many meanings – for he knows without reasoning whether or not the work is beautiful, before the mind begins to question what it is 'about'. Hindu writers say that the capacity to feel beauty (to taste *rasa*) cannot be acquired by study, but is the reward of merit gained in a past life; for many good men and would-be historians of art have never perceived it. The poet is born, not made; but so also is the *rasika*, whose genius differs in degree, not in kind, from that of the original artist. In western phraseology we should express this by saying that experience can only be bought by experience; opinions must be earned. We gain and feel nothing merely when we take it on authority that any particular works are beautiful. It is far better to be honest, and to admit that perhaps we cannot see their beauty. A day may come when we shall be better prepared.

The critic, as soon as he becomes an exponent, has to prove his case; and he cannot do this by any process of argument, but only by creating a new work of art, the criticism. His audience, catching the gleam at second-hand – but still the same gleam, for there is only one – has then the opportunity to approach the original work a second time, more reverently.

When I say that works of art are reminders, and the activity of the critic is one of reproduction, I suggest that the vision of even the original artist may be rather a discovery than a creation. If beauty awaits discovery everywhere, that is to say that it waits upon our recollection (in the sūfī sense and in Wordsworth's): in aesthetic contemplation as in love and knowledge, we momentarily recover the unity of our being released from individuality.

There are no degrees of beauty; the most complex and the simplest expression remind us of one and the same state. The sonata cannot be more beautiful than the simplest lyric, nor the painting than the drawing, merely because of their greater elaboration. Civilized art is not more beautiful than savage art, merely because of its possibly more attractive *ethos*. A mathematical analogy is found if we consider large and small circles; these differ only in their content, not in their circularity. In the same way, there cannot be any continuous progress in art. Immediately a given intuition has attained to perfectly clear expression, it remains only to multiply and repeat this expression. This repetition may be desirable for many reasons, but it almost invariably involves a gradual decadence, because we soon begin to take the experience for granted. The vitality of a tradition persists only so long as it is fed by intensity of imagination. What we mean by creative art, however, has no necessary connection with novelty of subject, though that is not excluded. Creative art is art that reveals beauty where we should have otherwise overlooked it, or more clearly than we have yet received. Beauty is sometimes overlooked just because certain expressions have become what we call 'hackneyed'; then the creative artist dealing with the same subject restores our memory. The artist is challenged to reveal the beauty of all experiences, new and old.

Many have rightly insisted that the beauty of a work of art is independent of its subject, and truly, the humility of art, which finds its inspiration everywhere, is identical with the humility of Love, which regards alike a dog and a Brahman – and of Science, to which the lowest form is as significant as the highest. And this is possible, because it is one and the same undivided all. 'If a beauteous form we view, 'Tis His reflection shining through.'

It will now be seen in what sense we are justified in speaking of Absolute Beauty, and in identifying this beauty with God. We do not imply by this that God (who is without parts) has a lovely form which can be the object of knowledge; but that in so far as we see and feel beauty, we see and are one with Him. That God is the first artist does not mean that He created forms, which might not have been lovely had the hand of the potter slipped: but that every natural object is an immediate realization of His being. This creative activity is comparable with aesthetic expression in its non-volitional character; no element of choice enters into that world of imagination and eternity, but there is always perfect identity of intuition-expression, soul and body. The human artist who discovers beauty here or there is the ideal ***guru*** of Kabīr, who 'reveals the Supreme Spirit wherever the mind attaches itself'.

Notes

1 Coomaraswamy's several references to Benedetto Croce are to his *The Aesthetic as the Science of Expression and of the Linguistic in General*, Cambridge: Cambridge University Press, 1992.

2 The meaning of 'in identity' in this remark of Viśvanātha's is that, in the case of ***rasa***, the distinction between the subject and object of experience is lost.

3 The author is here rejecting the 'non-duality' (***Advaita***) doctrine of Vedantic

philosophers like Śankara, according to which, since there is only Brahman, the empirical world must be an 'illusion' (*māyā*). Coomaraswamy's sympathies are with the 'qualified non-duality' doctrine of Rāmānuja, which holds that while things are indeed part of Brahman, they do not thereby lose their reality – no more than waves do just because they are part of the ocean.

4 '*Purusha*' and '*prakṛiti*' are ancient Sanskrit terms for 'soul' and 'nature' (or 'material substance') respectively.

5 These four propositions, as it happens, are a fair summary of Croce's view, repeated with qualifications by R. G. Collingwood (see chapter 16).

6 Hsieh Ho was a Wei dynasty (fourth to sixth century CE) author, whose doctrine of 'rhythmic vitality' had an immense influence on Chinese painting and aesthetics.

14 John Dewey, *Art as Experience*, Chapters 1–2

From John Dewey, *Art as Experience*. New York: Perigree, 1980, pp. 3–27 [footnotes, one passage and the second part of ch. 2 omitted].

For Bell and advocates of 'art for art's sake' such as Gautier and Pater,[1] but also for Schopenhauer and Coomaraswamy, art is of paramount importance through affording especially pure experiences that elevate us above ordinary life. When John Dewey (1859–1952) writes, in *Art as Experience* (1934), that 'esthetic experience is experience in its integrity', 'pure' and 'consummatory' (p. 274), it is tempting to add his name to that list – even if it is surprising to find a leading representative of American pragmatism, with its robust emphasis on the practical implications of experience, keeping such company. Our surprise would be justified, and the fact is that Dewey is at as far a remove from 'aestheticism' as Tolstoy or any Marxist. The very idea of 'art for art's sake', he writes, would have been unintelligible until recently, and is at once 'completely esoteric' and dangerous.

In the pages selected, Dewey argues that the pretence that there is, on a 'remote pedestal', a special class of objects, 'works of art', affording a *sui generis* kind of experience, has encouraged the formation of cliques of connoisseurs, thereby giving art a bad name among 'the mass of people' who then feel free to 'seek the cheap and the vulgar' instead. 'Works of art' anyway constitute an artificial category, a classification due not to any intrinsic, distinguishing properties of such objects, but to sociological factors such as the growth of museums and private collecting by prestige-seeking *nouveaux riches*. Properly understood, 'art' embraces countless human products, not just those canonized as 'works of art'. Similarly, 'aesthetic experience' is involved in many ordinary activities and is certainly not confined to visits to the museum or art gallery.

[1] See Théophile Gautier, *Madamoiselle de Maupin*, Preface, Harmondsworth: Penguin, 1981, and Walter Pater, *The Renaissance: studies in art and poetry*, Oxford: Oxford University Press, 1986, concluding chapter.

In short, art is thoroughly continuous with everyday life. (In Dewey's writings, almost all 'dualistic' categories, including art vs. life, blend into one another – 'like the ingredients of a Christmas pudding'.[2])

To understand this claim about continuity, and reconcile it with the insistence on the 'consummatory' character of aesthetic experience, it is essential to grasp that central concept in Dewey's thought – experience itself. Experience is not, for Dewey, something 'inner', such as sensation or feeling. Rather, as when one speaks of 'experiencing army life', it is 'the shared social activity of symbolically mediated behaviour'.[3] Such experience or activity has a characteristic 'rhythm', that of 'loss of integration with environment and recovery of union' (p. 15). In other words the 'live creature' is constantly challenged by its recalcitrant surroundings to act upon them, or reinterpret them, so as to recover a sense of 'harmony' with them, thereby relieving the 'tension' of discord. In the sense of harmony, of things fitting together with one another and oneself, resides aesthetic pleasure in the broadest sense. This fulfilling achievement of 'union' is 'art in its germ'. Art in a somewhat narrower sense is at work when human beings quite self-consciously aim to produce harmony and union out of discord. The 'idea of art' – 'the greatest intellectual achievement in the history of humanity' (p. 25) – is precisely the recognition that such self-conscious production is possible, and necessary for developing a meaningful existence. Art in its narrowest sense – 'works of art' – is only an especially 'pure' form of this wider activity. Great works of art – and it is not Dewey's aim to deny there are such – are paradigms of experience, 'consummatory' experiences, precisely because they maximally embody the achievement of union and harmony. What Bach accomplishes in his fugues is 'experience in its integrity', an epitome of what all we 'live creatures' strive for in our activities.

Art as Experience is a long book and many of its influential claims, concerning 'expression' for example, only emerge in later chapters. But chapters 1–2 have by themselves shaped much contemporary discussion, not always in ways Dewey could have approved. Doubtless he would praise many subsequent attempts to 'place' art both within the larger life of the community and within the still larger story of man's development as a species, where 'the idea of art' has been decisive. This one-time member of the board of the Barnes Foundation would surely have been less happy, however, at the way in which his remarks on 'works of art' as a socially constructed category have been exploited by elements within 'Cultural Studies' to excoriate 'high' culture and extol the virtues of what Dewey himself would have included in 'the cheap and the vulgar'.

[2] F. E. Sparshott, *The Structure of Aesthetics*, London: Routledge & Kegan Paul, 1963, p. 237.

[3] Thomas M. Alexander, 'John Dewey', in D. E. Cooper (ed.), *A Companion to Aesthetics*, Oxford: Blackwell, 1992, p. 119. See the same author's *John Dewey's Theory of Art, Experience, and Nature*, Albany, NY: State University of New York Press, 1987.

[1] The Live Creature

By one of the ironic perversities that often attend the course of affairs, the existence of the works of art upon which formation of an esthetic theory depends has become an obstruction to theory about them. For one reason, these works are products that exist externally and physically. In common conception, the work of art is often identified with the building, book, painting, or statue in its existence apart from human experience. Since the actual work of art is what the product does with and in experience, the result is not favorable to understanding. In addition, the very perfection of some of these products, the prestige they possess because of a long history of unquestioned admiration, creates conventions that get in the way of fresh insight. When an art product once attains classic status, it somehow becomes isolated from the human conditions under which it was brought into being and from the human consequences it engenders in actual life-experience.

When artistic objects are separated from both conditions of origin and operation in experience, a wall is built around them that renders almost opaque their general significance, with which esthetic theory deals. Art is remitted to a separate realm, where it is cut off from that association with the materials and aims of every other form of human effort, undergoing, and achievement. A primary task is thus imposed upon one who undertakes to write upon the philosophy of the fine arts. This task is to restore continuity between the refined and intensified forms of experience that are works of art and the everyday events, doings, and sufferings that are universally recognized to constitute experience. Mountain peaks do not float unsupported; they do not even just rest upon the earth. They *are* the earth in one of its manifest operations. It is the business of those who are concerned with the theory of the earth, geographers and geologists, to make this fact evident in its various implications. The theorist who would deal philosophically with fine art has a like task to accomplish.

If one is willing to grant this position, even if only by way of temporary experiment, he will see that there follows a conclusion at first sight surprising. In order to understand the meaning of artistic products, we have to forget them for a time, to turn aside from them and have recourse to the ordinary forces and conditions of experience that we do not usually regard as esthetic. We must arrive at the theory of art by means of a detour. For theory is concerned with understanding, insight, not without exclamations of admiration, and stimulation of that emotional outburst often called appreciation. It is quite possible to enjoy flowers in their colored form and delicate fragrance without knowing anything about plants theoretically. But if one sets out to ***understand*** the flowering of plants, he is committed to finding out something about the interactions of soil, air, water and sunlight that condition the growth of plants.

By common consent, the Parthenon is a great work of art. Yet it has esthetic standing only as the work becomes an experience for a human being. And, if one is to go beyond personal enjoyment into the formation of a theory about that large republic of art of which the building is one member, one has to be willing at some point in his reflections to turn from it to the bustling, arguing, acutely sensitive Athenian citizens, with civic sense identified with a civic religion, of whose experience the temple was an expression, and who built it not as a work of art but as a civic commemoration. The turning to them is as human beings who had needs that were a demand for the building and that were carried to fulfillment in it; it is not an examination such as might be carried on by a sociologist in search for material relevant to his purpose. The one who sets out to theorize about the esthetic experience embodied in the Parthenon must realize in thought what the people into whose lives it entered had in common, as creators and as those who were satisfied with it, with people in our own homes and on our own streets.

In order to ***understand*** the esthetic in its ultimate and approved forms, one must begin with it in the raw; in the events and scenes that hold the attentive eye and ear of man, arousing his interest and affording him enjoyment as he looks and listens: the sights that hold the crowd – the fire-engine rushing by; the machines excavating enormous holes in the earth; the human-fly climbing the steeple-side; the men perched high in air on girders, throwing and catching red-hot bolts. The sources of art in human experience will be learned by him who sees how the tense grace of the ball-player infects the onlooking crowd; who notes the delight of the housewife in tending her plants, and the intent interest of her goodman in tending the patch of green in front of the house; the zest of the spectator in poking the wood burning on the hearth and in watching the darting flames and crumbling coals. These people, if questioned as to the reason for their actions, would doubtless return reasonable answers. The man who poked the sticks of burning wood would say he did it to make the fire burn better; but he is none the less fascinated by the colorful drama of change enacted before his eyes and imaginatively partakes in it. He does not remain a cold spectator. What Coleridge said of the reader of poetry is true in its way of all who are happily absorbed in their activities of mind and body: 'The reader should be carried forward, not merely or chiefly by the mechanical impulse of curiosity, not by a restless desire to arrive at the final solution, but by the pleasurable activity of the journey itself.'

The intelligent mechanic engaged in his job, interested in doing well and finding satisfaction in his handiwork, caring for his materials and tools with genuine affection, is artistically engaged. The difference between such a worker and the inept and careless bungler is as great in the shop as it is in the studio. Oftentimes the product may not appeal to the esthetic sense of those who use the product. The fault, however, is oftentimes not so much with the worker as with the conditions of the market for which his product is designed. Were conditions and opportunities different, things as significant to the eye as those produced by earlier craftsmen would be made.

So extensive and subtly pervasive are the ideas that set Art upon a remote pedestal, that many a person would be repelled rather than pleased if told that he enjoyed his casual recreations, in part at least, because of their esthetic quality. The arts which today have most vitality for the average person are things he does not take to be arts: for instance, the movie, jazzed music, the comic strip, and, too frequently, newspaper accounts of love-nests, murders, and exploits of bandits. For, when what he knows as art is relegated to the museum and gallery, the unconquerable impulse towards experiences enjoyable in themselves finds such outlet as the daily environment provides. Many a person who protests against the museum conception of art, still shares the fallacy from which that conception springs. For the popular notion comes from a separation of art from the objects and scenes of ordinary experience that many theorists and critics pride themselves upon holding and even elaborating. The times when select and distinguished objects are closely connected with the products of usual vocations are the times when appreciation of the former is most rife and most keen. When, because of their remoteness, the objects acknowledged by the cultivated to be works of fine art seem anemic to the mass of people, esthetic hunger is likely to seek the cheap and the vulgar.

The factors that have glorified fine art by setting it upon a far-off pedestal did not arise within the realm of art nor is their influence confined to the arts. For many persons an aura of mingled awe and unreality encompasses the 'spiritual' and the 'ideal' while 'matter' has become by contrast a term of depreciation, something to be explained away or apologized for. The forces at work are those that have removed religion as well as fine art from the scope of the common or community life. The forces have historically produced so many of the dislocations and divisions of modern life and thought that art could not escape their influence. We do not have to travel to the ends of the earth nor return many millennia in time to find peoples for whom everything that intensifies the sense of immediate living is an object of intense admiration. Bodily scarification, waving feathers, gaudy robes, shining ornaments of gold and silver, of emerald and jade, formed the contents of esthetic arts, and, presumably, without the vulgarity of class exhibitionism that attends their analogues today. Domestic utensils, furnishings of tent and house, rugs, mats, jars, pots, bows, spears, were wrought with such delighted care that today we hunt them out and give them places of honor in our art museums. Yet in their own time and place, such things were enhancements of the processes of everyday life. Instead of being elevated to a niche apart, they belonged to display of prowess, the manifestation of group and clan membership, worship of gods, feasting and fasting, fighting, hunting, and all the rhythmic crises that punctuate the stream of living.

Dancing and pantomime, the sources of the art of the theater, flourished as part of religious rites and celebrations. Musical art abounded in the fingering of the stretched string, the beating of the taut skin, the blowing with reeds. Even in the caves, human habitations were adorned with colored pictures that kept alive to the senses experienes with the animals that were so closely bound with the lives of humans. Structures that housed their gods and the instrumentalities that facilitated commerce with the higher powers were wrought with especial fineness. But the arts of the drama, music, painting, and architecture thus exemplified had no peculiar connection with theaters, galleries, museums. They were part of the significant life of an organized community.

The collective life that was manifested in war, worship, the forum, knew no division between what was characteristic of these places and operations, and the arts that brought color, grace, and dignity, into them. Painting and sculpture were organically one with architecture, as that was one with the social purpose that buildings served. Music and song were intimate parts of the rites and ceremonies in which the meaning of group life was consummated. Drama was a vital reenactment of the legends and history of group life. Not even in Athens can such arts be torn loose from this setting in direct experience and yet retain their significant character. Athletic sports, as well as drama, celebrated and enforced traditions of race and group, instructing the people, commemorating glories, and strengthening their civic pride.

Under such conditions, it is not surprising that the Athenian Greeks, when they came to reflect upon art, formed the idea that it is an act of reproduction, or imitation. There are many objections to this conception. But the vogue of the theory is testimony to the close connection of the fine arts with daily life; the idea would not have occurred to any one had art been remote from the interests of life. For the doctrine did not signify that art was a literal copying of objects, but that it reflected the emotions and ideas that are associated with the chief institutions of social life. Plato felt this connection so strongly that it led him to his idea of the necessity of censorship of poets, dramatists, and musicians. Perhaps he exaggerated when he said that a change from the Doric to the Lydian mode in music would be the sure precursor of civic degeneration. But no contemporary would have doubted that music was an integral part of the ethos and the institutions of the community. The idea of 'art for art's sake' would not have been even understood.

There must then be historic reasons for the rise of the compartmental conception of fine art. Our present museums and galleries to which works of fine art are removed and stored illustrate some of the causes that have operated to segregate art instead of finding it an attendant of temple, forum, and other forms of associated life. An instructive history of modern art could be written in terms of the formation of the distinctively modern institutions of museum and exhibition gallery. I may point to a few outstanding facts. Most European museums are, among other things, memorials of the rise of nationalism and imperialism. Every capital must have its own museum of painting, sculpture, etc., devoted in part to exhibiting the greatness of its artistic past, and, in other part, to exhibiting the loot gathered by its monarchs in conquest of other nations; for instance, the accumulations of the spoils of Napoleon that are in the Louvre. They testify to the connexion between the modern segregation of art and nationalism and militarism. Doubtless this connexion has served at times a useful purpose, as in the case of Japan, who, when she was in the process of westernization, saved much of her art treasures by nationalizing the temples that contained them.

The growth of capitalism has been a powerful influence in the development of the museum as the proper home for works of art, and in the promotion of the idea that they are apart from the common life. The ***nouveaux riches***, who are an important by-product of the capitalist system, have felt especially bound to surround themselves with works of fine art which, being rare, are also costly. Generally speaking, the typical collector is the typical capitalist. For evidence of good standing in the realm of higher culture, he amasses paintings, statuary, and artistic *bijoux*, as his stocks and bonds certify to his standing in the economic world.

Not merely individuals, but communities and nations, put their cultural good taste in evidence by building opera houses, galleries, and museums. These show that a community is not wholly absorbed in material wealth, because it is willing to spend its gains in patronage of art. It erects these buildings and collects their contents as it now builds a cathedral. These things reflect and establish superior cultural status, while their segregation from the common life reflects that fact that they are not part of a native and spontaneous culture. They are a kind of counterpart of a holier-than-thou attitude, exhibited not toward persons as such but toward the interests and occupations that absorb most of the community's time and energy.

Modern industry and commerce have an international scope. The contents of galleries and museums testify to the growth of economic cosmopolitanism. The mobility of trade and of populations, due to the economic system, has weakened or destroyed the connexion between works of art and the *genius loci* of which they were once the natural expression. As works of art have lost their indigenous status, they have acquired a new one – that of being specimens of fine art and nothing else. Moreover, works of art are now produced, like other articles, for sale in the market. Economic patronage by wealthy and powerful individuals has at many times played a part in the encouragement of artistic production. Probably many a savage tribe had its Maecenas. But now even that much of intimate social connexion is lost in the impersonality of a world market. Objects that were in the past valid and significant because of their place in the life of a community now function in isolation from the conditions of their origin. By that fact they are also set apart from common experience, and serve as insignia of taste and certificates of special culture.

Because of changes in industrial conditions the artist has been pushed to one side from the main streams of active interest. Industry has been mechanized and an artist cannot work mechanically for mass production. He is less integrated than formerly in the normal flow of social services. A peculiar esthetic 'individualism' results. Artists find it incumbent upon them to betake themselves to their work as an isolated means of 'self-expression.' In order not to cater to the trend of economic forces, they often feel obliged to exaggerate their separateness to the point of eccentricity. Consequently artistic products take on to a still greater degree the air of something independent and esoteric.

Put the action of all such forces together, and the conditions that create the gulf which exists generally between producer and consumer in modern society operate to create also a chasm between ordinary and esthetic experience. Finally we have, as the record of this chasm, accepted as if it were normal, the philosophies of art that locate it in a region inhabited by no other creature, and that emphasize beyond all reason the merely contemplative character of the esthetic. Confusion of values enters in to accentuate the separation. Adventitious matters, like the pleasure of collecting, of exhibiting, of ownership and display, simulate esthetic values. Criticism is affected. There is much applause for the wonders of appreciation and the glories of the transcendent beauty of art indulged in without much regard to capacity for esthetic perception in the concrete.

My purpose, however, is not to engage in an economic interpretation of the history of the arts, much less to argue that economic conditions are either invariably or directly relevant to perception and enjoyment, or even to interpretation of individual works of art. It is to indicate that *theories* which isolate art and its appreciation by placing them in a realm of their own, disconnected from other modes of experiencing, are not inherent in the subject-matter but arise because of specifiable extraneous conditions. Embedded as they are in institutions and in habits of life, these conditions operate effectively because they work so unconsciously. Then the theorist assumes they are embedded in the nature of things. Nevertheless, the influence of these conditions is not confined to theory. As I have already indicated, it deeply affects the practice of living, driving away esthetic perceptions that are necessary ingredients of happiness, or reducing them to the level of compensating transient pleasurable excitations.

Even to readers who are adversely inclined to what has been said, the implications of the statements that have been made may be useful in defining the nature of the problem: that of recovering the continuity of esthetic experience with normal processes of living. The understanding of art and of its role in civilization is not furthered by setting out with eulogies of it nor by occupying ourselves exclusively at the outset with great works of art recognized as such. The comprehension which theory essays will be arrived at by a detour; by going back to experience of the common or mill run of things to discover the esthetic quality such experience possesses. Theory can start with and from acknowledged works of art only when the esthetic is already compartmentalized, or only when works of art are set in a niche apart instead of being celebrations, recognized as such, of the things of ordinary experience. Even a crude experience, if authentically an experience, is more fit to give a clue to the intrinsic nature of esthetic experience than is an object already set apart from any other mode of experience. Following this clue we can discover how the work of art develops and accentuates what is characteristically valuable in things of everyday enjoyment. The art product will then be seen to issue from the latter, when the full meaning of ordinary experience is expressed, as dyes come out of coal tar products when they receive special treatment.

Many theories about art already exist. If there is justification for proposing yet another philosophy of the esthetic, it must be found in a new mode of approach. Combinations and permutations among existing theories can easily be brought forth by those so inclined. But, to my mind, the trouble with existing theories is that they start from a ready-made compartmentalization, or from a conception of art that 'spiritualizes' it out of connexion with the objects of concrete experience. The alternative, however, to such spiritualization is not a degrading and Philistinish materialization of works of fine art, but a conception that discloses the way in which these works idealize qualities found in common experience. Were works of art placed in a directly human context in popular esteem, they would have a much wider appeal than they can have when pigeon-hole theories of art win general acceptance.

A conception of fine art that sets out from its connexion with discovered qualities of ordinary experience will be able to indicate the factors and forces that favor the normal development of common human activities into matters of artistic value. It will also be able to point out those conditions that arrest its normal growth. Writers on esthetic theory often raise the question of whether esthetic philosophy can aid in cultivation of esthetic appreciation. The question is a branch of the general theory of criticism, which, it seems to me, fails to accomplish its full office if it does not indicate what to look for and what to find in concrete esthetic objects. But, in any case, it is safe to say that a philosophy of art is sterilized unless it makes us aware of the function of art in relation to other modes of experience, and unless it indicates why this function is so inadequately realized, and unless it suggests the conditions under which the office would be successfully performed.

The comparison of the emergence of works of art out of ordinary experiences to the refining of raw materials into valuable products may seem to some unworthy, if not an actual attempt to reduce works of art to the status of articles manufactured for commercial purposes. The point, however, is that no amount of ecstatic eulogy of finished works can of itself assist the understanding or the generation of such works. Flowers can be enjoyed without knowing about the interactions of soil, air, moisture, and seeds of which they are the result. But they cannot be *understood* without taking just these interactions into account – and theory is a matter of understanding. Theory is concerned with discovering the nature of the production of works of art and of their enjoyment in perception. How is it that the everyday making of things grows into that form of making which is genuinely artistic? How is it that our everyday enjoyment of scenes and situations develops into the peculiar satisfaction that attends the experience which is emphatically esthetic? These are the questions theory must answer. The answers cannot be found, unless we are willing to find the germs and roots in matters of experience that we do not currently regard as esthetic. Having discovered these active seeds, we may follow the course of their growth into the highest forms of finished and refined art.

It is a commonplace that we cannot direct, save accidentally, the growth and flowering of plants, however lovely and enjoyed, without understanding their causal conditions. It should be just a commonplace that esthetic understanding – as distinct from sheer personal enjoyment – must start with the soil, air and light out of which things esthetically admirable arise. And these conditions are the conditions and factors that make an ordinary experience complete. The more we recognize this fact, the more we shall find ourselves faced with a problem rather than with a final solution. *If* artistic and esthetic quality is implicit in every normal experience, how shall we explain how and why it so generally fails to become explicit? Why is it that to multitudes art seems to be an importation into experience from a foreign country and the esthetic to be a synonym for something artificial?

We cannot answer these questions any more than we can trace the development of art out of everyday experience, unless we have a clear and coherent idea of what is meant when we say 'normal experience.' Fortunately, the road to arriving at such an idea is open and well marked. The nature of experience is determined by the essential conditions of life. While man is other than bird and beast, he shares basic vital functions with them and has to make the same basal adjustments if he is to continue the process of living. Having the same vital needs, man derives the means by which he breathes, moves, looks and listens, the very brain with which he coordinates his senses and his movements, from his animal forbears. The organs with which he maintains himself in being are not of himself alone, but by the grace of struggles and achievements of a long line of animal ancestry.

Fortunately a theory of the place of the esthetic in experience does not have to lose itself in minute details when it starts with experience in its elemental form. Broad outlines suffice. The first great consideration is that life goes on in an environment; not merely *in* it but because of it, through interaction with it. No creature lives merely under its skin; its subcutaneous organs are means of connexion with what lies beyond its bodily frame, and to which, in order to live, it must adjust itself, by accommodation and defense but also by conquest. At every moment, the living creature is exposed to dangers from its surroundings, and at every moment, it must draw upon something in its surroundings to satisfy its needs. The career and destiny of a living being are bound up with its interchanges with its environment, not externally but in the most intimate way.

The growl of a dog crouching over his food, his howl in time of loss and loneliness, the wagging of his tail at the return of his human friend are expressions of the implication of a living in a natural medium which includes man along with the animal he has domesticated. Every need, say hunger for fresh air or food, is a lack that denotes at least a temporary absence of adequate adjustment with surroundings. But it is also a demand, a reaching out into the environment to make good the lack and to restore adjustment by building at least a temporary equilibrium. Life itself consists of phases in which the organism falls out of step with the march of surrounding things and then recovers unison with it – either through effort or by some happy chance. And, in a growing life, the recovery is never mere return to a prior state, for it is enriched by the state of disparity and resistance through which it has successfully passed. If the gap between organism and environment is too wide, the creature dies. If its activity is not enhanced by the temporary alienation, it merely subsists. Life grows when a temporary falling out is a transition to a more extensive balance of the energies of the organism with those of the conditions under which it lives.

These biological commonplaces are something more than that; they reach to the roots of the esthetic in experience. The world is full of things that are indifferent and even hostile to life; the very processes by which life is maintained tend to throw it out of gear with its surroundings. Nevertheless, if life continues and if in continuing it expands, there is an overcoming of factors of opposition and conflict; there is a transformation of them into differentiated aspects of a higher powered and more significant life. The marvel of organic, of vital, adaptation through expansion (instead of by contraction and passive accommodation) actually takes place. Here in germ are balance and harmony attained through rhythm. Equilibrium comes about not mechanically and inertly but out of, and because of, tension.

There is in nature, even below the level of life, something more than mere flux and change. Form is arrived at whenever a stable, even though moving, equilibrium is reached. Changes interlock and sustain one another. Wherever there is this coherence there is endurance. Order is not imposed from without but is made out of the relations of harmonious interactions that energies bear to one another. Because it is active (not anything static because foreign to what goes on) order itself develops. It comes to include within its balanced movement a greater variety of changes.

Order cannot but be admirable in a world constantly threatened with disorder – in a world where living creatures can go on living only by taking advantage of whatever order exists about them, incorporating it into themselves. In a world like ours, every living creature that attains sensibility welcomes order with a response of harmonious feeling whenever it finds a congruous order about it.

For only when an organism shares in the ordered relations of its environment does it secure the stability essential to living. And when the participation comes after a phase of disruption and conflict, it bears within itself the germs of a consummation akin to the esthetic.

The rhythm of loss of integration with environment and recovery of union not only persists in man but becomes conscious with him; its conditions are material out of which he forms purposes. Emotion is the conscious sign of a break, actual or impending. The discord is the occasion that induces reflection. Desire for restoration of the union converts mere emotion into interest in objects as conditions of realization of harmony. With the realization, material of reflection is incorporated into objects as their meaning. Since the artist cares in a peculiar way for the phase of experience in which union is achieved, he does not shun moments of resistance and tension. He rather cultivates them, not for their own sake but because of their potentialities, bringing to living consciousness an experience that is unified and total. In contrast with the person whose purpose is esthetic, the scientific man is interested in problems, in situations wherein tension between the matter of observation and of thought is marked. Of course he cares for their resolution. But he does not rest in it; he passes on to another problem using an attained solution only as a stepping stone from which to set on foot further inquiries.

The difference between the esthetic and the intellectual is thus one of the place where emphasis falls in the constant rhythm that marks the interaction of the live creature with his surroundings. The ultimate matter of both emphases in experience is the same, as is also their general form. The odd notion that an artist does not think and a scientific inquirer does nothing else is the result of converting a difference of tempo and emphasis into a difference in kind. The thinker has his esthetic moment when his ideas cease to be mere ideas and become the corporate meanings of objects. The artist has his problems and thinks as he works. But his thought is more immediately embodied in the object. Because of the comparative remoteness of his end, the scientific worker operates with symbols, words and mathematical signs. The artist does his thinking in the very qualitative media he works in, and the terms lie so close to the object that he is producing that they merge directly into it.

The live animal does not have to project emotions into the objects experienced. Nature is kind and hateful, bland and morose, irritating and comforting, long before she is mathematically qualified or even a congeries of 'secondary' qualities like colors and their shapes. Even such words as long and short, solid and hollow, still carry to all, but those who are intellectually specialized, a moral and emotional connotation. The dictionary will inform any one who consults it that the early use of words like sweet and bitter was not to denote qualities of sense as such but to discriminate things as favorable and hostile. How could it be otherwise? Direct experience comes from nature and man interacting with each other. In this interaction, human energy gathers, is released, dammed up, frustrated and victorious. There are rhythmic beats of want and fulfillment, pulses of doing and being withheld from doing.

All interactions that effect stability and order in the whirling flux of change are rhythms. There is ebb and flow, systole and diastole: ordered change. The latter moves within bounds. To overpass the limits that are set is destruction and death, out of which, however, new rhythms are built up. The proportionate interception of changes establishes an order that is spatially, not merely temporally patterned: like the waves of the sea, the ripples of and where waves have flowed back and forth, the fleecy and the black-bottomed cloud. Contrast of lack and fullness, of struggle and achievement, of adjustment after consummated irregularity, form the drama in which action, feeling, and meaning are one. The outcome is balance and counterbalance. These are not static nor mechanical. They express power that is intense because measured through overcoming resistance. Environing objects avail and counteravail.

There are two sorts of possible worlds in which esthetic experience would not occur. In a world of mere flux, change would not be cumulative; it would not move toward a close. Stability and rest would have no being. Equally is it true, however, that a world that is finished, ended, would have no traits of suspense and crisis, and would offer no opportunity for resolution. Where everything is already complete, there is no fulfillment. We envisage with pleasure Nirvana and a uniform heavenly bliss only because they are projected upon the background of our present world of stress and conflict. Because the actual world, that in which we live, is a combination of movement and culmination, of breaks and re-unions, the experience of a living creature is capable of esthetic quality. The live being recurrently loses and reestablishes equilibrium with his surroundings. The moment of passage from disturbance into harmony is that of intensest life. In a finished world, sleep and waking could not be distinguished. In one wholly perturbed, conditions could not even be struggled with. In a world made after the pattern of ours, moments of fulfillment punctuate experience with rhythmically enjoyed intervals.

Inner harmony is attained only when, by some means, terms are made with the environment. When it occurs on any other than an 'objective' basis, it is illusory – in extreme cases to the point of insanity. Fortunately for variety in experience, terms are made in many ways – ways ultimately decided by selective interest. Pleasures may come about through chance contact and stimulation; such pleasures are not to be despised in a world full of pain. But happiness and delight are a different sort of thing. They come to be through a fulfillment that reaches to the depths of our being –

one that is an adjustment of our whole being with the conditions of existence. In the process of living, attainment of a period of equilibrium is at the same time the initiation of a new relation to the environment, one that brings with it potency of new adjustments to be made through struggle. The time of consummation is also one of beginning anew. Any attempt to perpetuate beyond its term the enjoyment attending the time of fulfillment and harmony constitutes withdrawal from the world. Hence it marks the lowering and loss of vitality. But, through the phases of perturbation and conflict, there abides the deep-seated memory of an underlying harmony, the sense of which haunts life like the sense of being founded on a rock.

Most mortals are conscious that a split often occurs between their present living and their past and future. Then the past hangs upon them as a burden; it invades the present with a sense of regret, of opportunities not used, and of consequences we wish undone. It rests upon the present as an oppression, instead of being a storehouse of resources by which to move confidently forward. But the live creature adopts its past; it can make friends with even its stupidities, using them as warnings that increase present wariness. Instead of trying to live upon whatever may have been achieved in the past, it uses past successes to inform the present. Every living experience owes its richness to what Santayana well calls 'hushed reverberations.'

To the being fully alive, the future is not ominous but a promise; it surrounds the present as a halo. It consists of possibilities that are felt as a possession of what is now and here. In life that is truly life, everything overlaps and merges. But all too often we exist in apprehensions of what the future may bring, and are divided within ourselves. Even when not overanxious, we do not enjoy the present because we subordinate it to that which is absent. Because of the frequency of this abandonment of the present to the past and future, the happy periods of an experience that is now complete because it absorbs into itself memories of the past and anticipations of the future, come to constitute an esthetic ideal. Only when the past ceases to trouble and anticipations of the future are not perturbing is a being wholly united with his environment and therefore fully alive. Art celebrates with peculiar intensity the moments in which the past reenforces the present and in which the future is a quickening of what now is.

To grasp the sources of esthetic experience it is, therefore, necessary to have recourse to animal life below the human scale. The activities of the fox, the dog, and the thrush may at least stand as reminders and symbols of that unity of experience which we so fractionize when work is labor, and thought withdraws us from the world. The live animal is fully present, all there, in all of its actions: in its wary glances, its sharp sniffings, its abrupt cocking of ears. All senses are equally on the *qui vive*. As you watch, you see motion merging into sense and sense into motion – constituting that animal grace so hard for man to rival. What the live creature retains from the past and what it expects from the future operate as directions in the present. The dog is never pedantic nor academic; for these things arise only when the past is severed in consciousness from the present and is set up as a model to copy or a storehouse upon which to draw. The past absorbed into the present carries on; it presses forward.

There is much in the life of the savage that is sodden. But, when the savage is most alive, he is most observant of the world about him and most taut with energy. As he watches what stirs about him, he, too, is stirred. His observation is both action in preparation and foresight of the future. He is as active through his whole being when he looks and listens as when he stalks his quarry or stealthily retreats from a foe. His senses are sentinels of immediate thought and outposts of action, and not, as they so often are with us, mere pathways along which material is gathered to be stored away for a delayed and remote possibility.

It is mere ignorance that leads then to the supposition that connexion of art and esthetic perception with experience signifies a lowering of their significance and dignity. Experience in the degree in which it *is* experience is heightened vitality. Instead of signifying being shut up within one's own private feelings and sensations, it signifies active and alert commerce with the world; at its height it signifies complete interpenetration of self and the world of objects and events. Instead of signifying surrender to caprice and disorder, it affords our sole demonstration of a stability that is not stagnation but is rhythmic and developing. Because experience is the fulfillment of an organism in its struggles and achievements in a world of things, it is art in germ. Even in its rudimentary forms, it contains the promise of that delightful perception which is esthetic experience.

[2] The Live Creature and 'Ethereal Things'

Why is the attempt to connect the higher and ideal things of experience with basic vital roots so often regarded as betrayal of their nature and denial of their value? Why is there repulsion when the high achievements of fine art are brought into connexion with common life, the life that we share with all living creatures? Why is life thought of as an affair of low appetite, or at its best a thing of gross sensation, and ready to sink from its best to the level of lust and harsh cruelty? A complete answer to the question would involve the writing of a history of morals that would set forth the conditions that have brought about contempt for the body, fear of the senses, and the opposition of flesh to spirit.

One aspect of this history is so relevant to our problem that it must receive at least passing notice. The institutional life of mankind is marked by disorganization. This disorder is often disguised by the fact that it takes the form of static division into classes, and this static separation is accepted as the very essence of order as long as it is so fixed and so accepted as not to generate open conflict. Life is compartmentalized and the institutionalized compartments are classified as high and as low; their values as profane and spiritual, as material and ideal. Interests are related to one another externally and mechanically, through a system of checks and balances. Since religion, morals, politics, business has each its own compartment, within which it is fitting each should remain, art, too, must have its peculiar and private realm. Compartmentalization of occupations and interests brings about separation of that mode of activity commonly called 'practice' from insight, of imagination from executive doing, of significant purpose from work, of emotion from thought and doing. Each of these has, too, its own place in which it must abide. Those who write the anatomy of experience then suppose that these divisions inhere in the very constitution of human nature.

Of much of our experience as it is actually lived under present economic and legal institutional conditions, it is only too true that these separations hold. Only occasionally in the lives of many are the senses fraught with the sentiment that comes from deep realization of intrinsic meanings. We undergo sensations as mechanical stimuli or as irritated stimulations, without having a sense of the reality that is in them and behind them: in much of our experience our different senses do not unite to tell a common and enlarged story. We see without feeling; we hear, but only a second-hand report, second-hand because not reenforced by vision. We touch, but the contact remains tangential because it does not fuse with qualities of senses that go below the surface. We use the senses to arouse passion but not to fulfill the interest of insight, not because that interest is not potentially present in the exercise of sense but because we yield to conditions of living that force sense to remain an excitation on the surface. Prestige goes to those who use their minds without participation of the body and who act vicariously through control of the bodies and labor of others.

Under such conditions, sense and flesh get a bad name. The moralist, however, has a truer sense of the intimate connexions of sense with the rest of our being than has the professional psychologist and philosopher, although his sense of these connexions takes a direction that reverses the potential facts of our living in relation to the environment. Psychologist and philosopher have in recent times been so obsessed with the problem of knowledge that they have treated 'sensations' as mere elements of knowledge. The moralist knows that sense is allied with emotion, impulse and appetition. So he denounces the lust of the eye as part of the surrender of spirit to flesh. He identifies the sensuous with the sensual and the sensual with the lewd. His moral theory is askew, but at least he is aware that the eye is not an imperfect telescope designed for intellectual reception of material to bring about knowledge of distant objects.

'Sense' covers a wide range of contents: the sensory, the sensational, the sensitive, the sensible, and the sentimental, along with the sensuous. It includes almost everything from bare physical and emotional shock to sense itself – that is, the meaning of things present in immediate experience. Each term refers to some real phase and aspect of the life of an organic creature as life occurs through sense organs. But sense, as meaning so directly embodied in experience as to be its own illuminated meaning, is the only signification that expresses the function of sense organs when they are carried to full realization. The senses are the organs through which the live creature participates directly in the ongoings of the world about him. In this participation the varied wonder and splendor of this world are made actual for him in the qualities he experiences. This material cannot be opposed to action, for motor apparatus and 'will' itself are the means by which this participation is carried on and directed. It cannot be opposed to 'intellect,', for mind is the means by which participation is rendered fruitful through sense; by which meanings and values are extracted, retained, and put to further service in the intercourse of the live creature with his surroundings.

Experience is the result, the sign, and the reward of that interaction of organism and environment which, when it is carried to the full, is a transformation of interaction into participation and communication. Since sense-organs with their connected motor apparatus are the means of this participation, any and every derogation of them, whether practical or theoretical, is at once effect and cause of a narrowed and dulled life-experience. Oppositions of mind and body, soul and matter, spirit and flesh all have their origin, fundamentally, in fear of what life may bring forth. They are marks of contraction and withdrawal. Full recognition, therefore, of the continuity of the organs, needs and basic impulses of the human creature with his animal forbears, implies no necessary reduction of man to the level of the brutes. On the contrary, it makes possible the drawing of a ground-plan of human experience upon which is erected the superstructure of man's marvelous and distinguishing experience. What is distinctive in man makes it possible for him to sink below the level of the beasts. It also makes it possible for him to carry to new and unprecedented heights that unity of sense and impulse, of brain and eye and ear, that is exemplified in animal life, saturating it with the conscious meanings derived from communication and deliberate expression.

Man excels in complexity and minuteness of differentiations. This very fact constitutes the necessity for many more comprehensive and exact relationships among the constituents of his being. Important as are the distinctions and relations thus made possible, the story does not end here. There are more opportunities for resistance and tension, more drafts upon experimentation and invention, and therefore more novelty in action, greater range and depth of insight and increase of poignancy in feeling. As an organism increases in complexity, the rhythms of struggle and consummation in its relation to its environment are varied and prolonged, and they come to include within themselves an endless variety of sub-rhythms. The designs of living are widened and enriched. Fulfillment is more massive and more subtly shaded.

Space thus becomes something more than a void in which to roam about, dotted here and there with dangerous things and things that satisfy the appetite. It becomes a comprehensive and enclosed scene within which are ordered the multiplicity of doings and undergoings in which man engages. Time ceases to be either the endless and uniform flow or the succession of instantaneous points which some philosophers have asserted it to be. It, too, is the organized and organizing medium of the rhythmic ebb and flow of expectant impulse, forward and retracted movement, resistance and suspense, with fulfillment and consummation. It is an ordering of growth and maturations – as [William] James said, we learn to skate in summer after having commenced in winter. Time as organization in change is growth, and growth signifies that a varied series of change enters upon intervals of pause and rest; of completions that become the initial points of new processes of development. Like the soil, mind is fertilized while it lies fallow, until a new burst of bloom ensues.

[. . .]

Art is thus prefigured in the very processes of living. A bird builds its nest and a beaver its dam when internal organic pressures cooperate with external materials so that the former are fulfilled and the latter are transformed in a satisfying culmination. We may hesitate to apply the word 'art,' since we doubt the presence of directive intent. But all deliberation, all conscious intent, grows out of things once performed organically through the interplay of natural energies. Were it not so, art would be built on quaking sands, nay, on unstable air. The distinguishing contribution of man is consciousness of the relations found in nature. Through consciousness, he converts the relations of cause and effect that are found in nature into relations of means and consequence. Rather, consciousness itself is the inception of such a transformation. What was mere shock becomes an invitation; resistance becomes something to be used in changing existing arrangements of matter; smooth facilities become agencies for executing an idea. In these operations, an organic stimulation becomes the bearer of meanings, and motor responses are changed into instruments of expression and communication; no longer are they mere means of locomotion and direct reaction. Meanwhile, the organic substratum remains as the quickening and deep foundation. Apart from relations of cause and effect in nature, conception and invention could not be. Apart from the relation of processes of rhythmic conflict and fulfillment in animal life, experience would be without design and pattern. Apart from organs inherited from animal ancestry, idea and purpose would be without a mechanism of realization. The primeval arts of nature and animal life are so much the material, and, in gross outline, so much the model for the intentional achievements of man, that the theologically minded have imputed conscious intent to the structure of nature – as man, sharing many activities with the ape, is wont to think of the latter as imitating his own performances.

The existence of art is the concrete proof of what has just been stated abstractly. It is proof that man uses the materials and energies of nature with intent to expand his own life, and that he does so in accord with the structure of his organism – brain, sense-organs, and muscular system. Art is the living and concrete proof that man is capable of restoring consciously, and thus on the plane of meaning, the union of sense, need, impulse and action characteristic of the live creature. The intervention of consciousness adds regulation, power of selection, and redisposition. Thus it varies the arts in ways without end. But its intervention also leads in time to the *idea* of art as a conscious idea – the greatest intellectual achievement in the history of humanity.

The variety and perfection of the arts in Greece led thinkers to frame a generalized conception of art and to project the ideal of an art of organization of human activities as such – the art of politics and morals as conceived by Socrates and Plato. The ideas of design, plan, order, pattern, purpose emerged in distinction from and relation to the materials employed in their realization. The conception of man as the being that uses art became at once the ground of the distinction of man from the rest of nature and of the bond that ties him to nature. When the conception of art as the distinguishing trait of man was made explicit, there was assurance that, short of complete relapse of humanity below even savagery, the possibility of invention of new arts would remain, along with use of old arts, as the guiding ideal of mankind. Although recognition of the fact still halts, because of traditions established before the power of art was adequately recognized, science itself is but a central art auxiliary to the generation and utilization of other arts.

It is customary, and from some points of view necessary, to make a distinction between fine art and useful or technological art. But the point of view from which it is necessary is one that is extrinsic to the work of art itself. The customary distinction is based simply on acceptance of certain existing social conditions. I suppose the fetiches of the negro sculptor were taken to be useful in the highest degree to his tribal group, more so even than spears and clothing. But now they are fine art, serving in the twentieth century to inspire renovations in arts that had grown conventional. But they are fine art only because the anonymous artist lived and experienced so fully during the process of production. An angler may eat his catch without thereby losing the esthetic satisfaction he experienced in casting and playing. It is this degree of completeness of living in the experience of making and of perceiving that makes the difference between what is fine or esthetic in art and what is not. Whether the thing made is put to use, as are bowls, rugs, garments, weapons, is, *intrinsically* speaking, a matter of indifference. That many, perhaps most, of the articles and utensils made at present for use are not genuinely esthetic happens, unfortunately, to be true. But it is true for reasons that are foreign to the relation of the 'beautiful' and 'useful' as such. Wherever conditions are such as to prevent the act of production from being an experience in which the whole creature is alive and in which he possesses his living through enjoyment, the product will lack something of being esthetic. No matter how useful it is for special and limited ends, it will not be useful in the ultimate degree – that of contributing directly and liberally to an expanding and enriched life. The story of the severance and final sharp opposition of the useful and the fine is the history of that industrial development through which so much of production has become a form of postponed living and so much of consumption a superimposed enjoyment of the fruits of the labor of others.

Martin Heidegger, 'The origin of the work of art', from Lectures 1 & 2

15

From Martin Heidegger, *Poetry, Language, Thought*, trans. A. Hofstadter. New York: Harper & Row, 1971, pp. 32–48.

The perspectives of those, like Dewey, who focus on art as 'part of the significant life of an organized community', and those, like Schopenhauer, who see it as a vehicle for conveying essences and truths, are rarely combined. One exception is Hegel: art could play a central part in the communal life of the Greeks precisely because it was the primary embodiment of dimly perceived metaphysical truths. An exception, too, is another German philosopher, Martin Heidegger (1889–1976), whose Epilogue to the three 1936 lectures 'On the origin of the work of art' makes clear their continuity with Hegel's lectures on art a century before. Like Hegel, he is concerned only with 'great art' – art which plays a vital role within a people's life and which owes its very identity to that role. (The Bamberg Cathedral has now 'gone by', along with the Gothic world to which it belonged.) Like Hegel, too, Heidegger is dismissive of 'aesthetics', construed as the study of properties like beauty and the pleasures they afford. 'Aesthetics' in this sense reflects the modern 'technological' perspective from which everything is viewed as so much 'equipment': caught up in the 'art business', artworks are treated as 'object[s] for our feelings', artifacts to yield pleasurable 'art experiences'.[1]

It is, however, in the course of discussing the nature of 'equipment' (clothing, tools etc.) that Heidegger – 'clandestinely', he says – approaches an answer to his question 'What and how is a work of art?' In his best-known book, *Being and Time* (1927), Heidegger had elaborated a distinction between two main kinds of being – that of 'mere' things of nature and of equipment, respectively – omitting any discussion of the kind of being enjoyed by works of

[1] *On the Way to Language*, San Francisco: Harper & Row, 1982, pp. 42ff.

art. This omission is made good in the lectures, and at the point where we join them Heidegger is about to follow up the 'clue' that equipment, such as shoes, occupies an 'intermediate position' between natural objects and artworks. During the subsequent analysis, the 'essence' of equipment is identified but not, ironically, through examining an actual pair of shoes. Instead, it is reflection on Van Gogh's famous painting of a peasant's shoes which has 'revealed' the true nature of shoes – notably by rendering vivid the integral relations of the shoes both to the social and domestic 'world' inhabited by the peasant and to the 'earth' on which she works and depends. 'Unwittingly', therefore, we have discovered something crucial about the artwork: its 'open[ing] up in its own way the Being of beings', in this instance of equipmental things.

When Heidegger turns, in the second lecture, to the example of a Greek temple, it emerges that great artworks have a still more crucial function than 'revealing' the world and earth in and on which people dwell. For the temple served to 'found' the world and earth of the Greeks. Put less dramatically, the great works of the Greeks – temples, tragedies, statues – played an indispensable part in shaping that view of themselves and the natural world around them which determined their identity as a people or nation. The great work of art is at once 'the setting up of a world and the setting forth of earth' (p.48). It is, so to speak, Janus-faced, with one side directed towards the network of meaningful activities that constitutes a people's communal world, and the other towards the earth from which its materials are drawn. This is why it is wrong for philosophers of art, as is their wont, exclusively to focus upon either the meaning or the material ingredients of artworks. The value and very 'Being of the work of art lies in its providing a domain within which the world of human purposes and meanings meets the non-human horizon [the earth] of any purposive activity'.[2]

Given Heidegger's unmatched impact upon continental European philosophy over the last half-century, it is unsurprising to find 'hermeneuticists', like his student Hans-Georg Gadamer, and 'postmodernists', such as Jacques Derrida, appealing to Heidegger in their writings on art. Notable contributions to literary and art criticism are also in debt to him: for example, George Steiner's theory of artworks as 'icons' in which things or their essences are 'real presences' is explicitly modelled on Heidegger's discussion of the Van Gogh painting mentioned above.[3] More generally, Heidegger has persuaded many readers to look at works of art in a new way, as items which both reveal and help to constitute our unarticulated senses of the interpersonal world and the material earth to which they belong. And not only at works of art, for in his later writings Heidegger argues that, appropriately regarded, things in general –

[2] Stephen Mulhall, *On Being in the World: Wittgenstein and Heidegger on seeing aspects*, London: Routledge, 1990, p. 170.

[3] See his *Real Presences: is there anything in what we say?*, London: Faber, 1989.

bridges, jugs, trees – can each play this dual role.[4] This should not be treated as a plea for 'ready-mades' or *art trouvé*: on the contrary, by recruiting things into the 'art business' and wrenching them out of their usual contexts, their identity and significance is lost.

... Equipment, having come into being through human making, is particularly familiar to human thinking. At the same time, this familiar being has a peculiar intermediate position between thing and [art] work. We shall follow this clue and search first for the equipmental character of equipment. Perhaps this will suggest something to us about the thingly character of the thing and the workly character of the work. We must only avoid making thing and work prematurely into subspecies of equipment. . . .

But what path leads to the equipmental quality of equipment? How shall we discover what a piece of equipment truly is? The procedure necessary at present must plainly avoid any attempts that again immediately entail the encroachments of the usual interpretations. We are most easily insured against this if we simply describe some equipment without any philosophical theory.

We choose as example a common sort of equipment – a pair of peasant shoes. We do not even need to exhibit actual pieces of this sort of useful article in order to describe them. Everyone is acquainted with them. But since it is a matter here of direct description, it may be well to facilitate the visual realization of them. For this purpose a pictorial representation suffices. We shall choose a well-known painting by Van Gogh, who painted such shoes several times. But what is there to see here? Everyone knows what shoes consist of. If they are not wooden or bast shoes, there will be leather soles and uppers, joined together by thread and nails. Such gear serves to clothe the feet. Depending on the use to which the shoes are to be put, whether for work in the field or for dancing, matter and form will differ.

Such statements, no doubt correct, only explicate what we already know. The equipmental quality of equipment consists in its usefulness. But what about this usefulness itself? In conceiving it, do we already conceive along with it the equipmental character of equipment? In order to succeed in doing this, must we not look out for useful equipment in its use? The peasant woman wears her shoes in the field. Only here are they what they

[4] See the essays 'Building, dwelling, thinking' and 'The thing', also in *Poetry, Language, Thought*. I try to explain these later views in my *Heidegger*, London: Claridge, 1996, ch. 6.

are. They are all the more genuinely so, the less the peasant woman thinks about the shoes while she is at work, or looks at them at all, or is even aware of them. She stands and walks in them. That is how shoes actually serve. It is in this process of the use of equipment that we must actually encounter the character of equipment.

As long as we only imagine a pair of shoes in general, or simply look at the empty, unused shoes as they merely stand there in the picture, we shall never discover what the equipmental being of the equipment in truth is. From Van Gogh's painting we cannot even tell where these shoes stand. There is nothing surrounding this pair of peasant shoes in or to which they might belong – only an undefined space. There are not even clods of soil from the field or the field-path sticking to them, which would at least hint at their use. A pair of peasant shoes and nothing more. And yet –

From the dark opening of the worn insides of the shoes the toilsome tread of the worker stares forth. In the stiffly rugged heaviness of the shoes there is the accumulated tenacity of her slow trudge through the far-spreading and ever-uniform furrows of the field swept by a raw wind. On the leather lie the dampness and richness of the soil. Under the soles slides the loneliness of the field-path as evening falls. In the shoes vibrates the silent call of the earth, its quiet gift of the ripening grain and its unexplained self-refusal in the fallow desolation of the wintry field. This equipment is pervaded by uncomplaining anxiety as to the certainty of bread, the wordless joy of having once more withstood want, the trembling before the impending childbed and shivering at the surrounding menace of death. This equipment belongs to the *earth*, and it is protected in the *world* of the peasant woman. From out of this protected belonging the equipment itself rises to its resting-within-itself.

But perhaps it is only in the picture that we notice all this about the shoes. The peasant woman, on the other hand, simply wears them. If only this simple wearing were so simple. When she takes off her shoes late in the evening, in deep but healthy fatigue, and reaches out for them again in the still dim dawn, or passes them by on the day of rest, she knows all this without noticing or reflecting. The equipmental quality of the equipment consists indeed in its usefulness. But this usefulness itself rests in the abundance of an essential being of the equipment. We call it reliability. By virtue of this reliability the peasant woman is made privy to the silent call of the earth; by virtue of the reliability of the equipment she is sure of her world. World and earth exist for her, and for those who are with her in her mode of being, only thus – in the equipment. We say 'only' and therewith fall into error; for the reliability of the equipment first gives to the simple world its security and assures to the earth the freedom of its steady thrust.

The equipmental being of equipment, reliability, keeps gathered within itself all things according to their manner and extent. The usefulness of equipment is nevertheless only the essential consequence of reliability. The former vibrates in the latter and would be nothing without it. A single piece of equipment is worn out and used up; but at the same time the use itself also falls into disuse, wears away, and becomes usual. Thus equipmentality wastes away, sinks into mere stuff. In such wasting, reliability vanishes. This dwindling, however, to which use-things owe their boringly obtrusive usualness, is only one more testimony to the original nature of equipmental being. The worn-out usualness of the equipment then obtrudes itself as the sole mode of being, apparently peculiar to it exclusively. Only blank usefulness now remains visible. It awakens the impression that the origin of equipment lies in a mere fabricating that impresses a form upon some matter. Nevertheless, in its genuinely equipmental being, equipment stems from a more distant source. Matter and form and their distinction have a deeper origin.

The repose of equipment resting within itself consists in its reliability. Only in this reliability do we discern what equipment in truth is. But we still know nothing of what we first sought: the thing's thingly character. And we know nothing at all of what we really and solely seek: the workly character of the work in the sense of the work of art.

Or have we already learned something unwittingly, in passing so to speak, about the work-being of the work?

The equipmental quality of equipment was discovered. But how? Not by a description and explanation of a pair of shoes actually present; not by a report about the process of making shoes; and also not by the observation of the actual use of shoes occurring here and there; but only by bringing ourselves before Van Gogh's painting. This painting spoke. In the vicinity of the work we were suddenly somewhere else than we usually tend to be.

The art work let us know what shoes are in truth. It would be the worst self-deception to think that our description, as a subjective action, had first depicted everything thus and then projected it into the painting. If anything is questionable here, it is rather that we experienced too little in the neighborhood of the work and that we expressed the experience too crudely and too literally. But above all, the work did not, as it might seem at first, serve merely for a better visualizing of what a piece of equipment is. Rather, the equipmentality of equipment first genuinely arrives at its appearance through the work and only in the work.

What happens here? What is at work in the work? Van Gogh's painting is the disclosure of what the equipment, the pair of peasant shoes, *is* in truth. This entity emerges into the unconcealedness of its being. The Greeks called the unconcealedness of beings *aletheia*. We say 'truth' and think little enough in using this word. If there occurs in the work a disclosure of a particular being, disclosing what and how it is, then there is here an occurring, a happening of truth at work.[1]

In the work of art the truth of an entity has set itself to work. 'To set' means here: to bring to a stand. Some particular entity, a pair of peasant shoes, comes in the work to stand in the light of its being. The being of the being comes into the steadiness of its shining.

The nature of art would then be this: the truth of beings setting itself to work. But until now art presumably has had to do with the beautiful and beauty, and not with truth. The arts that produce such works are called the beautiful or fine arts, in contrast with the applied or industrial arts that manufacture equipment. In fine art the art itself is not beautiful, but is called so because it produces the beautiful. Truth, in contrast, belongs to logic. Beauty, however, is reserved for esthetics.

But perhaps the proposition that art is truth setting itself to work intends to revive the fortunately obsolete view that art is an imitation and depiction of reality? The reproduction of what exists requires, to be sure, agreement with the actual being, adaptation to it; the Middle Ages called it *adaequatio*; Aristotle already spoke of *homoiosis*. Agreement with what *is* has long been taken to be the essence of truth. But then, is it our opinion that this painting by Van Gogh depicts a pair of actually existing peasant shoes, and is a work of art because it does so successfully? Is it our opinion that the painting draws a likeness from something actual and transposes it into a product of artistic production? By no means.

The work, therefore, is not the reproduction of some particular entity that happens to be present at any given time; it is, on the contrary, the reproduction of the thing's general essence. But then where and how is this general essence, so that art works are able to agree with it? With what nature of what thing should a Greek temple agree? Who could maintain the impossible view that the Idea of Temple is represented in the building? And yet, truth is set to work in such a work, if it is a work. Or let us think of Hölderlin's hymn, 'The Rhine.' What is pregiven to the poet, and how is it given, so that it can then be regiven in the poem? And if in the case of this hymn and similar poems the idea of a copy-relation between something already actual and the art work clearly fails, the view that the work is a copy is confirmed in the best possible way by a work of the kind presented in C. F. Meyer's poem 'Roman Fountain.'

Roman Fountain

The jet ascends and falling fills
The marble basin circling round;
This, veiling itself over, spills
Into a second basin's ground.
The second in such plenty lives,
Its bubbling flood a third invests,
And each at once receives and gives
And streams and rests.

This is neither a poetic painting of a fountain actually present nor a reproduction of the general essence of a Roman fountain. Yet truth is put into the work. What truth is happening in the work? Can truth happen at all and thus be historical? Yet truth, people say, is something timeless and supertemporal.

We seek the reality of the art work in order to find there the art prevailing within it. The thingly substructure is what proved to be the most immediate reality in the work. But to comprehend this thingly feature the traditional thing-concepts are not adequate; for they themselves fail to grasp the nature of the thing. The currently predominant thing-concept, thing as formed matter, is not even derived from the nature of the thing but from the nature of equipment. It also turned out that equipmental being generally has long since occupied a peculiar preeminence in the interpretation of beings. This preeminence of equipmentality, which however did not actually come to mind, suggested that we pose the question of equipment anew while avoiding the current interpretations.

We allowed a work to tell us what equipment is. By this means, almost clandestinely, it came to light what is at work in the work: the disclosure of the particular being in its being, the happening of truth. If, however, the reality of the work can be defined solely by means of what is at work in the work, then what about our intention to seek out the real art work in its reality? As long as we supposed that the reality of the work lay primarily in its thingly substructure we were going astray. We are now confronted by a remarkable result of our considerations – if it still deserves to be called a result at all. Two points become clear:

First: the dominant thing-concepts are inadequate as means of grasping the thingly aspect of the work.

Second: what we tried to treat as the most immediate reality of the work, its thingly substructure, does not belong to the work in that way at all.

As soon as we look for such a thingly substructure in the work, we have unwittingly taken the work as equipment, to which we then also ascribe a superstructure supposed to contain its artistic quality. But the work is not a piece of equipment that is fitted out in addition with an aesthetic value that adheres to it. The work is no more anything of the kind than the bare thing is a piece of equipment that merely lacks the specific equipmental characteristics of usefulness and being made.

Our formulation of the question of the work has been shaken because we asked, not about the work but half about a thing and half about equipment. Still, this formulation of the question was not first developed by us. It is the formulation native to esthetics. The way in which esthetics views the art work from the outset is dominated by the traditional interpretation of all beings. But the shaking of this accustomed formulation is not the essential point. What matters is a first opening of our vision to the fact that what is workly in the work, equipmental in equipment, and thingly in the thing comes closer to us only when we think the Being of beings. To this end it is necessary beforehand that the barriers of our preconceptions fall away and that the current pseudo concepts be set aside. That is why we had to take this detour. But it brings us directly to a road that may lead to a determination of the thingly feature in the work. The thingly feature in the work should not be denied; but if it belongs admittedly to the work-being of the work, it must be conceived by way of the work's workly nature. If this is so, then the road toward the determination of the thingly reality of the work leads not from thing to work but from work to thing.

The art work opens up in its own way the Being of beings. This opening up, i.e., this deconcealing, i.e., the truth of beings, happens in the work. In the art work, the truth of what is has set itself to work. Art is truth setting itself to work. What is truth itself, that it sometimes comes to pass as art? What is this setting-itself-to-work?

The Work and Truth

The origin of the art work is art. But what is art? Art is real in the art work. Hence we first seek the reality of the work. In what does it consist? Art works universally display a thingly character, albeit in a wholly distinct way. The attempt to interpret this thing-character of the work with the aid of the usual thing-concepts failed – not only because these concepts do not lay hold of the thingly feature, but because, in raising the question of its thingly substructure, we force the work into a preconceived framework by which we obstruct our own access to the work-being of the work. Nothing can be discovered about the thingly aspect of the work so long as the pure self-subsistence of the work has not distinctly displayed itself.

Yet is the work ever in itself accessible? To gain access to the work, it would be necessary to remove it from all relations to something other than itself, in order to let it stand on its own for itself alone. But the artist's most peculiar intention already aims in this direction. The work is to be released by him to its pure self-subsistence. It is precisely in great art – and only such art is under consideration here – that the artist remains inconsequential as compared with the work, almost like a passageway that destroys itself in the creative process for the work to emerge.

Well, then, the works themselves stand and hang in collections and exhibitions. But are they here in themselves as the works they themselves are, or are they not rather here as objects of the art industry? Works are made available for public and private art appreciation. Official agencies assume the care and maintenance of works. Connoisseurs and critics busy themselves with them. Art dealers supply the market. Art-historical study makes the works the objects of a science. Yet in all this busy activity do we encounter the work itself?

The Aegina sculptures in the Munich collection, Sophocles' *Antigone* in the best critical edition, are, as the works they are, torn out of their own native sphere. However high their quality and power of impression, however good their state of preservation, however certain their interpretation, placing them in a collection has withdrawn them from their own world. But even when we make an effort to cancel or avoid such displacement of works – when, for instance, we visit the temple in Paestum at its own site or the Bamberg cathedral on its own square – the world of the work that stands there has perished.

World-withdrawal and world-decay can never be undone. The works are no longer the same as they once were. It is they themselves, to be sure, that we encounter there, but they themselves are gone by. As bygone works they stand over against us in the realm of tradition and conservation. Henceforth they remain merely such objects. Their standing before us is still indeed a consequence of, but no longer the same as, their former self-subsistence. This self-subsistence has fled from them. The whole art industry, even if carried to the extreme and exercised in every way for the sake of works themselves, extends only to the object-being of the works. But this does not constitute their work-being.

But does the work still remain a work if it stands outside all relations? Is it not essential for the work to stand in relations? Yes, of course – except that it remains to ask in what relations it stands.

Where does a work belong? The work belongs, as work, uniquely within the realm that is opened up by itself. For the work-being of the work is present in, and only in, such opening up. We said that in the work there was a happening of truth at work. The reference to Van Gogh's picture tried to point to this happening. With regard to it there arose the question as to what truth is and how truth can happen.

We now ask the question of truth with a view to the work. But in order to become more familiar with what the question involves, it is necessary to make visible once more the happening of truth in the work. For this attempt let us deliberately select a work that cannot be ranked as representational art.

A building, a Greek temple, portrays nothing. It simply stands there in the middle of the rock-cleft valley. The building encloses the figure of the god, and in this concealment lets it stand out into the holy precinct through the open portico. By means of the temple, the god is present in the temple. This presence of the god is in itself the extension and delimitation of the precinct as a holy precinct. The temple and its precinct, however, do not fade away into the indefinite. It is the temple-work that first fits together and at the same time gathers around itself the unity of those paths and relations in which birth and death, disaster and blessing, victory and disgrace, endurance and decline acquire the shape of destiny for human being. The all-governing expanse of this open relational context is the world of this historical people. Only from and in this expanse does the nation first return to itself for the fulfillment of its vocation.

Standing there, the building rests on the rocky ground. This resting of the work draws up out of the rock the mystery of that rock's clumsy yet spontaneous support. Standing there, the building holds its ground against the storm raging above it and so first makes the storm itself manifest in its violence. The luster and gleam of the stone, though itself apparently glowing only by the grace of the sun, yet first brings to light the light of the day, the breadth of the sky, the darkness of the night. The temple's firm towering makes visible the invisible space of air. The steadfastness of the work contrasts with the surge of the surf, and its own repose brings out the raging of the sea. Tree and grass, eagle and bull, snake and cricket first enter into their distinctive shapes and thus come to appear as what they are. The Greeks early called this emerging and rising in itself and in all things *phusis*. It clears and illuminates, also, that on which and in which man bases his dwelling. We call this ground the *earth*. What this word says is not to be associated with the idea of a mass of matter deposited somewhere, or with the merely astronomical idea of a planet. Earth is that whence the arising brings back and shelters everything that arises without violation. In the things that arise, earth is present as the sheltering agent.

The temple-work, standing there, opens up a world and at the same time sets this world back again on earth, which itself only thus emerges as native ground. But men and animals, plants and things, are never present and familiar as unchangeable objects, only to represent incidentally also a fitting environment for the temple, which one fine day is added to what is already there. We shall get closer to what *is*, rather, if we think of all this in reverse order, assuming of course that we have, to begin with, an eye for how differently everything then faces us. Mere reversing, done for its own sake, reveals nothing.

The temple, in its standing there, first gives to things their look and to men their outlook on themselves. This view remains open as long as the work is a work, as long as the god has not fled from it. It is the same with the sculpture of the god, votive offering of the victor in the athletic games. It is not a portrait whose purpose is to make it easier to realize how the god looks; rather, it is a work that lets the god himself be present and thus *is* the god himself. The same holds for the linguistic work. In the tragedy nothing is staged or displayed theatrically, but the battle of the new gods against the old is being fought. The linguistic work, originating in the speech of the people, does not refer to this battle; it transforms the people's saying so that now every living word fights the battle and puts up for decision what is holy and what unholy, what great and what small, what brave and what cowardly, what lofty and what flighty, what master and what slave (cf. Heraclitus, Fragment 53).

In what, then, does the work-being of the work consist? Keeping steadily in view the points just crudely enough indicated, two essential features of the work may for the moment be brought out more distinctly. We set out here, from the long familiar foreground of the work's being, the thingly character which gives support to our customary attitude toward the work.

When a work is brought into a collection or placed in an exhibition we say also that it is 'set up.' But this setting up differs essentially from setting up in the sense of erecting a building, raising a statue, presenting a tragedy at a holy festival. Such setting up is erecting in the sense of dedication and praise. Here 'setting up' no longer means a bare placing. To dedicate means to consecrate, in the sense that in setting up the work the holy is opened up as holy and the god is invoked into the openness of his presence. Praise belongs to dedication as doing honor to the dignity and splendor of the god. Dignity and splendor are not properties beside and behind which the god, too, stands as something distinct, but it is rather in the dignity, in the splendor that the god is present. In the reflected glory of this splendor there glows, i.e., there lightens itself, what we called the world. To e-rect means: to open the right in the sense of a guiding measure, a form in which what belongs to the nature of being gives guidance. But why is the setting up of a work an erecting that consecrates and praises? Because the work, in its work-being, demands it. How is it that the work comes to demand such a setting up? Because it itself, in its own work-being, is something that sets up. What does the work, as work, set up? Towering up within itself, the work opens up a *world* and keeps it abidingly in force.

To be a work means to set up a world. But what is it to be a world? The answer was hinted at when we referred to the temple. On the path we must follow here, the nature of world can only be indicated. What is more, this indication limits itself to warding off anything that might at first distort our view of the world's nature.

The world is not the mere collection of the countable or uncountable, familiar and unfamiliar things that are just there. But neither is it a merely imagined framework added by our representation to the sum of such given things. The *world worlds*, and is more fully in being than the tangible and perceptible realm in which we believe ourselves to be at home.[2] World is never an object that stands before us and can be seen. World is the ever-nonobjective to which we are subject as long as the paths of birth and death, blessing and curse keep us transported into Being. Wherever those decisions of our history that relate to our very being are made, are taken up and abandoned by us, go unrecognized and are rediscovered by new inquiry, there the world worlds. A stone is worldless. Plant and animal likewise have no world; but they belong to the covert throng of a surrounding into which they are linked. The peasant woman, on the other hand, has a world because she dwells in the overtness of beings, of the things that are. Her equipment, in its reliability, gives to this world a necessity and nearness of its own. By the opening up of a world, all things gain their lingering and hastening, their remoteness and nearness, their scope and limits. In a world's worlding is gathered that spaciousness out of which the protective grace of the gods is granted or withheld. Even this doom of the god remaining absent is a way in which world worlds.

A work, by being a work, makes space for that spaciousness. 'To make space for' means here especially to liberate the Open and to establish it in its structure. This in-stalling occurs through the erecting mentioned earlier. The work as work sets up a world. The work holds open the Open of the world. But the setting up of a world is only the first essential feature in the work-being of a work to be referred to here. Starting again from the foreground of the work, we shall attempt to make clear in the same way the second essential feature that belongs with the first.

When a work is created, brought forth out of this or that work-material – stone, wood, metal, color, language, tone – we say also that it is made, set forth out of it. But just as the work requires a setting up in the sense of a consecrating-praising erection, because the work's work-being consists in the setting up of a world, so a setting forth is needed because the work-being of the work itself has the character of setting forth. The work as work, in its presencing, is a setting forth, a making. But what does the work set forth? We come to know about this only when we explore what comes to the fore and is customarily spoken of as the making or production of works.

To work-being there belongs the setting up of a world. Thinking of it within this perspective, what is the nature of that in the work which is usually called the work material? Because it is determined by usefulness and serviceability, equipment takes into its service that of which it consists: the matter. In fabricating equipment – e.g., an ax – stone is used, and used up. It disappears into usefulness. The material is all the better and more suitable the less it resists perishing in the equipmental being of the equipment. By contrast the temple-work, in setting up a world, does not cause the material to disappear, but rather causes it to come forth for the very first time and to come into the Open of the work's world. The rock comes to bear and rest and so first becomes rock; metals come to glitter and shimmer, colors to glow, tones to sing, the word to speak. All this comes forth as the work sets itself back into the massiveness and heaviness of stone, into the firmness and pliancy of wood, into the hardness and luster of metal, into the lighting and darkening of color, into the clang of tone, and into the naming power of the word.

That into which the work sets itself back and which it causes to come forth in this setting back of itself we called the earth. Earth is that which comes forth and shelters. Earth, self-dependent, is effortless and untiring. Upon the earth and in it, historical man grounds his dwelling in the world. In setting up a world, the work sets forth the earth. This setting forth must be thought here in the strict sense of the word. The work moves the earth itself into the Open of a world and keeps it there. *The work lets the earth be an earth.*

But why must this setting forth of the earth happen in such a way that the work sets itself back into it? What is the earth that it attains to the unconcealed in just such a manner? A stone presses downward and manifests its heaviness. But while this heaviness exerts an opposing pressure upon us it denies us any penetration into it. If we attempt such a penetration by breaking open the rock, it still does not display in its fragments anything inward that has been disclosed. The stone has instantly withdrawn again into the same dull pressure and bulk of its fragments. If we try to lay hold of the stone's heaviness in another way, by placing the stone on a balance, we merely bring the heaviness into the form of a calculated weight. This perhaps very precise determination of the stone remains a number, but the weight's burden has escaped us. Color shines and wants only to shine. When we analyze it in rational terms by measuring its wavelengths, it is gone. It shows itself only when it remains undisclosed and unexplained. Earth thus shatters every attempt to penetrate into it. It causes every merely calculating importunity upon it to turn into a destruction. This destruction may herald itself under the appearance of mastery and of progress in the form of the technical-scientific objectivation of nature, but this mastery nevertheless remains an impotence of will. The earth appears openly cleared as itself only when it is perceived and preserved as that which is by nature undisclosable, that which shrinks from every disclosure and constantly keeps itself closed up. All things of earth, and the earth itself as a whole, flow together into a reciprocal accord. But this confluence is not a blurring of their outlines. Here there flows the stream, restful within itself, of the setting of bounds, which delimits everything present within its presence. Thus in each of the self-secluding things there is the same not-knowing-of-one-another. The earth is essentially self-secluding. To set forth the earth means to bring it into the Open as the self-secluding.

This setting forth of the earth is achieved by the work as it sets itself back into the earth. The self-seclusion of earth, however, is not a uniform, inflexible staying under cover, but unfolds itself in an inexhaustible variety of simple modes and shapes. To be sure, the sculptor uses stone just as the mason uses it, in his own way. But he does not use it up. That happens in a certain way only where the work miscarries. To be sure, the painter also uses pigment, but in such a way that color is not used up but rather only now comes to shine forth. To be sure, the poet also uses the word – not, however, like ordinary speakers and writers who have to use them up, but rather in such a way that the word only now becomes and remains truly a word.

Nowhere in the work is there any trace of a work-material. It even remains doubtful whether, in the essential definition of equipment, what the equipment consists of is properly described in its equipmental nature as matter.

The setting up of a world and the setting forth of earth are two essential features in the work-being of the work. They belong together, however, in the unity of work-being. This is the unity we seek when we ponder the self-subsistence of the work and try to express in words this closed, unitary repose of self-support. . . .

Notes

1 In many writings, Heidegger emphasizes the etymology of the Greek word ***aletheia*** (*a*-(not), *-lath-* (to be concealed), usually translated as 'truth', as evidence that the Greeks recognized a more basic notion than that of truth as 'correspondence'. For statements or beliefs to correspond to how things are, things must first be un-concealed or revealed. The point in the present essay is that truth belongs to 'great art' in this more basic sense.

2 'The ***world worlds***' is a characteristic Heideggerean invention. Its point in the present context is the primarily negative one of discouraging less tautologous descriptions of the world, as a collection of objects, say, or a series of events. Such descriptions are misleading since objects and events can only be identified within the context provided by the world in Heidegger's sense.

16 R. G. Collingwood, *The Principles of Art*, Chapter 7

From R. G. Collingwood, *The Principles of Art*. Oxford: Clarendon Press, 1938, pp. 125–52 [some passages and footnotes omitted].

A thriving sector of aesthetics in recent years has been 'the ontology of artworks', the enquiry into the kind(s) of existence which works of art have. Take a Beethoven symphony: is this a musical score, the sum total of its performances, an abstract object 'realized' in performances, or what? Questions of this type were rarely raised until this century when, in pursuing the implications for the status of artworks of wider philosophical positions – notably, idealism and phenomenology – they were addressed by continental thinkers such as Croce and Ingarden and by the unmistakably British historian and philosopher, Robin George Collingwood (1889–1943), an Oxford Professor of Metaphysics.[1] In his own way, as we have seen, such questions were addressed by Heidegger, but the contrast with Collingwood could hardly be greater. Whereas for Heidegger the being of the artwork is defined in terms of its role in a community and its special relation to its material, for Collingwood the artwork is at once profoundly private and non-material.

Collingwood proposes a version of 'expressionism': 'artistic activity is the experience of expressing one's emotions . . . the same thing as becoming conscious of [them]' (pp. 275, 282). Art is valuable in itself, for it is a 'corruption of consciousness' to fail to express, and thereby become aware of, one's emotions. It is not, however, with this expressionism *per se*, but with its ontological implications that chapter 7 of *The Principles of Art* is concerned. The main implication is that an artwork is not any kind of actual physical object at all,

[1] See Benedetto Croce, *The Aesthetic as the Science of Expression and of the Linguistic in General*, Cambridge: Cambridge University Press, 1992; Roman Ingarden, *The Literary Work of Art*, Evanston, Ill.: Northwestern University Press, 1973. On the ontology of art more generally, see Nicholas Wolterstoff, *Works and Worlds of Art*, Oxford: Clarendon Press, 1980.

not even in the widest sense of 'physical object'. To think otherwise is to confuse art with mere craft, which differs from art in having practical purposes, in applying a preconceived plan and in shaping raw materials. (The words and sounds which the poet or composer may employ are not, argues Collingwood, analogous to the stone used in building a bridge.)

If artistic creation is to be compared with anything, it is not with the building of a bridge, nor even with the engineer's sketches for the bridge, but with the conception of it 'in his head'. In short, the work of art itself is something mental, an imaginative experience or activity, which may or may not result in the production of a physical object. Typically it will, but only because most artists need to put something down on paper or canvas in order for their imaginative experience – the work of art itself – to articulate their emotions. In Collingwood's view, this mentalistic treatment of the artwork is supported by everyday convictions: all of us, for instance, distinguish between the tune itself and its being scored or sung.

Unfortunately Collingwood thinks it 'unnecessary' to spell this point out for the plastic arts, thereby leaving it unclear how painting, say, might dispense with any physical embodiment. But in §6, where attention turns to the 'total imaginative experience' of the listener or viewer, a rather different reason for distinguishing the artwork from any physical object emerges. While he was as much 'carried off his feet' by Cézanne as was Clive Bell, Collingwood emphasizes the great feat of imaginative empathy which the viewer must perform to see this artist's pictures properly. The implication is that one can hardly identify the pictures with objects hanging on a wall if so much in them is contributed by us, the viewers.

It is regrettable that this section of chapter 7 has received much less attention than the previous ones: for in it we find not only an early version of the now fashionable 'role of the reader' doctrine that works of art are partly constituted by their audience, but a clear indication of how far Collingwood is from the crude expressionism usually, if unfairly, associated with Tolstoy. For Collingwood, an artwork is not a response to, an outburst of, an emotion, but an often difficult effort to cognize that emotion. Nor, we now see, is the audience simply 'infected' with the artist's emotion, for it too must be capable of a rich cognitive effort in order to grasp the emotion that is articulated in the work. The ontological thesis that artworks are 'ideal' or 'mental' entities may have stimulated much recent discussion of the status of artworks; but perhaps the more enduring contribution of Croce and Collingwood is their appreciation that art is intimately connected with the whole of our mental life – intellectual, affective, imaginative – and not just a device for exercising some hived-off faculty called 'taste' or 'the aesthetic sense'.[2]

[2] See Roger Scruton, *Art and Imagination: a study in the philosophy of mind*, London: Routledge & Kegan Paul, 1982, c. p. 4.

Art Proper: (2) As Imagination

§ 1. The Problem Defined

What is a work of art, granted that there is something in art proper (not only in art falsely so called) to which that name is applied, and that, since art is not craft, this thing is not an artifact? It is something made by the artist, but not made by transforming a given raw material, nor by carrying out a preconceived plan, nor by way of realizing the means to a preconceived end. What is this kind of making?

Here are two questions which, however closely they are connected, we shall do well to consider separately. We had better begin with the artist, and put the second question first. I shall therefore begin by asking: What is the nature of this making which is not technical making, or, if we want a one-word name for it, not fabrication? It is important not to misunderstand the question. When we asked what expression was, in the preceding chapter, it was pointed out that the writer was not trying to construct an argument intended to convince the reader, nor to offer him information, but to remind him of what . . . he knows already. So here. We are not asking for theories but for facts. And the facts for which we are asking are not recondite facts. They are facts well known to the reader. The order of facts to which they belong may be indicated by saying that they are the ways in which all of us who are concerned with art habitually think about it, and the ways in which we habitually express our thoughts in ordinary speech.

By way of making this clearer, I will indicate the kind of way in which our question cannot be answered. A great many people who have put to themselves the question 'What is this making, characteristic of the artist, which is not a fabrication?' have sought an answer in some such way as the following: 'This non-technical making is plainly not an accidental making, for works of art could not be produced by accident. Something must be in control. But if this is not the artist's skill, it cannot be his reason or will or consciousness. It must therefore be something else; either some controlling force outside the artist, in which case we may call it inspiration, or something inside him but other than his will and so forth. This must be either his body, in which case the production of a work of art is at bottom a physiological activity, or else it is something mental but unconscious, in which case the productive force is the artist's unconscious mind.'

Many imposing theories of art have been built on these foundations. The first alternative, that the artist's activity is controlled by some divine or at least spiritual being that uses him as its mouthpiece, is out of fashion today, but that is no reason why we should refuse it a hearing. It does at least fit the facts better than most of the theories of art nowadays current. The second alternative, that the artist's work is controlled by forces which, though part of himself and specifically part of his mind, are not voluntary and not conscious, but work in some mental cellar unseen and unbidden by the dwellers in the house above, is extremely popular; not among artists, but among psychologists and their numerous disciples, who handle the theory with a great deal of confidence and seem to believe that by its means the riddle of art has at last been solved. . . .

It would be waste of time to criticize these theories. The question about them is not whether they are good or bad, considered as examples of theorizing; but whether the problem which they are meant to solve is one that calls for theorizing in order to solve it. A person who cannot find his spectacles on the table may invent any number of theories to account for their absence. They may have been spirited away by a benevolent deity, to prevent him from overworking, or by a malicious demon, to interfere with his studies, or by a neighbouring mahatma, to convince him that such things can be done. He may have unconsciously made away with them himself, because they unconsciously remind him of his oculist, who unconsciously reminds him of his father, whom he unconsciously hates. Or he may have pushed them off the table while moving a book. But these theories, however ingenious and sublime, are premature if the spectacles should happen to be on his nose.

Theories professing to explain how works of art are constructed by means of hypotheses like these are based on recollecting that the spectacles are not on the table, and overlooking the fact that they are not on the nose. Those who put them forward have not troubled to ask themselves whether we are in point of fact familiar with a kind of activity productive of results and under the agent's voluntary control, which has none of the special characteristics of craft. If they had asked the question, they must have answered it in the affirmative. We are perfectly familiar with activities of this kind; and our ordinary name for them is creation.

§ 2. Making and Creating

Before we ask what in general are the occasions on which we use this word, we must forestall a too probable objection to the word itself. Readers suffering from theophobia will certainly by now have taken offence. Knowing as they do that theologians use it for describing the relation of God to the world, victims of this disease smell incense whenever they hear it spoken, and think it a point of honour that it shall never sully their lips or ears. They will by now have on the tips of their tongues all the familiar protests against an aesthetic mysticism that raises the function of art to the level of something divine and identifies the artist with God. Perhaps some day, with an eye on the Athanasian Creed, they will pluck up courage to excommunicate an arithmetician who uses the word 'three'. Meanwhile, readers willing to understand words instead of shying at them will recollect that the word 'create' is daily used in contexts that offer no valid ground for a fit of *odium theologicum*. If a witness in court says that a drunken man was creating a noise, or that a dance club has created a nuisance, . . . if a publicist says that secret diplomacy creates international distrust, . . . no one expects a little man at the back of the room to jump up and threaten to leave unless the word is withdrawn. If he did, the stewards would throw him out for creating a disturbance.

To create something means to make it non-technically, but yet consciously and voluntarily. Originally, *creare* means to generate, or make offspring, for which we still use its compound 'procreate', and the Spaniards have *criatura*, for a child. The act of procreation is a voluntary act, and those who do it are responsible for what they are doing; but it is not done by any specialized form of skill. It need not be done (as it may be in the case of a royal marriage) as a means to any preconceived end. It need not be done (as it was by Mr. Shandy senior) according to any preconceived plan. It cannot be done (whatever Aristotle may say) by imposing a new form on any pre-existing matter. It is in this sense that we speak of creating a disturbance or a demand or a political system. The person who makes these things is acting voluntarily; he is acting responsibly; but he need not be acting in order to achieve any ulterior end; he need not be following a preconceived plan; and he is certainly not transforming anything that can properly be called a raw material. It is in the same sense that Christians asserted, and neo-Platonists denied, that God created the world.

This being the established meaning of the word, it should be clear that when we speak of an artist as making a poem, or a play, or a painting, or a piece of music, the kind of making to which we refer is the kind we call creating. For, as we already know, these things, in so far as they are works of art proper, are not made as means to an end; they are not made according to any preconceived plan; and they are not made by imposing a new form upon a given matter. Yet they are made deliberately and responsibly, by people who know what they are doing, even though they do not know in advance what is going to come of it.

The creation which theologians ascribe to God is peculiar in one way and only one. The peculiarity of the act by which God is said to create the world is sometimes supposed to lie in this, that God is said to create the world 'out of nothing', that is to say, without there being previously any matter upon which he imposes a new form. But that is a confusion of thought. In that sense, all creation is creation out of nothing. The peculiarity which is really ascribed to God is that in the case of his act there lacks not only a prerequisite in the shape of a matter to be transformed, but any prerequisite of any kind whatsoever. This would not apply to the creation of a child, or a nuisance, or a work of art. In order that a child should be created, there must be a whole world of organic and inorganic matter, not because the parents fabricate the child out of this matter, but because a child can come into existence, as indeed its parents can exist, only in such a world. In order that a nuisance should be created, there must be persons capable of being annoyed, and the person who creates the nuisance must already be acting in a manner which, if modified this way or that, would annoy them. In order that a work of art should be created, the prospective artist . . . must have in him certain unexpressed emotions, and must also have the wherewithal to express them. In these cases, where creation is done by finite beings, it is obvious that these beings, because finite, must first be in circumstances that enable them to create. Because God is conceived as an infinite being, the creation ascribed to him is conceived as requiring no such conditions.

Hence, when I speak of the artist's relation to his works of art as that of a creator, I am not giving any excuse to unintelligent persons who think, whether in praise or dispraise of my notions, that I am raising the function of art to the level of something divine or making the artist into a kind of God.

§ 3. Creation and Imagination

We must proceed to a further distinction. All the things taken above as examples of things created are what we ordinarily call real things. A work of art need not be what we should call a real thing. It may be what we call an imaginary thing. A disturbance, or a nuisance, or a navy, or the like, is not created at all until it is created as a thing having its place in the real world. But a work of art may be completely created when it has been created as a thing whose only place is in the artist's mind.

Here, I am afraid, it is the metaphysician who will take offence. He will remind me that the distinction between real things and things that exist only in our minds is one to which he and his fellows have given a great deal of attention. They have thought about it so long and so intently that it has lost all meaning. Some of them have decided that the things we call real are only in our minds; others that the things we describe as being in our minds are thereby implied to be just as real as anything else. These two sects, it appears, are engaged in a truceless war, and any one who butts in by using the words about which they are fighting will be set upon by both sides and torn to pieces.

I do not hope to placate these gentlemen. I can only cheer myself up by reflecting that even if I go on with what I was saying they cannot eat me. If an engineer has decided how to build a bridge, but has not made any drawings or specifications for it on paper, and has not discussed his plan with any one or taken any steps towards carrying it out, we are in the habit of saying that the bridge exists only in his mind, or (as we also say) in his head. When the bridge is built, we say that it exists not only in his head but in the real world. A bridge which 'exists only in the engineer's head' we also call an imaginary bridge; one which 'exists in the real world' we call a real bridge.

This may be a silly way of speaking; or it may be an unkind way of speaking, because of the agony it gives to metaphysicians; but it is a way in which ordinary people do speak, and ordinary people who speak in that way know quite well what kind of things they are referring to. The metaphysicians are right in thinking that difficult problems arise from talking in that way; and I shall spend the greater part of Book II in discussing these problems. Meanwhile, I shall go on 'speaking with the vulgar'; if metaphysicians do not like it they need not read it.

The same distinction applies to such things as music. If a man has made up a tune but has not written it down or sung it or played it or done anything which could make it public property, we say that the tune exists only in his mind, or only in his head, or is an imaginary tune. If he sings or plays it, thus making a series of audible noises, we call this series of noises a real tune as distinct from an imaginary one.

When we speak of making an artifact we mean making a real artifact. If an engineer said that he had made a bridge, and when questioned turned out to mean that he had only made it in his head, we should think him a liar or a fool. We should say that he had not made a bridge at all, but only a plan for one. If he said he had made a plan for a bridge and it turned out that he had put nothing on paper, we should not necessarily think he had deceived us. A plan is a kind of thing that can only exist in a person's mind. As a rule, an engineer making a plan in his mind is at the same time making notes and sketches on paper; but the plan does not consist of what we call the 'plans', that is, the pieces of paper with these notes and sketches on them. Even if he has put complete specifications and working drawings on paper, the paper with these specifications and drawings on it is not the plan; it only serves to tell people (including himself, for memory is fallible) what the plan is. If the specifications and drawings are published, for example in a treatise on civil engineering, any one who reads the treatise intelligently will get the plan of that bridge into his head. The plan is therefore public property, although by calling it public we mean only that it can get into the heads of many people; as many as read intelligently the book in which the specifications and drawings are published.

In the case of the bridge there is a further stage. The plan may be 'executed' or carried out; that is to say, the bridge may be built. When that is done, the plan is said to be 'embodied' in the built bridge. It has begun to exist in a new way, not merely in people's heads but in stone or concrete. From being a mere plan existing in people's heads, it has become the form imposed on certain matter. Looking back from that point of view, we can now say that the engineer's plan was the form of the bridge without its matter, or that when we describe him as having the plan in his mind we might equally have described him as having in mind the form of the finished bridge without its matter.

The making of the bridge is the imposing of this form on this matter. When we speak of the engineer as making the plan, we are using the word 'make' in its other sense, as equivalent to create. Making a plan for a bridge is not imposing a certain form on a certain matter; it is a making that is not a transforming, that is to say, it is a creation. It has the other characteristics, too, that distinguish creating from fabricating. It need not be done as means to an end, for a man can make plans (for example, to illustrate a text-book of engineering) with no intention of executing them. In such a case the making of the plan is not means to composing the text-book, it is part of composing the text-book. It is not means to anything. Again, a person making a plan need not be carrying out a plan to make that plan. He may be doing this; he may for instance have planned a text-book for which he needs an example of a reinforced concrete bridge with a single span of 150 feet, to carry a two-track railway with a roadway above it, and he may work out a plan for such a bridge in order that it may occupy that place in the book. But this is not a necessary condition of planning. People sometimes speak as if everybody had, or ought to have, a plan for his whole life, to which every other plan he makes is or ought to be subordinated; but no one can do that.

Making an artifact, or acting according to craft, thus consists of two stages. (1) Making the plan, which is creating. (2) Imposing that plan on certain matter, which is fabricating. Let us now consider a case of creating where what is created is not a work of art. A person creating a disturbance need not be, though of course he may be, acting on a plan. He need not be, though of course he may be, creating it as means to some ulterior end, such as causing a government to resign. He cannot be transforming a pre-existing material, for there is nothing out of which a disturbance can be made; though he is able to create it only because he already stands, as a finite being always does stand, in a determinate situation; for example, at a political meeting. But what he creates cannot be something that exists only in his own mind. A disturbance is something in the minds of the people disturbed.

Next, let us take the case of a work of art. When a man makes up a tune, he may and very often does at the same time hum it or sing it or play it on an instrument. He may do none of these things, but write it on paper. Or he may both hum it or the like, and also write it on paper at the same time or afterwards. Also he may do these things in public, so that the tune at its very birth becomes public property, like the disturbance we have just considered. But all these are accessories of the real work, though some of them are very likely useful accessories. The actual making of the tune is something that goes on in his head, and nowhere else.

I have already said that a thing which 'exists in a person's head' and nowhere else is alternatively called an imaginary thing. The actual making of the tune is therefore alternatively called the making of an imaginary tune. This is a case of creation, just as much as the making of a plan or a disturbance, and for the same reasons, which it would be tedious to repeat. Hence the making of a tune is an instance of imaginative creation. The same applies to the making of a poem, or a picture, or any other work of art.

The engineer, as we saw, when he made his plan in his own head, may proceed to do something else which we call 'making his plans'. His 'plans', here, are drawings and specifications on paper, and these are artifacts made to serve a certain purpose, namely to inform others or remind himself of the plan. The making of them is accordingly not imaginative creation; indeed, it is not creation at all. It is fabrication, and the ability to do it is a specialized form of skill, the craft of engineer's draughtsmanship.

The artist, when he has made his tune, may go on to do something else which at first sight seems to resemble this: he may do what is called publishing it. He may sing or play it aloud, or write it down, and thus make it possible for others to get into their heads the same thing which he has in his. But what is written or printed on music-paper is not the tune. It is only something which when studied intelligently will enable others (or himself, when he has forgotten it) to construct the tune for themselves in their own heads.

The relation between making the tune in his head and putting it down on paper is thus quite different from the relation, in the case of the engineer, between making a plan for a bridge and executing that plan. The engineer's plan is embodied in the bridge: it is essentially a form that can be imposed on certain matter, and when the bridge is built the form is there, in the bridge, as the way in which the matter composing it is arranged. But the musician's tune is not there on the paper at all. What is on the paper is not music, it is only musical notation. The relation of the tune to the notation is not like the relation of the plan to the bridge; it is like the relation of the plan to the specifications and drawings; for these, too, do not embody the plan as the bridge embodies it, they are only a notation from which the abstract or as yet unembodied plan can be reconstructed in the mind of a person who studies them.

§ 4. *Imagination and Make-believe*

Imagination, like art itself, is a word with proper and improper meanings. For our present purpose it will be enough to distinguish imagination proper from one thing that is often improperly so called: a thing already referred to under the name of make-believe.

Make-believe involves a distinction between that which is called by this name and that which is called real; and this distinction is of such a kind that the two exclude one another. A make-believe situation can never be a real situation, and vice versa. If, being hungry, I 'imagine' myself to be eating, this 'bare imagination of a feast' is a make-believe situation which I may be said to create for myself imaginatively; but this imaginative creation has nothing to do with art proper, though it has much to do with certain kinds of art falsely so called. It is the motive of all those sham works of art which provide their audiences or addicts with fantasies depicting a state of things in which their desires are satisfied. Dreaming consists to a great extent (some psychologists say altogether) of make-believe in which the dreamer's desires are thus satisfied; day-dreaming even more obviously so; and the sham works of art of which I am speaking are perhaps best understood as an organized and commercialized development of day-dreaming. A story is told of a psychologist who issued a questionnaire to all the girl students in a college, asking them how they spent their time, and learnt from their replies that I forget what vast percentage of it was spent in day-dreaming. He is said to have come to the conclusion that great results could be achieved if all this day-dreaming could be co-ordinated. Quite right; but he overlooked the fact that the thing had already been done, and that Hollywood was there to prove it.

Imagination is indifferent to the distinction between the real and the unreal. When I look out of the window, I see grass to right and left of the mullion that stands immediately before me; but I also imagine the grass going on where this mullion hides it from my sight. It may happen that I also imagine a lawn-mower standing on that part of the lawn. Now, the hidden part of the lawn is really there, the lawn-mower is not; but I can detect nothing, either in the way in which I imagine the two things, or in the ways in which they respectively appear to my imagination, which at all corresponds to this distinction. The act of imagining is of course an act really performed; but the imagined object or situation or event is something which need not be real and need not be unreal, and the person imagining it neither imagines it as real or unreal, nor, when he comes to reflect on his act of imagining, thinks of it as real or unreal. Make-believe, too, is a thing which can be done without reflecting on it. When it is so done, the person who does it is unaware that he is constructing for himself unreal objects or situations or events; but when he reflects, he either discovers that these things are unreal, or else falls into the error of taking them for realities.

There is probably always a motive behind any act of make-believe, namely, the desire for something which we should enjoy or possess if the make-believe were truth. It implies a felt dissatisfaction with the situation in which one actually stands, and an attempt to compensate for this dissatisfaction not by practical means, by bringing a more satisfactory state of things into existence, but by imagining a more satisfactory state of things and getting what satisfaction one can out of that. For imagination proper there is no such motive. It is not because I am dissatisfied with the match-box lying before me on the table that I imagine its inside, whether as full or as empty; it is not because I am dissatisfied with an interrupted grass-plot that I imagine it as continuing where the mullion hides it from my view. Imagination is indifferent, not only to the distinction between real and unreal, but also to the distinction between desire and aversion.

Make-believe presupposes imagination, and may be described as imagination operating in a peculiar way under the influence of peculiar forces. Out of the numerous things which one imagines, some are chosen, whether consciously or unconsciously, to be imagined with peculiar completeness or vividness or tenacity, and others are repressed, because the first are things whose reality one desires, and the second things from whose reality one has an aversion. The result is make-believe, which is thus imagination acting under the censorship of desire; where desire means not the desire to imagine, nor even the desire to realize an imagined situation, but the desire that the situation imagined were real.

A good deal of damage has been done to aesthetic theory by confusing these two things. The connection between art and imagination has been a commonplace for at least two hundred years; but the confusion between art and amusement has been both reflected and reinforced by a confusion between imagination and make-believe, which culminates in the attempt of the psycho-analysts to subsume artistic creation under their theory (certainly a true theory) of 'fantasies' as make-believe gratifications of desire. This attempt is admirably successful so long as it deals with the art, falsely so called, of the ordinary popular novel or film; but it could not conceivably be applied to art proper. When the attempt is made to base an aesthetic upon it (a thing which has happened lamentably often) the result is not an aesthetic but an anti-aesthetic. This may be because the psychologists who have tried to explain artistic creation by appeal to the notion of 'fantasy' have no idea that there is any such distinction as that between amusement art and art proper, but are merely perpetuating in their own jargon a vulgar misconception, common in the nineteenth century, according to which the artist is a kind of dreamer or day-dreamer, constructing in fancy a make-believe world which if it existed would be, at least in his own opinion, a better or more pleasant one than that in which we live. Competent artists and competent aestheticians have again and again protested against this misconception; but the protest has naturally had no effect on the many people whose experience of so-called art, being limited to the 'art' of organized and commercialized day-dreaming, it faithfully describes. And to this class it would seem that our psycho-analyst aestheticians belong. Or perhaps it is their patients that belong to it. An excessive indulgence in day-dreaming would certainly tend to produce moral diseases like those from which their patients suffer.

§ 5. The Work of Art as Imaginary Object

If the making of a tune is an instance of imaginative creation, a tune is an imaginary thing. And the same applies to a poem or a painting or any other work of art. This seems paradoxical; we are apt to think that a tune is not an imaginary thing but a real thing, a real collection of noises; that a painting is a real piece of canvas covered with real colours; and so on. I hope to show, if the reader will have patience, that there is no paradox here; that both these propositions express what we do as a matter of fact say about works of art; and that they do not contradict one another, because they are concerned with different things.

When, speaking of a work of art (tune, picture, &c.), we mean by art a specific craft, intended as a stimulus for producing specific emotional effects in an audience, we certainly mean to designate by the term 'work of art' something that we should call real. The artist as magician or purveyor of amusement is necessarily a craftsman making real things, and making them out of some material according to some plan. His works are as real as the works of an engineer, and for the same reason.

But it does not at all follow that the same is true of an artist proper. His business is not to produce an emotional effect in an audience, but, for example, to make a tune. This tune is already complete and perfect when it exists merely as a tune in his head, that is, an imaginary tune. Next, he may arrange for the tune to be played before an audience. Now there comes into existence a real tune, a collection of noises. But which of these two things is the work of art? Which of them is the music? The answer is implied in what we have already said: the music, the work of art, is not the collection of noises, it is the tune in the composer's head. The noises made by the performers, and heard by the audience, are not the music at all; they are only means by which the audience, if they listen intelligently (not otherwise), can reconstruct for themselves the imaginary tune that existed in the composer's head.

This is not a paradox. It is not something *παρὰ λόξαν*, contrary to what we ordinarily believe and express in our ordinary speech. We all know perfectly well, and remind each other often enough, that a person who hears the noises the instruments make is not thereby possessing himself of the music. Perhaps no one can do that unless he does hear the noises; but there is something else which he must do as well. Our ordinary word for this other thing is listening; and the listening which we have to do when we hear the noises made by musicians is in a way rather like the thinking we have to do when we hear the noises made, for example, by a person lecturing on a scientific subject. We hear the sound of his voice; but what he is doing is not simply to make noises, but to develop a scientific thesis. The noises are meant to assist us in achieving what he assumes to be our purpose in coming to hear him lecture, that is, thinking this same scientific thesis for ourselves. The lecture, therefore, is not a collection of noises made by the lecturer with his organs of speech; it is a collection of scientific thoughts related to those noises in such a way that a person who not only hears but thinks as well becomes able to think these thoughts for himself. We may call this the communication of thought by means of speech, if we like; but if we do, we must think of communication not as an 'imparting' of thought by the speaker to the hearer, the speaker somehow planting his thought in the hearer's receptive mind, but as a 'reproduction' of the speaker's thought by the hearer, in virtue of his own active thinking.

The parallel with listening to music is not complete. The two cases are similar at one point, dissimilar at another. They are dissimilar in that a concert and a scientific lecture are different things, and what we are trying to 'get out of' the concert is a thing of a different kind from the scientific thoughts we are trying to 'get out of' the lecture. But they are similar in this: that just as what we get out of the lecture is something other than the noises we hear proceeding from the lecturer's mouth, so what we get out of the concert is something other than the noises made by the performers. In each case, what we get out of it is something which we have to reconstruct in our own minds, and by our own efforts; something which remains for ever inaccessible to a person who cannot or will not make efforts of the right kind, however completely he hears the sounds that fill the room in which he is sitting.

This, I repeat, is something we all know perfectly well. And because we all know it, we need not trouble to examine or criticize the ideas of aestheticians (if there are any left to-day – they were common enough at one time) who say that what we get out of listening to music, or looking at paintings, or the like, is some peculiar kind of sensual pleasure. When we do these things, we certainly may, in so far as we are using our senses, enjoy sensual pleasures. It would be odd if we did not. A colour, or a shape, or an instrumental timbre may give us an exquisite pleasure of a purely sensual kind. It may even be true (though this is not so certain) that no one would become a lover of music unless he were more susceptible than other people to the sensual pleasure of sound. But even if a special susceptibility to this pleasure may at first lead some people towards music, they must, in proportion as they are more susceptible, take the more pains to prevent that susceptibility from interfering with their power of listening. For any concentration on the pleasantness of the noises themselves concentrates the mind on hearing, and makes it hard or impossible to listen. There is a kind of person who goes to concerts mainly for the sensual pleasure he gets from the sheer sounds; his presence may be good for the box-office, but it is as bad for music as the presence of a person who went to a scientific lecture for the sensual pleasure he got out of the tones of the lecturer's voice would be for science. And this, again, everybody knows.

It is unnecessary to go through the form of applying what has been said about music to the other arts. We must try instead to make in a positive shape the point that has been put negatively. Music does not consist of heard noises, paintings do not consist of seen colours, and so forth. Of what, then, do these things consist? Not, clearly, of a 'form', understood as a pattern or a system of relations between the various noises we hear or the various colours we see. Such 'forms' are nothing but the perceived structures of bodily 'works of art', that is to say, 'works of art' falsely so called; and these formalistic theories of art, popular though they have been and are, have no relevance to art proper and will not be further considered in this book. The distinction between form and matter, on which they are based, is a distinction belonging to the philosophy of craft, and not applicable to the philosophy of art.

The work of art proper is something not seen or heard, but something imagined. But what is it that we imagine? We have suggested that in music the work of art proper is an imagined tune. Let us begin by developing this idea.

Everybody must have noticed a certain discrepancy between what we actually see when looking at a picture or statue or play and what we see imaginatively; what we actually see when listening to music or speech and what we imaginatively hear. To take an obvious example: in watching a puppet-play we could (as we say) swear that we have seen the expression on the puppets' faces change with their changing gestures and the puppet-man's changing words and tones of voice. Knowing that they are only puppets, we know that their facial expression cannot change; but that makes no difference; we continue to see imaginatively the expressions which we know that we do not see actually. The same thing happens in the case of masked actors like those of the Greek stage.

In listening to the pianoforte, again, we know from evidence of the same kind that we must be hearing every note begin with a *sforzando*, and fade away for the whole length of time that it continues to sound. But our imagination enables us to read into this experience something quite different. As we seem to see the puppets' features move, so we seem to hear a pianist producing a *sostenuto* tone, almost like that of a horn; and in fact notes of the horn and the pianoforte are easily mistaken one for the other. Still stranger, when we hear a violin and pianoforte playing together in the key, say, of G, the violin's F sharp is actually played a great deal sharper than the pianoforte's. Such a discrepancy would sound intolerably out of tune except to a person whose imagination was trained to focus itself on the key of G, and silently corrected every note of the equally tempered pianoforte to suit it. The corrections which imagination must thus carry out, in order that we should be able to listen to an entire orchestra, beggar description. When we listen to a speaker or singer, imagination is constantly supplying articulate sounds which actually our ears do not catch. In looking at a drawing in pen or pencil, we take a series of roughly parallel lines for the tint of a shadow. And so on.

Conversely, in all these cases imagination works negatively. We disimagine, if I may use the word, a great deal which actually we see and hear. The street noises at a concert, the noises made by our breathing and shuffling neighbours, and even some of the noises made by the performers, are thus shut out of the picture unless by their loudness or in some other way they are too obtrusive to be ignored. At the theatre, we are strangely able to ignore the silhouettes of the people sitting in front of us, and a good many things that happen on the stage. Looking at a picture, we do not notice the shadows that fall on it or, unless it is excessive, the light reflected from its varnish.

All this is commonplace. And the conclusion has already been stated by Shakespeare's Theseus: 'the best in this kind ['works of art', as things actually perceived by the senses] are but shadows, and the worst are no worse if imagination amend them'. The music to which we listen is not the heard sound, but that sound as amended in various ways by the listener's imagination, and so with the other arts.

But this does not go nearly far enough. Reflection will show that the imagination with which we listen to music is something more, and more complex, than any inward ear; the imagination with which we look at paintings is something more than 'the mind's eye'. Let us consider this in the case of painting.

§ 6. *The Total Imaginative Experience*

The change which came over painting at the close of the nineteenth century was nothing short of revolutionary. Every one in the course of that century had supposed that painting was 'a visual art'; that the painter was primarily a person who used his eyes, and used his hands only to record what the use of his eyes had revealed to him. Then came Cézanne, and began to paint like a blind man. His still-life studies, which enshrine the essence of his genius, are like groups of things that have been groped over with the hands; he uses colour not to reproduce what he sees in looking at them but to express almost in a kind of algebraic notation what in this groping he has felt. So with his interiors; the spectator finds himself bumping about those rooms, circumnavigating with caution those menacingly angular tables, coming up to the persons that so massively occupy those chairs and fending himself off them with his hands. It is the same when Cézanne takes us into the open air. His landscapes have lost almost every trace of visuality. Trees never looked like that; that is how they feel to a man who encounters them with his eyes shut, blundering against them blindly. A bridge is no longer a pattern of colour . . . ; it is a perplexing mixture of projections and recessions, over and round which we find ourselves feeling our way as one can imagine an infant feeling its way, when it has barely begun to crawl, among the nursery furniture. And over the landscape broods the obsession of Mont Saint-Victoire, never looked at, but always felt, as a child feels the table over the back of its head.

Of course Cézanne was right. Painting can never be a visual art. A man paints with his hands, not with his eyes. The Impressionist doctrine that what one paints is light was a pedantry which failed to destroy the painters it enslaved only because they remained painters in defiance of the doctrine: men of their hands, men who did their work with fingers and wrist and arm, and even (as they walked about the studio) with their legs and toes. What one paints is what can be painted; no one can do more; and what can be painted must stand in some relation to the muscular activity of painting it. Cézanne's practice reminds one of Kant's theory that the painter's only use for his colours is to make shapes visible. But it is really quite different. Kant thought of the painter's shapes as two-dimensional shapes visibly traced on the canvass; Cézanne's shapes are never two-dimensional, and they are never traced on the canvass; they are solids, and we get at them through the canvass. In this new kind of painting the 'plane of the picture' disappears; it melts into nothing, and we go through it.*

Vernon Blake, who understood all this very well from the angle of the practising artist, and could explain himself in words like the Irishman he was, told draughtsmen that the plane of the picture was a mere superstition. Hold your pencil vertical to the paper, said he; don't stroke the paper, dig into it; think of it as if it were the surface of a slab of clay in which you were going to cut a relief, and of your pencil as a knife. Then you will find that you can draw something which is not a mere pattern on paper, but a solid thing lying inside or behind the paper.

In Mr. [Bernard] Berenson's hands the revolution became retrospective. He found that the great Italian painters yielded altogether new results when approached in this manner. He taught his pupils (and every one who takes any interest in Renaissance painting nowadays is Mr. Berenson's pupil) to

* The 'disappearance' of the picture-plane is the reason why, in modern artists who have learnt to accept Cézanne's principles and to carry their consequences a stage further than he carried them himself, perspective . . . has disappeared too. The man in the street thinks that this has happened because these modern fellows can't draw; which is like thinking that young men of the Royal Air Force career about in the sky because they can't walk.

look in paintings for what he called 'tactile values'; to think of their muscles as they stood before a picture, and notice what happened in their fingers and elbows. He showed that Masaccio and Raphael, to take only two outstanding instances, were painting as Cézanne painted, not at all as Monet or Sisley painted; not squirting light on a canvass, but exploring with arms and legs a world of solid things where Masaccio stalks giant-like on the ground and Raphael floats through serene air.

In order to understand the theoretical significance of these facts, we must look back at the ordinary theory of painting current in the nineteenth century. This was based on the conception of a 'work of art', with its implication that the artist is a kind of craftsman producing things of this or that kind, each with the characteristics proper to its kind, according to the difference between one kind of craft and another. The musician makes sounds; the sculptor makes solid shapes in stone or metal; the painter makes patterns of paint on canvass. What there is in these works depends, of course, on what kind of works they are; and what the spectator finds in them depends on what there is in them. The spectator in looking at a picture is simply seeing flat patterns of colour, and he can get nothing out of the picture except what can be contained in such patterns.

The forgotten truth about painting which was rediscovered by what may be called the Cézanne–Berenson approach to it was that the spectator's experience on looking at a picture is not a specifically visual experience at all. What he experiences does not consist of what he sees. It does not even consist of this as modified, supplemented, and expurgated by the work of the visual imagination. It does not belong to sight alone, it belongs also (and on some occasions even more essentially) to touch. We must be a little more accurate, however. When Mr. Berenson speaks of tactile values, he is not thinking of things like the texture of fur and cloth, the cool roughness of bark, the smoothness or grittiness of a stone, and other qualities which things exhibit to our sensitive finger-tips. As his own statements abundantly show, he is thinking, or thinking in the main, of distance and space and mass: not of touch sensations, but of motor sensations such as we experience by using our muscles and moving our limbs. But these are not actual motor sensations, they are imaginary motor sensations. In order to enjoy them when looking at a Masaccio we need not walk straight through the picture, or even stride about the gallery; what we are doing is to imagine ourselves as moving in these ways. In short: what we get from looking at a picture is not merely the experience of seeing, or even partly seeing and partly imagining, certain visible objects; it is also, and in Mr. Berenson's opinion more importantly, the imaginary experience of certain complicated muscular movements.

Persons especially interested in painting may have thought all this, when Mr. Berenson began saying it, something strange and new; but in the case of other arts the parallels were very familiar. It was well known that listening to music we not only hear the noises of which the 'music', that is to say the sequences and combinations of audible sounds, actually consists; we also enjoy imaginary experiences which do not belong to the region of sound at all, notably visual and motor experiences. Everybody knew, too, that poetry has the power of bringing before us not only the sounds which constitute the audible fabric of the 'poem', but other sounds, and sights, and tactile and motor experiences, and at times even scents, all of which we possess, when we listen to poetry, in imagination.

This suggests that what we get out of a work of art is always divisible into two parts. (I) There is a specialized sensuous experience, an experience of seeing or hearing as the case may be. (2) There is also a non-specialized imaginative experience, involving not only elements homogeneous, after their imaginary fashion, with those which make up the specialized sensuous experience, but others heterogeneous with them. So remote is this imaginative experience from the specialism of its sensuous basis, that we may go so far as to call it an imaginative experience of total activity.

At this point the premature theorist lifts up his voice again. 'See', he exclaims, 'how completely we have turned the tables on the old-fashioned theory that what we get out of art is nothing but the sensual pleasure of sight or hearing! The enjoyment of art is no merely sensuous experience, it is an imaginative experience. A person who listens to music, instead of merely hearing it, is not only experiencing noises, pleasant though these may be. He is imaginatively experiencing all manner of visions and motions; the sea, the sky, the stars; the falling of the rain-drops, the rushing of the wind, the storm, the flow of the brook; the dance, the embrace, and the battle. A person who looks at pictures, instead of merely seeing patterns of colour, is moving in imagination among buildings and landscapes and human forms. What follows? Plainly this: the value of any given work of art to a person properly qualified to appreciate its value is not the delightfulness of the sensuous elements in which as a work of art it actually consists, but the delightfulness of the imaginative experience which those sensuous elements awake in him. Works of art are only means to an end; the end is this total imaginative experience which they enable us to enjoy.'

This attempt to rehabilitate the technical theory depends on distinguishing what we find in the work of art, its actual sensuous qualities, as put there by the artist, from something else which we do not strictly find in it, but rather import into it from our own stores of experience and powers of imagination. The first is conceived as objective, really belonging to the work of art: the second as subjective, belonging not to it but to activities which go on in us when we contemplate it. The peculiar value of this contemplation, then, is conceived as lying not in the first thing but in the second. Any one having the use of his senses could see all the colours and shapes that a picture contains, and hear all the sounds which together make up a symphony; but he would not on that account be enjoying an aesthetic experience. To do that he must use his imagination, and so proceed from the first part of the experience, which is given in sensation, to the second part, which is imaginatively constructed.

This seems to be the position of the 'realistic' philosophers who maintain that what they call 'beauty' is 'subjective'. The peculiar value which belongs to an experience such as that of listening to music or looking at pictures arises, they think, not from our getting out of these things what is really in them, or 'apprehending their objective nature', but from our being stimulated by contact with them to certain free activities of our own. It is in these activities that the value really resides; and although (to use Professor [Samuel] Alexander's word) we may 'impute' it to the music or the picture, it actually belongs not to them but to us.

But we cannot rest in this position. The distinction between what we find and what we bring is altogether too naïve. Let us look at it from the point of view of the artist. He presents us with a picture. According to the doctrine just expounded, he has actually put into this picture certain colours which, by merely opening our eyes and looking at it, we shall find there. Is this all he did in painting the picture? Certainly not. When he painted it, he was in possession of an experience quite other than that of seeing the colours he was putting on the canvass; an imaginary experience of total activity more or less like that which we construct for ourselves when we look at the picture. If he knew how to paint, and if we know how to look at a painting, the resemblance between this imaginary experience of his and the imaginary experience which we get from looking at his work is at least as close as that between the colours he saw in the picture and those we see; perhaps closer. But if he paints his picture in such a way that we, when we look at it using our imagination, find ourselves enjoying an imaginary experience of total activity like that which he enjoyed when painting it, there is not much sense in saying that we bring this experience with us to the picture and do not find it there. The artist, if we told him that, would laugh at us and assure us that what we believed ourselves to have read into the picture was just what he put there.

No doubt there is a sense in which we bring it with us. Our finding of it is not something that merely happens to us, it is something we do, and do because we are the right kind of people to do it. The imaginary experience which we get from the picture is not merely the kind of experience the picture is capable of arousing, it is the kind of experience we are capable of having. But this applies equally to the colours. He has not put into the pictures certain colours which we passively find there. He has painted, and seen certain colours come into existence as he paints. If we, looking at his picture afterwards, see the same colours, that is because our own powers of colour-vision are like his. Apart from the activity of our senses we should see no colours at all.

Thus the two parts of the experience are not contrasted in the way in which we fancied them to be. There is no justification for saying that the sensuous part of it is something we find and the imaginary part something we bring, or that the sensuous part is objectively 'there' in the 'work of art', the imaginary part subjective, a mode of consciousness as distinct from a quality of a thing. Certainly we find the colours there in the painting; but we find them only because we are actively using our eyes, and have eyes of such a kind as to see what the painter wanted us to see, which a colour-blind person could not have done. We bring our powers of vision with us, and find what they reveal. Similarly, we bring our imaginative powers with us, and find what they reveal: namely, an imaginary experience of total activity which we find in the picture because the painter had put it there.

In the light of this discussion let us recapitulate and summarize our attempt to answer the question, what is a work of art? What, for example, is a piece of music?

(1) In the pseudo-aesthetic sense for which art is a kind of craft, a piece of music is a series of audible noises. The psychological and 'realistic' aestheticians, as we can now see, have not got beyond this pseudo-aesthetic conception.

(2) If 'work of art' means work of art proper, a piece of music is not something audible, but something which may exist solely in the musician's head (§ 3).

(3) To some extent it must exist solely in the musician's head (including, of course, the audience as well as the composer under that name), for his imagination is always supplementing, correcting, and expurgating what he actually hears (§ 4).

(4) The music which he actually enjoys as a work of art is thus never sensuously or 'actually' heard at all. It is something imagined.

(5) But it is not imagined sound (in the case of painting, it is not imagined colour-patterns, &c.). It is an imagined experience of total activity (§ 5).

(6) Thus a work of art proper is a total activity which the person enjoying it apprehends, or is conscious of, by the use of his imagination.

§ 7. Transition to Book II

Putting together the conclusions of this chapter and the last, we get the following result.

By creating for ourselves an imaginary experience or activity, we express our emotions; and this is what we call art.

What this formula means, we do not yet know. We can annotate it word by word; but only to forestall misunderstandings, thus. 'Creating' refers to a productive activity which is not technical in character. 'For ourselves' does not exclude 'for others'; on the contrary, it seems to include that; at any rate in principle. 'Imaginary' does not mean anything in the least like 'make-believe', nor does it imply that what goes by that name is private to the person who imagines. The 'experience or activity' seems not to be sensuous, and not to be in any way specialized: it is some kind of general activity in which the whole self is involved. 'Expressing' emotions is certainly not the same thing as arousing them. There is emotion there before we express it. But as we express it, we confer upon it a different kind of emotional colouring; in one way, therefore, expression creates what it expresses, for exactly this emotion, colouring and all, only exists so far as it is expressed. Finally, we cannot say what 'emotion' is, except that we mean by it the kind of thing which, on the kind of occasion we are talking about, is expressed.

Index

Made in the USA
San Bernardino, CA
05 January 2018